M

ENVIRONMENTAL ACCOUNTING
FOR THE
SUSTAINABLE CORPORATION

ENVIRONMENTAL ACCOUNTING
— F O R   T H E —
SUSTAINABLE CORPORATION

Strategies and Techniques

Daniel Blake Rubenstein

Q
Quorum Books
Westport, Connecticut • London

Library of Congress Cataloging-in-Publication Data

Rubenstein, Daniel Blake.
  Environmental accounting for the sustainable corporation :
strategies and techniques / Daniel Blake Rubenstein.
        p.   cm.
  Includes bibliographical references and index.
  ISBN 0–89930–866–X
  1. Natural resources — Accounting.   2. Sustainable development.
  3. Corporations — Accounting.   I. Title.
  HF5686.N3R8   1994
  651 — dc20   93–50066

British Library Cataloguing in Publication Data is available.

Library of Congress Catalog Card Number: 93–50066
ISBN: 0–89930–866–X

First published in 1994

Quorum Books, 88 Post Road West, Westport, CT 06881
An imprint of Greenwood Publishing Group, Inc.

Printed in the United States of America

The paper used in this book complies with the
Permanent Paper Standard issued by the National
Information Standards Organization (Z39.48 — 1984).

10 9 8 7 6 5 4 3 2 1

Contents

Figures and Tables

FIGURES

TABLES

Guide for Readers

The objective of this book is to demonstrate how the newly emerging field of environmental accounting *could* serve the needs of corporations aspiring to be sustainable over the coming decades. The book is then intended to provide an initial road map of what accounting *could* be, rather than describe what is actually in place today. The concepts introduced are new and necessarily of an innovative nature. The accounting systems proposed are virtually nonexistent today. Therefore, to achieve my objective, I chose to write the book in the genre of what I would call a "fictional documentary."

In order not to mislead the reader, it is important to distinguish between fact and fiction. First, while the issues confronted by the characters are real, all the characters are fictitious. Any resemblance with living persons is purely incidental. The material in Chapters 2 through 6 is based on interviews, a review of current literature, and documentation on industry practices in the forestry sector. The material on accounting for natural capital in Chapter 7 is of my own creation, based on the observations I made about forest ecology, with the exception of the material on waste minimization. Chapters 8 and 10 are based on in-depth interviews with a leading forestry management company and reflect an enlightened industry perspective of the options for sustainable forestry management and sustainable pulp operations. The numerical data presented were based on historical data of a representative company, modified to remove any proprietary information. An attempt was made to retain basic relationships. This database of representative data for forestry operations in the northern boreal forest was used to explore unit cost variations under different forestry options. The methodology for computing the commercial value of the forest proposed in Chapter 9 was developed by an industry cost accountant. The numbers presented are deemed representative of those found in a northern boreal forest, subject to the caveats in the text.

The approach to computing the noncommercial values of the forest, intergenerational liabilities, and the risk-management principles proposed for costing natural capital are of my own invention. When doing my initial research, I was unable to find any precedent for calculating intergenerational liabilities for a living forest at the corporate level. My objective was to focus on expanding the traditional definition of an asset, then to compute some rough estimates of the value of the forest ecosystem. The focus was always on developing potential reporting formats. My work is in no way definitive but rather intended to give tangible form to some of the new concepts.

With the exception of Figure 12.1, the material in Chapter 12 was based on a case study on the sustainable development of a northern boreal forest, developed for the United Nations Conference on Trade and Development. (In the text, when I refer to the work done by the United Nations, I am referring to the final drafts of the case study I created for the United Nations between 1991 and 1993. This case study is not yet published.) Given the focus on exploring reporting formats, the fuller cost calculations are in large part for illustrative purposes. It is my hope that with future research, accountants will someday be able to compute fuller cost estimates with a much higher degree of certainty and general acceptance. Today, the methodologies proposed in this text are the first tentative steps in a long journey; at this time there are no generally accepted approaches, from a corporate accounting perspective. Chapters 13 and 14 are both original, reflecting my aspirations for where accounting could go in the coming decade.

My hope is that readers will attain an appreciation of the potential of environmental accounting and the attitudes that will be required for this emerging discipline to achieve this full potential. This book is intended to be a depiction of how accounting could help today's corporations become sustainable.

Preface

I am deeply indebted to the United Nations Conference on Trade and Development for funding the research that resulted in the model environmental accounts that are the focal point of this book. The case study presented is based on these model accounts but contains modifications developed by the author after the completion of the contract with the United Nations. Special recognition must go to the project leader, Lorraine Ruffing, whose enthusiasm kept the project moving through the shoals of bureaucracy. I am also very grateful to the Office of the Auditor General of Canada for allowing me to take the leave from work as a legislative auditor that enabled me to complete the research.

Accounting for sustainable development, as with any open-ended research project, was filled with individual encounters that in their own way shaped the final product. I am deeply indebted to member industries of the Canadian Pulp and Paper Association that participated in this project. Participating companies provided honesty, expertise in forestry management, and a deeper appreciation of the challenges of managing the diverse interests of stakeholder groups. Participating companies provided experts in cost accounting, silviculture, environmental management, and marketing without which this book would have never been possible. I would also like to acknowledge the support and loyal friendship of my colleague on this project, Gord Clifford. Many thanks to Slvyie Lepage who helped manage the typing of an overstuffed manuscript.

I would like to acknowledge the invaluable assistance provided by experts who kindly volunteered to review drafts of the book. Their attention to matters of fact and interpretation was critical, given the multidisciplinary nature of the book. Rodney Anderson, FCA, helped crystallize the sections dealing with what was wrong with traditional accounting. His insights and creativity helped shape the final product. Dr. Ole Hendrickson from Forestry

Canada helped me get the ecology down. Dr. Crandall Benson from the School of Forestry at Lakehead University helped me ensure that the sections dealing with forestry management were accurate. The carefully thought out suggestions of the reviewers were incorporated in the final draft. Dr. Eamonn Walsh of the Leonard N. Stern School of Business, New York University, provided invaluable help, as well as encouragement and insightful comments on draft manuscripts. I am indebted to Anthony Cassils and David Runnalls, formerly with the Institute for Research on Public Policy, for their help in understanding the origins of the concept of sustainable development.

Throughout the process, my family was constant in their support and interest. As always, my parents' and my sister's interest and my mother's probing questions helped focus some of the writing. From my parents I learned how to research a topic, as well as how to take the germ of an idea and through disciplined effort develop it to its fullest potential. Special thanks go to Marcy Weiner who patiently walked me through the arduous process of getting a book published. As I neared the end of the task, the support of family and, most important, my wife made the difference between a finished manuscript and an unfulfilled dream.

Introduction

Accounting is at least 5,000 years old, depending on when a scribbled clay tablet became an artifact — a record of what one merchant owed to his neighbor in the next stall in the marketplace. Throughout this long history, the focus of accounting has been wealth. Wealth is the accumulation of goods beyond immediate human needs. In the history of accounting for wealth, there have been three epochs.

In the period from 4000 B.C. to A.D. 1300, the record keeping aspect of accounting was dominant. Accumulation of commercial wealth required some form of control and notation. For this, accounting for individual transactions was essential. During the second epoch, from 1300 to about 1850, accounting had to adapt to the change in scale and qualitative nature of commercial enterprise. With far-flung trading empires, larger commercial ventures, and growing cadres of owners, the need for adequate record keeping grew. This second epoch can be characterized as one of systemized bookkeeping where accountants learned to deal with a much larger volume of transactions. Accountants had to develop conventions for summarizing this growing mass of data into reporting formats comprehendible to the merchant class.

The last epoch, the Age of Profits, was spurred on by the Industrial Revolution. During this period accountants saw the emergence of financial reporting as the key communications document between investors, creditors, the emerging managerial class, and others divorced from internal management but entitled to an accounting for the use of corporate funds and progress. The separation of ownership from management, with the birth of the joint stock company, created a greater need for business communications that accounting had to serve.

During these 5,000 years, there have been some common threads. Accounting values what society values. As these values change over time, accounting changes. During the beginning of the third epoch, the thought of accruing liabilities for health care, severance pay, or pensions was inconceivable; today such accruals spiral into the billions of dollars. Throughout this history, the place of commercial enterprise, its role in society, its rights and obligations have evolved. During the medieval period, the Church forbade usury, the place of commerce was circumscribed. In the transition between the medieval period and the Industrial Revolution, the role and place of a strong new business class changed significantly. From the Industrial Revolution to today, the role of business has again changed dramatically.

The interpretation of basic accounting tenets has evolved to respond to the changing accountability contract between business and society. In response to these changes, the definition of assets, those things a business owns, and liabilities, those amounts it owes, have continued to expand in their scope and breadth. During this period there was a shift from a focus on the balance sheet (wealth accumulation) to a focus on the income statement (earnings power). It would be fair to say that in the last hundred years the definition of asset and a liability has probably changed more profoundly than in the previous 4,900 years. Some argue that this came about because reporting companies wanted earnings per share to move in smooth trend lines, rather than "bumps." Today, assets include goodwill, deferred expenses, intellectual property, and other intangibles such as patents and licenses.

What is unique about the present is that the rate of change in society's values and the accountability contract between business and society have continued to accelerate. Accounting is scrambling to develop new valuation techniques to correspond to newly emerging social values, for values drive valuation. This suggests that accounting is on the verge of a transformation as profound as the one that occurred between the second and third epochs, a transformation that could cause accountants to rethink 5,000 years of conventions.

Accounting will have to respond to new values that have emerged the postwar period. The first such value is the need to recognize the limits to the tools, or the technology, of the industrial era. The next value is that natural resources and the natural habitat that supports them must be conserved. Human consumption has escalated exponentially, and humans are now forced to recognize the limits and complexities of the land organism that is the source of these natural resources. As so well articulated by Aldo Leopold in *A Sand County Almanac,* "The outstanding scientific discovery of the twentieth century is not television, or radio, but rather the complexity of the land organism. Only those who know the most about it can appreciate how little is known about it."

The third emerging value is that ownership is much more diffused than it was in the previous epoch. Title to land no longer provides exclusive, unfettered rights. The last concept is that of place, a sense of order, connectedness. This current epoch of accounting, which could be characterized as the

Age of Accounting for Other Values, will need to respond to the challenge of reflecting "nonbusiness values" (i.e., values other than making money).

There is no doubt that the ancient profession of accounting will adapt to the Age of Other Values. Its 5,000-year track record of survival and gradual adaptation suggests a resiliency and potential for adaptation. In the past three epochs of its history, however, adaptation and change were leisurely. Accountants muddled along in relative obscurity, behaving as most fellow members of their species. They reacted to the needs of their job, focusing on their own short-term requirements.

During the conversion from a postmedieval world to the new age of industry, exploration, exploitation, and plunder, certain major costs were never booked — species annihilated, indigenous peoples slaughtered, the human misery of slavery. Society recorded human chattel as assets of the plantation. Accurate record keeping was an integral part of the slave trade, branding irons, ownership records, rights to title were essential. In short, accounting, like any profession, is driven by prevailing social values.

Today, at this unique hinge of history between the Age of Profits and the Age of Other Values, accounting, if left to its own devices, would probably follow its passive, undemonstrative mode of adaptation. In five or six generations, it might be a very different beast. Yet, alas, independent assessments of the well-being of the fragile, small blue dot in a vast universe suggest that profound change must occur in less than half a generation. The swelling global population, the exponential growth in both the scale of production and the environmental impact of the technology employed, the environmental debt built up during World War II and the postwar period suggest that tomorrow was yesterday.

For the first time in accounting's sleepy history, there is a growing recognition among accountants and nonaccountants alike that accounting, that value-free, balanced system of double entries may be sending dangerously incomplete signals to business, to consumers, to regulators, and to bankers. The imperative to reconsider 5,000 years of accounting conventions is not a passing fad. What is fundamentally different today is that human enterprise and population have expanded to the point where they have bumped up against the limits of a finite planet.

The situation today is perhaps analogous to a protracted transpolar flight. The plane and its crew have now passed the halfway point, the point of no return. A sighting of a well-known peak confirms that the inertial navigational system is sending the wrong signals. Every minute of flying time, the plane is drifting farther off course. Urgently, the navigator tries to recalibrate the system, then override the system, resorting to more primitive navigational aids. The clock is ticking; every minute of flight time the plane's huge fan-jets consume hundreds of pounds of fuel. A leisurely search for true north is no longer an option.

Chapter 1

Charting a Middle Course

AN INDUSTRY WORRIED ABOUT ITS SUSTAINABILITY

The year 1991 was an awful year for Canada's forest industry. It was an industry cut down by red ink. Canadian forest companies had collectively lost $2.5 billion. Five plants had closed. Canada's exports had plummeted. The price of softwood pulp, the industry's main export, had fallen dramatically. In newsprint, North America had a tremendous overcapacity as a lingering recession dampened demand, forcing some prices down by as much as 40 percent. The push for more recycled content in newsprint had forced companies to consider the idea of building new mills far from Canada's northern forests, in the "urban forests" of large recycling depots near large cities.

On top of that, there has been one of the biggest bloodlettings in corporate history. Jack Carruthers was a survivor. He had been with Blackmore and Price, a medium-sized forestry management company, for 25 years; but many of the other senior managers of the forest industry were out, replaced by new types who talked about sustainable development and stakeholder management (see Chapter 5).

THE TWIN SOLITUDES OF BUSINESS AND WILDERNESS

Jack could deal with the red ink. There had been booms and busts for as long as there had been a forest industry in Canada. It was the debate about Caramanah Valley, Clayquot Sound, South Moresby, and Red Squirrel Road, with the bitter, sometimes violent confrontations between environmental activists and loggers that was hard to manage. And every time the environmental activists were on the news, Neil Thompson, from the Coalition for a Sustainable Tomorrow, was there, talking about clear-cutting, the devastation of the wilderness, the greed of the logging companies, and how the loggers couldn't see the forest for the trees.

When Jack was first asked to sit in the New Round Table group he was initially reluctant to be in the same room as Neil, talking face to face with one of his worst critics. The objective of the New Round Table was precisely that — to put industry and environmental activists in the same room and encourage a productive dialogue.

The moderator was supposed to arbitrate. After a few beers, Jack had let Neil have it. "Damn it Neil, what the hell do you expect of me and my company. We're struggling like hell to make money, to keep 2,500 people at work and you just won't get off my back. Every damn month it's a new demand. First it was to plant trees. We planted 35 million trees. Then you start on the perils of mono-culture. Then it was biodiversity. And now you're into genetic diversity. I don't know how the hell I can make any money, keep my people at work, and meet all your demands."

As the night wore on, Neil shot back, "You really don't give a damn about the forest. You don't give a damn about anything other than quarterly earnings. The health of the forest is a totally foreign concept. You've got this fixation that if you plant one tree for every tree you harvest, you are keeping the forest intact. You don't understand the forest is a living, breathing organism, a web of life with an infinite value, something that took ten thousand years to create — and you're chopping it down in a decade or two."

The moderator, a university professor, intervened. He focused their discussion on the Brundtland Commission Report, *Our Common Future,* which had popularized the term *sustainable development.* He explained that in his view, sustainable development was a marriage between business and the environment that allowed business to make a reasonable return *and* ensure that natural resources were preserved for future generations. Neil, Jack, and the moderator all agreed that while they put in long hours at work or research, they did it all for their children. That was their real bottom line.

In a fit of passion, Jack thumped the table and added, "I practice sustainable development. It's a black and white issue that I don't need to debate for three days with a bunch of tree huggers and academics. I'm leaving the next generation as well off as we are when it comes to forest wealth."

"Let me see if you really practice sustainable development," Neil challenged. "What are you doing about old growth stands, natural regeneration, the use of herbicides and smaller clear-cuts? Damn it, you are not practicing sustainable development. You have to reduce the size of your clear-cuts by a third. What are you doing about moose habitat and the nesting areas for blue herons and ospreys? When are you going to switch to chlorine-free paper and stop dumping toxins into the streams?"

Jack couldn't take it any more. "What are you doing, Neil, to create 2,500 jobs, to keep a whole community in Northern Ontario off the dole? You talk about the size of clear-cuts, about cutting one tree per acre. You're living in a dream-world."

At the next meeting they agreed to put the rhetoric aside. What they needed was more information. They needed a concrete definition of what sustainable development meant for the 6,500 square miles of forest under Jack's stewardship. Neil wanted Jack to define exactly what he was accountable for, what the forestry management options were, and when he would move from the "business-as-usual" mode to the sustainable development option. Jack wanted to discuss how much it was going to cost and who was going to pay for the conversion.

Soon after his first bout with Neil, Jack enlisted the help of his corporate controller, Walker Stone. "Walker, of course I would never admit it to Neil, but maybe we are going to have to change course, move ahead of the regulators to find alternatives to the use of herbicides and of chlorine gas in our pulp operations. I want to explore changing the way we do business. But I'm going to steer a middle course between business as usual and investing in the latest environmental flavor of the month. And I'm going to need you, Walker, to help me figure how much it is going to cost to change course."

According to Walker, "Traditional accounting is limited when it comes to measuring natural wealth. Accountants measure assets, earnings, one year behind the times. You know, jet pilots don't use rearview mirrors. If we want to account for the environment, we have to look forward. Accountants need to develop new ways to account for natural resources."

This was not good enough for Jack, "Walker, we've worked together for years. I know how creative you can be when it comes to year end. Expand accounting beyond these limitations. Reinvent it if you have to, but get me those numbers" (see Chapter 2).

Walker searched the literature and found that some forestry-management companies were providing shareholders with increased environmental disclosure in corporate state-of-the-environment reports. Such reports talked about sustainability of operations, the number of trees replanted, and compliance with municipal or provincial effluent regulations. Walker pointed out, "State-of-the-environment reports won't tell you whether a company is depleting natural capital instead of living off the interest, respecting ecological limits" (see Chapter 3).

Walker read *Our Common Future,* the Brundtland Commission Report that had popularized the term sustainable development. He gave excerpts to Jack to read. According to Jack, "The 'B' book reads like Karl Marx when it talks about poverty, wilderness, sharing the wealth! There's no bloody way I can run a business and do all that. It's impossible!" (See Chapter 4.)

"Walker, I want to be seen as a sustainable forest company that is competent and thrifty in the way it transforms forest wealth into wood and paper products. I want people to see us as a company that manages the waste it generates, measures its footprint on the environment, and manages its socio-economic impact on the community and the region. We contribute jobs, we contribute to our workers' education and training."

THE ESSENCE OF ACCOUNTING FOR
SUSTAINABLE DEVELOPMENT

Jack and Walker tried to interpret *Our Common Future*. According to Jack, "Managing for sustainable development means operating our business to meet the expectations of this generation and the next. And looking at my kids, God only knows what they'll expect!" Jack and Walker realized that to meet the demands of Neil and his ilk they had to address five fundamental questions:

1. *Who are the stakeholders?* Who benefits from the forest, and what is our corporation's accountability to them for sustaining the business *and* the forest?
2. *What is our accountability contract?* What is the company "contract" for maintaining the living forest that Neil had talked about, including the diversity of natural capital and habitat preservation? And what about the people—the jobs of loggers and the return to shareholders?
3. *What are the limits?* What are the social and ecological limits that define business's tradeoff options about the scale and technology of development?
4. *What are our options?* What kinds of tradeoff options do we have when it comes to balancing business limits and biological limits; how much will they cost and who is going to pay for them?
5. *What are the costs of doing nothing?* What are the potential costs of proceeding with a business-as-usual strategy?

Walker and Jack began to realize that the honeymoon had ended at the Earth Summit in Rio and that there was a big difference between talking about sustainable development and living it. "It's like the difference between love and marriage. After a few years of marriage, you get down to who's going to take out the garbage or pick up the kids, and there's heat over who leaves the toothpaste uncapped."

MANAGEMENT'S OPTIONS ARE TO DENY, CONFRONT,
OR WORK WITH STAKEHOLDERS

Jack and Walker realized that information was the currency necessary to bridge the gap in understanding between "the tree cutters and the tree huggers"; between the world of business and the world of nature. They recognized they could deny Neil's demands for a sustainable corporation or they could try to manage his request. Neil was trying to represent "invisible" stakeholders such as future generations, other species, and third-world nations (see Chapter 6).

Walker said, "I'm not sure what the activists mean by a sustainable corporation, but in my mind a sustainable corporation is simply one that follows enlightened self-interest. Sustainable development, in today's world, is just another term for managing what's best for us in the long haul." Walker recognized that to do the kind of accounting that would give Jack the information he needed to chart a middle course he would be required both to develop some new concepts and to rework some old concepts, such as the asset-maintenance concept. Then he would need to expand the definition of assets to include this natural capital that Neil kept talking about. His starting point was a model recently developed by the United Nations. Walker used the basic U.N. model for accounting for sustainable development, field testing it, and tailoring it to his company's unique circumstances.

NATURAL CAPITAL IS THE PRINCIPAL:
THE TREES ARE THE INTEREST

The starting point for Walker's accounting was the forest the company harvested. Walker recognized both the similarities and the profound differences between accounting for natural capital, such as a living forest, and accounting for a fixed asset, such as the corporate jet. "We practice regular, scheduled preventive maintenance to maximize its useful life to the corporation. We practice preventive maintenance with the forest because if there is a failure in the life of a northern boreal forest we might have to wait 10,000 years for a new one, given its complexity and the eons required to create fertile soil out of the northern shield!" The approach Walker took to valuing a forest is the approach he took when he bought life insurance. Walker did not know what his life was worth, but he did know how much it would cost to give his family economic security if something happened to him. He applied these basic concepts to valuing intangibles—nontimber values such as biodiversity. He started by calculating the maintenance and remediation costs required to maintain soil fertility. The last step would be to generate the "insurance cost" associated with higher-risk forest development options (see Chapter 8).

WHAT'S THE COMMERCIAL VALUE OF
THE FOREST IN 60 YEARS?

Walker knew that during the recession there would be extreme pressure to cut back on silvicultural investments such as tree planting. The change in direction Jack was talking about could require an incremental investment of up to $20 million a year. The company would find it necessary to compete for funds with other subsidiaries in real estate and mining. Walker knew that his challenge would be to prepare a submission that presented the costs of changing course, as well as the risks of steaming ahead in the business-as-usual mode. He would also need to develop some way to measure the benefits of following enlightened self-interest, as well as the quest for smooth earnings in the first quarter.

Using basic present-value techniques, Walker projected anticipated levels of harvesting and regeneration over the next 60 years, valuing stands of new growth over time. His analysis demonstrated the economic benefits of sustained-yield harvesting. Increasing the annual investment in silviculture would significantly increase the commercial value of the forest in 60 years. Walker calculated that the commercial value of the forest was $40 million and the value of the ecosystem itself was at least $530 million. In 60 years, Walker estimated, the total value of the forest would approach $3 billion (see Chapters 9 and 11). Walker developed some risk management principles for natural capital. They were built on the Superfund principle that in the long run the deepest pocket pays, even if the surviving company dumped only a small percentage of the toxins in a landfill site 50 years ago. Walker developed some "fuzzy" numbers for the board to illustrate the potential future costs of today's business-as-usual mode.

THE BOARD NEEDS TO KNOW WHY
BUSINESS AS USUAL IS NO LONGER AN OPTION

Walker prepared a stewardship report for the board. The condensed stewardship accounts presented in Table 1.1 summarized his analysis of the fuller costs and benefits of practicing sustainable development. This report contained the fuller costs of producing lumber and paper, costs that included a rough estimate of the potential damage to the forest ecosystem upon which the company was economically dependent (see Chapter 12).

The information in these stewardship accounts could be used to demonstrate to Neil, to consumers, and to shareholders the cost implications of different environmental options. Instead of taking a confrontational stance with environmental activists, Jack would now have the information to say, "We're all environmentalists, Neil. The issue is who's going to pay for the environment?" Jack could now outline for Neil what it would cost to withdraw productive forest, such as heritage stands of red and white pine, from production. Jack could also outline the costs of lower-impact development that involved smaller clear-cuts, natural rather than artificial regeneration, greater preservation of fish habitat, more extensive wildlife corridors for moose, more extensive landscape management that included aesthetics and preservation of heritage sites, and the total elimination of herbicides (see Chapter 9).

Table 1.1
Blackmore and Price Forest Products Ltd.: Condensed Stewardship Accounts

Option 1 Timber Is Primary Consideration	Option 2 Enhanced Nonwood Values		Option 3 Environment Is Equal: Nonwood Values Are of Equal Consideration	
Full compliance with all guidelines established by the Ministry of Natural Resources.	Full compliance plus selective response to public concerns.		The volume of production, the technology employed are to be determined by ecological rather than economic criteria.	
Sustained economic yield with regeneration equal to harvest with acceptance of a risk that guidelines may not be ecologically sustainable in the long run.	Commitment to sustained economic yield. Commitment to explore public concerns about the forest's ecological sustainability and accommodation of the long–term needs of all forest users.		Emulation of natural forest processes of disturbance, regeneration and succession. The sustainable use of the forest means sustainable use of the tree species and ecosystems found there not simply replacing one felled tree with another.	
	Price Increases		**Price Increases**	
Incremental price increases to offset increased production costs:	**Pulp**	**Lumber**	**Pulp**	**Lumber**
Silvicultural enhancements	4.5%	3%	11.0%	9%
Zero–impact pulp mill	2.5%	N/A	2.5%	N/A
	7.0%		13.5%	

Rate of Return on Environmental Investments (ROI)

	Range of Sustainability of Forestry Operations		
Levels of Pulp Mill Sustainability	Timber Is Primary Consideration (Option 1)	Enhanced Nonwood Values (Option 2)	Environment Is Equal (Option 3)
Below Average Pulp Mill	27% (23.7%) ROI	24.4% (23.0%) ROI	22.2% (21.4%) ROI
Average Pulp Mill	22.7% (19.7%) ROI	20.9% (19.9%) ROI	18.9% (18.2%) ROI
	Blackmore and Price (Now)		
Industry leader	18.4% (15.8%) ROI	17.3% (16.1 %) ROI	15.6% (14.8%) ROI

In North America and Germany, environmental activists had been pushing for chlorine-free paper. Walker included an analysis of what it would cost to move to a zero-impact pulp mill, a mill that did not discharge persistent toxins into the rivers. The analysis looked at the price implications. He computed the following rates of returns on investments primarily made to enhance and protect the environment. These percentages reflected projected long-term rates of return on capital employed. When the project team recomputed these rates of return on investment, using the fuller costs that reflected the higher-risk costs of the business-as-usual option, the gap between Option 1 and Option 2 narrowed to almost 1 percent (see Chapter 10).

As they neared the end of the project, Jack said to Walker, "We started this project in part because of the prodding of Neil. But you know, the information you generated on the rate of return on a zero-impact mill was new to me. It showed me I was in for a jolt on return of investment if I changed course too fast. But it also told me something else, something that I need to tell the board—the potential costs of not changing the way we do business. It helps to explain why I must change course, move toward creating a sustainable corporation."

Now that the project was over, Jack mused, "Walker demonstrated that he could expand the definitions of assets to extend almost two generations into the future. His estimates of the benefits of enlightened self-interest were necessarily imprecise, but they conveyed a rough order of magnitude to the board. To have included nothing, however fuzzy the numbers, would have been more misleading.

"I know that Walker was thinking about the relationship between accounting and the environment, long before I roped him into this project. I think those images of the *Exxon Valdez* leaking millions of gallons of crude oil into the pristine waters off Alaska added a sense of urgency and highlighted the limitations of traditional accounting when it comes to accounting for the environment" (see Chapter 2).

"Now Walker tells me he is convinced that the basic conventions, principles, and underlying concepts of accounting are sound and can be extended to encompass accounting for natural capital. Accountants can provide a bridge between business and other stakeholders, such as environmental activists, as accounting looks further into the future and takes a much broader view in defining assets."

Chapter 2

The Limitations of Traditional Accounting

STATEMENTS OUT OF BALANCE

Black Oil, Red Ink

Sometime between 12:08 A.M. and 12:14 A.M. on March 24, 1989, the *Exxon Valdez* struck a reef in Alaska's Prince William Sound and began leaking 11 million gallons of crude oil into the cold, pristine waters. Thousands of miles away, at Exxon's corporate headquarters, a nightmare began taking shape: How to stem the leak? Who was going to talk to the press? How soon could a cleanup crew be assembled? What sort of money were we talking about? Eventually, the corporation would spend an unprecedented amount of money trying to mop up the damage — setting, in turn, a major accounting precedent.

It was not the first major oil spill — witness the Ashland Oil Inc. spill in the Mississippi River in 1988. But Ashland's $400-million insurance policy covered the cleanup costs. Exxon's senior financial officers must have realized soon after the *Valdez* cleanup went into operation (complete with the U.S. Coast Guard and a cast of thousands) that its insurance wouldn't cover the estimated billion-dollar cleanup cost. Clearly, even for a company the size of Exxon, this was going to be more than an "unusual" item, an extraordinary expense.

Although in several respects this spill was unique (its size, the publicity it generated, and the degree of responsibility the corporation accepted), environmentally sensitive transactions are not rare. The question of settlements to victims of large-scale pollution had already arisen in Japanese fishing villages hit by mercury poisoning and, more recently, in the Union Carbide chemical accident in Bhopal, India. Most industries in the petrochemical field and some in other sectors have already come face to face with escalating public expectations about environmental protection.

Exxon must have known that to retain its place at the gas pumps of North America it had no alternative but to respond immediately and comprehensively to the spill. But what alternatives do accountants have when it comes to accounting for something like the *Valdez* oil spill? How can they account for environmentally sensitive transactions?

After the spill, Exxon's accountants might have wondered whether they had overlooked an unrecorded liability for all the years oil was being pumped out of Valdez, Alaska. It is unlikely that the "implicit" social contract between Exxon and the residents of Prince William Sound was based on the assumption that a major environmental accident was probable. At most, this contract assumed that Exxon would take responsibility for cleaning up *if,* not *when,* this happened. Otherwise, a regular accounting accrual would have been made. Such accruals are common in the mining industry, where a company knows it will be required to restore the land once a mine is finally shut down.

But Exxon's accountants must have known that every shipment of North Shore crude carried with it an associated risk and potential liability. In 1989, the risk became reality and the potential liability a real cost — a net cost of $850 million. For the 1989 financial statements, they found themselves stuck with a poor solution that some might say allowed for no real matching of past profits and deferred costs.[1]

In short, the images of the thick gooey black oil spreading across the fiords and inlets of Alaska were inescapable and disturbing at many levels. There was no accounting for the *Exxon Valdez* by any definition of accounting. Investors concerned about black ink faced a lot of red ink.

Walker and thousands of other accountants found these images disturbing. From an accounting perspective, Walker recognized that the spill was a classic example of how traditional accounting had real difficulty dealing with what he called "gigantic low-probability risks." He recognized that these risks were inherently difficult to account for. He wondered whether accountants could ever develop an approach to measure the "Exxon Expectation" (the product of risk times magnitude or, more rigorously, the sum of all products of the probabilities of alternative outcomes times their associated magnitudes). In Walker's view this was like trying to account for an "act of God." Yet in the litigious North American culture there almost seemed to be a presumption that if something unexpected happens and there was another party in proximity that could be sued, that party would be liable. Walker had to wonder about the limits to this chain of liability.

Clearly there were inherent risks in shipping millions of gallons of oil. When single-hulled ships slip through passages where sharp jagged rocks may at times be only a few feet from a thin layer of steel, a thin membrane between millions of gallons of thick oil and an ocean of pristine water, clearly there is a risk. To account properly for the inherent risks of transporting oil via a marine medium, accountants would need to take a long-term view over a 15- or 20-year time span. A rate of incidence would need to be predicted and anticipated. Accountants could assign costs for these inherent risks and account for them over a 15-year period, apportioning the costs associated with these risks to each year's financial results. The point is they don't.

If according to statistical odds an unfavorable occurrence such as a spill is likely to occur once every 15 or 20 years on average, then logically accountants should accrue for it over the 30-year risk period. What if the odds were once in 60 years but the magnitude at risk was twice as much? What if the risk was once in 300 years but the magnitude of the risk was tenfold? Intuitively, there was some notional threshold of remoteness of risk beyond which it made no sense to accrue, even though the statistician's theoretical expectation might be roughly the same. To Walker, however, the risks associated with shipping oil were not in this category of extreme remoteness. Another risk associated with the cost of doing business was the risk that regulations would be tighter 20 or 40 years from now and would be applied retroactively to the practices of today. This type of risk was illustrated by the lessons of Love—the story of the Love Canal.

ENVIRONMENTAL OBLIGATIONS
ARE DIFFICULT TO ACCOUNT FOR

Lessons of the Love Canal

Throughout World War II and into the early 1950s, the Hooker Chemical Company buried thousands of drums containing chemical waste—mainly dioxins—in a landfill site by the Love Canal in upper New York State. Some 25 years later, the drums had corroded, and toxic gases were rising to the surface. It was a nightmare, not only for the residents of the housing project that had been built on the site but also for the Occidental Chemical Corporation which had taken over Hooker in the late 1960s.

Many of Occidental's senior managers were probably war veterans, raised in an era and business culture that held productivity and prosperity next to godliness. Their obligation to society was to produce and do it profitably. There was no clause that even mentioned the environment.

In the 1980s, however, largely in reaction to Love Canal and other disasters, the U.S. courts began to question the very premise of the contract. For their part, Occidental's lawyers said the hazards had always been greatly exaggerated. Their main defense, though, was that back in the 1940s and 1950s Hooker's disposal techniques were "state of the art." Accordingly, it would be wrong to measure the company's actions then by what is now known about toxic chemicals. As Thomas Truitt, Occidental's chief lawyer, put it, "You cannot be judging the conduct of people 40 years ago by today's standards, especially when half of them are gone and they can't explain anything."

Walker and other accountants recognized that judges, juries, legislators, and the general public *are* now doing just that — judging the past by today's standards. In fact, for more than a decade now, the courts have been hearing an ever-increasing number of environmental lawsuits and defining an entirely new contract between business and society. A new concept of corporate accountability is emerging, one that is being updated and revised daily by new precedents. It is a worldwide phenomenon, and its magnitude would be difficult to exaggerate. The Environmental Protection Agency initially identified some 27,000 hazardous waste sites, with an estimated average cleanup cost of $25 million each, or a total possible cost of $675 billion. In more recent times, some accountants have estimated these liabilities as high as $7 trillion. In Western Europe, the cleanup bill is expected to be at least $65 billion. From Eastern Europe, accountants are now getting reports of major environmental crises there that will also cost billions to remedy.

In all, the world is now probably facing a multitrillion-dollar environmental obligation for which society is trying to sort out responsibility, trying to determine who's going to pay for what. One of the key problems here is that the accountants of the world do not yet really know how to account for cleanup costs and the related liabilities in a reasonable way.[2]

Contingent Costs or Hidden Costs? To a large extent, thinking the unthinkable means coming to terms with a central premise of the new social contract that is emerging. That is, there is now a new class of invisible "stakeholders," including people yet unborn, who can exercise common property rights in a company without ever investing a dime in it. This has quite accurately been described as an accounting nightmare. The only way out of it is to rethink current definitions of asset and liability that have been drummed into accountants in business schools and presented in accounting texts.

Consider the Hooker example. In 1940, the company bought the steel drums that later corroded from a local supplier. The purchase was accounted for in monetary terms, was conducted according to a well-defined contractual relationship, and all the parties to the transaction were clearly identifiable. The same applied in the purchase of the landfill site, which was recorded as an asset, at historical cost.

Ross M. Skinner, in his *Accounting Standards in Evolution* defines an asset as "a potential future benefit obtainable by a particular entity resulting from past transactions or events," which is fine for describing steel drums and such. Under this traditional definition, however, common-use property (that is, such "natural capital" as air, lakes, and so forth; and in this particular case, the sustainable, productive capability of the land where Hooker dumped its waste) would not be recorded. This occurs because the definition does not encompass future economic benefit obtainable by someone outside the particular entity.[3]

The same problem arises in our traditional definition of a liability. As Ross Skinner puts it, "A liability is a potential requirement on the part of the entity to sacrifice economic resources in future because of past transactions or events." Again, there is an inequity in that a future economic sacrifice by someone outside the entity will not be recognized.

Under the current accounting definition, only explicit contractual obligations to shareholders, suppliers, and so on can be recorded as liabilities. But, because there is no transaction with future generations, the potential liability of dumping toxic wastes at a landfill site cannot be recognized at the time of dumping. The real nexus of the problem becomes evident when we consider definitions that flow from our basic definitions of assets and liabilities. An example of this is equity, which Skinner defines as "the residual interest in the assets of an entity that remains after deducting the amounts of its liabilities."

The problem here is a failure to recognize the natural capital contributed by society in the form of free goods such as air, water, and other prerequisites for industrial activity, which are lent to businesses for use rather than consumption. This is the basis of the judgments the courts are now handing down. As a result, Occidental may face a quarter-billion-dollar liability to homeowners and the other stakeholders who suffered as a result of the Love Canal contamination. That is, the courts may establish that these hitherto "invisible" stakeholders had an interest in Hooker's operations, even though it went unrecognized during the 1940s and 1950s.

The unfortunate fact is that, as accountants enter the mid-1990s, such interests are to all intents and purposes *still* largely unrecognized by accountants. At present, the key pronouncements governing the accounting for hazardous waste and similar items are the rules for contingent liabilities, and the limitations of these are obvious to anyone who cares to look at Occidental Petroleum's consolidated financial statements. For instance, in the statements for 1989, disclosure of contingent liabilities associated with the Love Canal cleanup rates only about half a page. There is no real disclosure of the estimated loss or range of losses. The statements are largely silent on whether any accruals have been booked and even on whether an estimate of loss is possible. This is but one of many possible examples of the great need to find a better way to account for the trillion-dollar Superfund environmental obligation. Regulators such as the Securities and Exchange Commission and institutional and other investors are concerned because only a relatively small fraction of this multitrillion-dollar obligation is reported in the financial statements of publicly traded companies.

As illustrated in Figure 2.1, environmental obligations are inherently difficult to account for under any accounting rules. They take a very long time to settle, involve a high degree of interdependence with other users of com-

Figure 2.1
The Difficulties of Accounting for Environmental Obligations

	Traditional Obligations	Environmental Obligations
Time span involved	• Relatively well defined, short to medium term	• Ill–defined, more long term (intergenerational)
Interdependence	• "Self–contained" liability	• High degree of interdependence
Ease of estimation	• Relatively easy to estimate	• Inherently difficult to estimate
Stewardship concept	• Traditional private property, shareholder stewardship concept	• Common property, stakeholder stewardship concept
Contractual basis	• "Explicit" contract between known transacting parties	• Implicit social contract with unknown, "invisible" parties
Valuation basis	• Fair–market transaction values	• Court–arbitrated values
Philosophy	• Economic orientation • Anthropocentric (centred on human beings)	• Recognition of noneconomic impact on other habitats • Multi species orientation
Entity	• Entity specific	• Ecosystem specific

mon-use property, entail a great deal of uncertainty, and require complex estimations where there is no accepted basis of valuation. However, are they so much more difficult to account for than pension liabilities based on complex actuarial calculations?

In Walker's mind, they were not. In his experience there was a fairly wide spectrum of long-term, undefined liabilities, such as warranty obligations, that presented many of the same difficulties as environmental obligations. There appeared to be a conceptual weak spot in the traditional accounting model posed by long-term, ill-defined risks with lower probabilities of occurrence but high dollar figures associated with their occurrence. In the past, the cases where this defect surfaced were relatively few — until trillion-dollar environmental obligations came along. Now this long-standing defect had become more serious.

Another accounting issue was related to the "risk defect." That was the matter of the going-concern assumption. A reporting company is assumed to be a viable, robust business unless there is persuasive evidence to the contrary. In that case the assets would have to be written down to reflect realization values, rather than the amounts the company originally paid for them (their historical costs). Walker felt that the either-or, black-or-white nature of the application of the concept was another defect in the traditional accounting model. In his view this was one of the contributing factors that inhibited both accountants and auditors from providing an early warning of the savings and loan failures. This defect would also hamper accounting for economic and environmental sustainability.

The financial press has been full of examples that illustrate the limitations of traditional accounting when it comes to giving investors a preview of coming attractions. In recent years, the most glaring example was that of IBM. Few readers of the annual financial statements of Big Blue were provided with any early warnings of the massive downsizing and restructuring that would become the norm. How may readers of the annual report of General Motors during the boom years had any inkling of the pain and billion-dollar losses that lay around the corner?

In Walker's view the either-or nature of the going-concern assumption appeared defective. It was not a matter of either deciding a company was continuing business as usual with assets valued at historical cost, or reckoning a company was close to bankruptcy. Rather, there were a great many in-between situations that a robust accounting model should deal with. Just because a company was a going concern today, it would not be exempt from future risks that could be reflected in the accounts.

For Walker, the common thread in these cases was the defects in the traditional accounting model when it came to going-concern risks and low-probability–high-magnitude risks. What the *Exxon Valdez,* Love Canal, and the going-concern assumption had in common were hundred-million-dollar surprises for which shareholders and management as well received little in the way of an early warning, a preview of coming attractions. To begin to address these defects, accountants should start with the limitations in the traditional accounting model.

SIX LIMITATIONS IN ACCOUNTING

Traditional financial accounting as currently practiced suffers from six limitations when it comes to accounting for profit and accounting for the environment.

- *First,* accounting is restricted to dealing with legislated social costs, such as environmental fines, a company must pay. Traditional accounting rules do not account for the full costs of production, including natural capital such as air, water, or fertile land because society has not legislated that it should.
- *Second,* traditional accounting rules record the costs of environmental investments in the costs of production, but there is no recognition of their less tangible benefits. Without "putting-it-right" accruals (i.e., accruals to decommission a mine), current application of the rules can penalize rather than encourage the environmentally responsible corporation.
- *Third,* accounting has not yet dealt with the notion of inherent limits to economic activity.

- *Fourth,* environmental concerns require a long-term view. Accounting's definition of an asset is forward looking, but is it sufficiently forward looking?

- *Fifth,* the traditional accounting entity is the firm. To properly account for air and water, the entity would have to be the firm in the context of the natural capital upon which it is economically dependent but may not own in the conventional sense of private property.

- *Sixth,* and perhaps most important, accountants see both profit and all the thorny equity questions implicit in profit as a return on risk. The critical question is whether going-concern and low-occurrence–high-magnitude risks should be recognized before the traditional residual profit is calculated.

In reviewing these limitations upon and opportunities to expand accounting's intellectual underpinnings, Walker reflected on the origins of accounting.

Medieval Roots

Single-entry accounting evolved from simple notations on clay or stone tablets, recording goods traded and debts owed — a record of tangible transactions. Readers see these clay tablets when they go to the museums in London, Paris, Cairo, Toronto, and other large cities. These stone tablets kept track of who owes what to whom.

During the medieval period, commercial activity became more extensive and complex. Double-entry accounting, born in the medieval era, addressed this complexity. A basic principle was one of offsetting financial entries, matching an acquired asset against an asset reduction or incurred liability. Double entry worked well in the ordered, contractual world of the middle ages. A world with a social contract between the lord of the manor and the serfs and between the merchants and the church was fairly well established and static. Then came the Renaissance, the Age of Exploration of the New World, and the Industrial Revolution and the Age of Profits. With the Industrial Revolution came the corporation, a unique organizational structure that allowed the benefits of partnership without the risks of unlimited liability. Double-entry accounting expanded to encompass increasingly complex estimates and accruals and deferred charges. Thus far, it has not expanded to the point where the accountants of Exxon had to estimate liabilities that reflected the risks of shipping oil through Prince William Sound.

However, the *Exxon Valdez* case helped to reinforce an important precedent, a precedent that social costs can become corporate costs if there is sufficient public pressure and an enforceable legal liability under legislation, such as that covering the transport of dangerous goods in a marine environment. Provisions in the company's annual reports reflected the corporation's expenses for cleanup, restoration, litigation, claims, and other costs related to the accident, net of estimated insurance recoveries, including estimates for future spending. Walker's interpretation of this precedent was that the distance between traditional internal company costs and the external social costs that economists talked about was narrowing. Walker visualized two circles—one for internal corporate costs and one for external social costs—with an area of overlap. The costs in the area of overlap were the social costs that increasingly companies were having to internalize. In his view, this area of overlap had expanded dramatically since the *Exxon Valdez* spill.

Walker believed this case illustrated the first limitation in traditional accounting as it is currently practiced. These risk costs, which some could argue are an intrinsic part of shipping oil, were not estimated *before* the spill, on the basis of operations of prior periods. The root cause of this failure is that accountants define both assets and the related liabilities too narrowly. Air, rivers, the fertility of the soil, and other components of the environment are not considered assets.

First, accountants do not account for the full costs of production, including the costs of consuming central natural resources such as air, water, fertile land, and (in this case of the *Exxon Valdez*) salmon runs in Alaska. Accountants do not account for them until there is a monetary value assigned to them. Double-entry accounting efforts, based on almost 500 years of practice, are geared primarily to measuring financial transactions rather than resource consumption. However, in Walker's view, the traditional model could be modified to better account for the risks of damage to these assets. It would be like accounting for pensions on a grand scale—future events surrounded by a high degree of uncertainty as to whether and when they might occur.

Second, accounting rules penalize rather than encourage the environmentally responsible corporation. The more Exxon spent on prevention and cleanup, the less earnings per share it recorded in the short run. Accountants currently lack a vehicle for recording "green assets" and monitoring their use, for distinguishing between the costs of renewable and nonrenewable resources, and for recognizing the more intangible benefits of investing in environmental projects below corporate profit targets.

Third, traditional accounting has yet to deal with the concept of limits to economic growth imposed by ecological or social limits. There is growing evidence of limits to exponential economic growth imposed by the fragility, or vulnerability, of the ecosystem upon which an enterprise is economically dependent. For example, there may be limits to the fiber a forest could produce, generation after generation, without some impact on soil fertility.

In short, accounting can deal with "more or less"—more revenue or less revenue, more expenses or fewer expenses—but it needs to develop a way of dealing with the concept of "sufficiency." In the aftermath of the *Exxon Valdez* spill, the Canadian government established a public review panel on tanker safety and marine spills response capability. The major findings of the panel suggested that there may be inherent limits to how much oil can safely be transported with existing technology within Canadian inland and offshore waters. The study found that the capability to respond affectively to a spill of any significant magnitude did not exist at present anywhere in Canada.[4]

These and other studies suggest that there may be inherent limits to business activity for which business will be required to account. Walker believed traditional accounting could be expanded to deal with such limits. For example, it is possible to assume that a forest is "perfectly self-sustaining" provided a set percentage of old-growth timber is left to rot on the forest floor and replenish soil nutrients. If old-growth timber is removed in excess of some set percentage (i.e., limit), the "infinite" life of the forest is reduced to a finite one of say 500 years. Perhaps the accounting model could be modified to account for this loss in forest productivity.

Fourth, environmental concerns require a long-term view. Traditional financial statements focus on both the short and long run, within certain limitations. The problem here is not with accounting theory, but with its application. The service-life concept that is the foundation of the traditional balance-sheet accounting is inherently long term. Accountants record as assets buildings with useful lives up to 40 years. The very concept of an asset is forward looking. According to the Financial Accounting Standards Board, "assets are probable future economic benefits obtained or controlled by a particular entity, as a result of past transactions or events." In Walker's view the theory was fine. The application problems arose with business people whose planning horizon did not extend beyond next quarter's earnings.

Fifth, the traditional accounting entity for both financial statements and the organization that is the focus of a financial report has traditionally been a business, not-for-profit organization, or government. The focus is on those things the entity has paid for, on the entity's private property and rights. In other words, the accounting is from the perspective of the owners of the assets. Assets that the entity does not own are not included. Traditional accounting measures an owner's legal earnings. The dilemma traditional accountants face is how to record the consumption of assets such as air or water if the proprietor does not own them.

Accountants could define the accounting entity, however, not from the perspective of the owner but from the perspective of the planet earth. In other words, the basic limitation in traditional accounting is the exclusive focus on ownership interests. If there were an ideal set of environmental laws in place, then "ownership profits" (after deducting all legally imposed environmental costs) and "profit for a fragile blue planet" would be the same. As long as "perfect" environmental laws are not in place, "profit for a fragile blue planet" could be a useful agent for change until the legislation changes.

There is nothing precluding the definition of an accounting entity that included the company, not-for-profit organization, or government in the context of the natural resources and natural capital upon which it was economically dependent. The profit recorded would include a wider spectrum of costs that included costs traditionally treated as "externalities." This would lead to a different concept of profit, one separate from "ownership profit." The obvious question is "What is profit?"

PROFIT IS A RETURN ON RISK

The *sixth* limitation is that accountants tend to view profit as a leftover. The problem with understanding profit is that owners or shareholders cannot see it, smell it, or taste it — it exists largely on paper, created by accounting conventions. Regardless of whether these conventions are right or wrong, what makes the system work is that accountants follow the same basic conventions. The auditors try to ensure that accountants produce numbers that are more or less consistent.

One of the hardest tasks for an accountant is explaining to his or her client where the profit is hiding. In many cases, the client will show a healthy bottom line, but there will be nothing in the bank. He or she will be strapped for cash. "Where is my profit?" the client asks. The accountant will know that profit, this illusory creature, may be invested in inventories, invested in fixed assets, hidden in a reduction in the banker's loans, or buried in intangibles such as research and development or trademarks. The issue here is not the virtues of cash-flow accounting but the intangible, hard-to-define nature of profit. Accounting theory has moved well beyond seeing cash flow as a good surrogate for profit. The very point of accrual accounting is to cure the limitations and myopia of cash-flow accounting.

The concept of an asset leads to a more forward-looking perspective that encourages investment in tomorrow amortized to income over the asset's useful life. The accountant's profit figure is both meaningful and explainable. It is meaningful because it disentangles earning activities from investment activities. However, Walker believed it could be made even more meaningful if it were expanded to account for long-term risks, even if short-sighted entrepreneurs did not want to recognize these costs, which are now an integral part of doing business. To better understand what profit is, or is not, it is useful again to return to an era before the rise of capitalism — the medieval period.

The Medieval Concept of a Just Return

In the theological framework of the medieval world, profit did not exist. There was a clear concept of a *just return,* not that of an opportunistic profit. "Just price" was based on the principle that a craft should supply each man a livelihood and a fair return but no more.[5]

For the medieval accountant practicing double-entry bookkeeping the concept of any sort of residual would have been anathema. His natural inclination would have been to try to allocate the residual to some other factor of production, to wages or raw material cost.

Since then, accountants' thinking has evolved. In economic terms profit is now seen as the sum of economic rent of capital and reward for risk. Because the risks fluctuate wildly, the rewards fluctuate wildly as well, hence the concept of profit as a residual. In Walker's view, what was missing from the calculation was the economic rent on natural capital that should be factored in before calculating the reward for risk. In contrast to the traditional ownership profit, there could also be a definition of profit that put the accounting in the context of the natural capital a company depended upon for continued prosperity. In his search for answers and ways to respond to the CEO's request for new types of information, Walker reviewed the current literature on the burgeoning subject of "green," or environmental, accounting.

NOTES

1. Daniel B. Rubenstein, "Black Oil, Red Ink," *CA Magazine* (November 1989): 30–35.

2. Daniel B. Rubenstein, "Lessons of Love," *CA Magazine* (March 1991): 35–40.

3. Ross M. Skinner, *Accounting Standards in Evolution* (Toronto: Holt, Reinhart and Winston, 1989).

4. Public Review Panel on Tanker Safety and Marine Spills Response Capability, *Protecting Our Waters* (Ottawa, 1990), p. 8.

5. Barbara W. Tuchman, *A Distant Mirror: The Calamitous Fourteenth Century* (New York: Ballantine Books, 1978), p. 37.

Chapter 3

A Guide to
Environmental Accounting

WORLDWIDE INTEREST IN GREEN ACCOUNTING

Accountants around the world are concerned about the limitations in traditional accounting when it comes to accounting for the environment. They recognize the need to explore the potential of environmental accounting or green accounting. Accounting magazines in North America or Europe devote considerable space to environmental issues. Typical articles deal with sustainable development and competitiveness, the need for balancing nature's books, the deficiencies of traditional cost accounting, the need for better risk analysis, or the need for better environmental disclosure in annual reports. As in any emerging field, there are few definitive answers. Rather, there is a great deal of earnest searching for a new vision of accounting.

There is a wide spectrum of views and philosophies. There are the "light green" accountants who see that there is a need to tinker with the present accounting model. At the other end of the spectrum there are the "deep greens" who urge nothing less than a revolutionary new form of accounting. The dark greens talk about accounting and the ecological crisis, about new ethics and new corporate responsibilities toward the commons or shared resources.

Amidst all this creativity, in a profession that is said to be staid, are some emerging themes. The first is that accounting, the score card of business, may be sending dangerously incomplete signals to corporate decision makers. The second is the need to figure a better way to measure and account for environmental obligations. The third is the quest for full costs that begin to include the costs of natural capital.

Relative to the first point, that accounting is sending incomplete and misleading signals, there is some debate whether the preparers or the users of financial reports are to blame for the preoccupation with quarterly earnings.

Some say it is the concept of smooth earnings that is the villain. Accountants have injected the underlying presumption of smooth earnings into their accounting model by not revaluing long-term depreciable or depletable assets every quarter because of the "bumpiness" in earnings that would result. It is argued that long-term asset lives and values should be kept "constant" so that quarterly and annual earnings are "meaningful" for comparative purposes (i.e., the "smooth income paradigm"). Walker had to wonder whether it was so meaningful to keep accounting estimates relatively frozen, even though accountants' best guesses as to future conditions kept changing. Others say it is management's focus on short-term gain, at perhaps the expense of long-term corporate pain that is the problem. They say current accounting rules for cleanup costs promote a pollute now, pay later mentality.

A second theme is the need to better account for environmental liabilities such as those of Love Canal. Even the most traditional of accountants agree that the current rules on contingent liabilities need to be fixed. A third theme is the need for full costs that include the costs of consumption of essential natural resources such as air, water, or soil.

While there is general agreement on what needs to be fixed, there is less agreement on how to fix it. There are at least four major schools of thought. Some advocate tinkering with the present model while letting the market make the major adjustments; some suggest creating a new discipline; some favor redefining accounting; and others promote disclosing more information on environmental performance.

Tinkering with the Present Accounting Model

It is clear to many accountants that the way they account for cleanup costs is just plain poor accounting. The traditional model is defective when it comes to dealing with low-probability–high-magnitude events. The tinkerers believe the answer to accounting for the environment is to find a better way to account for contingent liabilities. The objective here is to fix today's accounting rules for known deficiencies or shortcomings. In a nutshell, under the current rules companies generally do not "book" liabilities for cleanup but disclose the potential of some future costs, subject to an external event such as a court order. Contingent liabilities involve a high degree of uncertainty both in terms of the occurrence of the event that will trigger payment and in estimating the amount of ultimate payment.

Lender liability under the Superfund in the United States has promoted increased interest in accounting for contingent liabilities. The fundamental issue for society is differentiating between negligence and ignorance. Is it that companies cannot estimate these liabilities or that they will not estimate and disclose them? The Securities and Exchange Commission appears to be pushing harder for estimating a range of potential cleanup costs. Their operant philosophy appears to be that an inability to precisely estimate potential costs does not mean "zero cost."

Increasing numbers of accountants recognize that the profession can make significant strides in improving its estimating techniques. They note that many of the statistical methods used to estimate actuarial liabilities for pensions can be modified to estimate a range of potential cleanup costs. They also note that with the Superfund experience, there is a large database of actual costs to use in estimating potential cleanup costs. There is growing support for estimating a range of costs and disclosing this range, recognizing the imprecision that is an inherent part of calculating these estimates. Accountants might find solace in the words of the late Howard Ross, "that it is better to be approximately right than precisely wrong."

The Market Will Adjust

Many of the tinkerers feel that ultimately the problem with accounting for the environment is a political problem. If society set fines commensurate with the "true costs" of the depletion of natural resources, accountants would have no problem computing full costs. This group also notes how fast the market has responded to "green" concerns. For example, Fleet Financial Group Inc. became the first major banking concern in the United States to require nearly all commercial real estate borrowers to get environmental liability insurance before they obtain loans. Requiring borrowers to get insurance causes the costs of inadequate environmental protection measures to be factored into a company's income statements. Poor environmental performers will pay higher premiums in the same way that poor drivers pay higher premiums. This school of thought also notes that there are tradable, marketable permits to pollute that have again brought environmental costs into the traditional income statement. Even so, the "dark green" accountants urge more radical solutions.

Creating a New Discipline

Another group of accountants feels that traditional financial accounting can never be adapted to encompass environmental accounting; environmental matters are inherently incompatible with traditional accounting. There's a need for a new multidisciplinary approach to accounting for the environment. For example, the Danish Steel Works Ltd. developed a green account that was included in the annual report. The company wanted to show a "true and fair" view of the company's production. One way to do this is to prepare a "mass balance sheet" or eco-balance. Such an account would show inputs in the form of materials supplied, energy consumed, and outputs in the form of finished goods, emissions, recycled waste products, and other waste. To prepare such an account, the first step was to identify all the materials that enter into the production process. The accounting was made in physical terms, not monetary units. The analysis resulted in the determination of an ecological "footprint" for the steel products.

Another approach is that developed by Professor Soren Bergstrom at Stockholm University. His accounts include key indicators in three areas — effectiveness indicators, thrift indicators, and margin indicators — which are illustrated for a construction project. Effectiveness indicators include access to green space, clean air, and relative freedom from radon — to name a few. Thrift indicators include physical support capacity, nature cost, and cleanness of the investment. Margin indicators include the relative change in water flows, the effect on ground acidity, or oxygen in the lake. Bergstrom's accounts focus on physical units and nonmonetary values in part because of the risk of monetary values not reflecting true scarcity values.

Walker also reviewed the work done by the International Network for Environmental Management (INEM) in Europe. The INEM model examines the environmental impact of a company's own operations, including everything a company owns, leases, or rents. The core accounting includes an analysis of energy use and the disposal of waste products. The focus appears to be on natural resource thrift.

Walker was now getting the general drift of these new models. He could easily visualize preparing an input–output analysis for the forestry operations with which he was very familiar. Inputs during the harvesting phase would include the natural capital of the forest, diesel fuel used in the fellerbunchers and trucks, manpower, machinery, and equipment. Outputs would include logs ready for further processing, air emissions, compaction of the soil, and impact on the microclimate. Walker could see that this could be done for the whole productive process. Theoretically, it could be expanded to include an accounting for the energy required to transport product to market and the ultimate deposit of some paper products in landfill. Walker liked the concept and decided to try to incorporate as much as possible in the work he would be doing.

Theoretically, there could be some bridge between these new environmental accounts and traditional financial statements — perhaps in terms of a charge to income. Given Walker's two decades of professional life as an industry accountant, he was naturally most interested in the next school of thought.

Define Accounting to Meet Present and Future Needs

This school of thought says that the inability to account for the environment is the most extreme example of other more profound deficiencies in traditional financial accounting. By going back to basics, redefining what accounting is all about, this group suggests, researchers can come up with a discipline that will meet the needs both of traditional investors and of those who care about the environment. The ideal is an accounting regime that meets the information needs of the owners, as well as all those with an "invisible stake" in a company's operations.

This group sees a wide spectrum of potential economic information that could be included in annual reports. This spectrum encompasses the need for accounting for both natural resources and nonnatural resources (i.e., what is manufactured by man). The focus is on wealth — wealth created and wealth preserved. To this school of thought, accounting could be defined as follows:

Accounting measures the economic, intellectual, and natural capital consumed in producing goods and services for trade and for promoting public welfare, as well as the natural and intellectual capital preserved and the wealth created for future use, according to the conventions mutually agreed upon by the stewards of these resources and the stakeholders, in this and future generations, to whom they are accountable.[1]

This group says it is the concept of the accounting entity that must change. Accountants should not be limited by the notions of private property as the basis of assets and liabilities to be accounted for.

Disclose Our Way Out

The last school of thought believes companies can and should create supplemental reports on environmental performance that will both motivate management to solve problems and create good corporate public relations. These companies note that their financial results are largely transparent. They feel that their environmental stewardship should be just as transparent.

This push for expanded disclosure reflects the reality of heightened environmental awareness in Canada, the rest of North America, and the world at large. Consumers, politicians, lenders, and investors have reacted by placing new demands on business. They have increased their scrutiny of the environmental performance of individual companies. Reporting a good financial bottom line may no longer be sufficient. How results are achieved is taking on greater importance. Corporations have responded by changing their extraction, manufacturing, distribution, transportation, and servicing processes. They are trying to adapt their products. The enhanced awareness of these issues has created a widespread demand for more information on, and improved public disclosure about, corporate environmental performance.

The next section describes what such an improved public disclosure report might look like and why companies will need to go beyond such disclosure to provide both senior management and external readers of reports with the information they need for informed decisions.

ANNUAL REPORT ABOUT THE ENVIRONMENT

How Should Shareholders Interpret These Reports?

Next spring, along with the annual reports and financial statements for the year ended December 31, shareholders may receive glossy, supplementary reports on the environment. They could be from a utility company, a logging company, a mineral company, a seafood products company, a chemical company, or even an ice cream company.

Perhaps a shareholder is curious about what the company is doing to and for the environment. The challenge is to interpret the information. Typically a report starts with a mission statement, a vision of where the company has been and where it would like to go. The vision will be one of a company with a sustainable future. It is likely to talk of sustainable development, of using resources today without impairing what will be available to future generations, and of the company's commitment to achieving this goal. It may talk about sustained economic yield.

The report on environmental performance will certainly include the corporation's environmental policy and objectives. In most cases, the environmental report will also talk about compliance with regulatory requirements, energy management, material and waste management, water and air management, and social responsibility. There may be specific data on goals for waste management, energy efficiency, minimization of pollution, and product safety, as well as some information on recent performance against these goals.

The challenge to the reader will be to sift through the pictures and the charts and determine whether the company's performance is good news or bad news for the environment in *real* terms, not relative terms. Is the company on a benign path or merely a less harmful path? Readers are generally provided with a mass of data. But nowhere will they generally be told whether they can drink the water, breathe the air, eat the fish, or swim downstream from the plant. A useful analogy is that of a simple measure of human health—a thermometer. Until a user knows that 98.6 degrees Fahrenheit denotes a healthy temperature, a list of thermometer readings is largely useless.

In board rooms, there are two polarities on a spectrum of environmental concern. At one extreme are corporate leaders who feel that nature is resilient or "fixable"; they use natural resources as endlessly renewable resources. Natural resources are to be owned and exploited, and rights of extraction are paramount and exclusive. At the other end of the spectrum are corporate managers who believe natural resources are shared resources, common property, for which a company has a stewardship role on behalf of present and future generations. These managers recognize natural limits. Expanded environmental disclosure does not deal with the question of ecological limits, does not disclose whether a company is respecting these limits. This would be the information a reader would need to assess a company's environmental stewardship.

The main drawback of the environmental disclosure option is that while there is limited reporting of environmental impacts, there's no accounting for the *full costs* of products or services (i.e., product costs that include the costs of natural resources such as air, water, or arable land consumed in production). This a major deficiency in a market-driven economy.

WHY FULL COSTS ARE SO IMPORTANT

Full costs are critical in a market-driven economy where resources are allocated to the most efficient use in the capital markets and the supermarkets. The economy self-adjusts. Implicit in anything we do in the market place is the risk of failure. Entrepreneurs bite their fingernails, worry about the timing of loan payments, whether to expand or contract, how to weather business ups and downs. Risk management is nothing to be taken lightly. Anyone in business knows there is always the chance, the specter of going bankrupt, getting caught in the squeeze between rising costs and dropping prices. According to traditional economic theory, risk of failure leads to efficiency.

In business, knowledge of the comprehensive costs of an activity is critical for survival. In traditional cost accounting, full costs include all variable costs that change with volume of production, all fixed costs (such as the costs of plant and equipment), and other overheads. To many accountants it is only natural to extend these basic principles to include natural resource costs.

Walker had little problem accepting the importance of full costs. Most of his professional life had been spent producing relevant cost information. Thinking about the four schools of thought, Walker was supportive of the need for better accounting for environmental liabilities. Once a year, he had to work with the actuaries to arrive at complex pension obligations. Based on this experience he was confident accountants could come up with better measurement techniques for the liabilities associated with such past sins as Love Canal. He believed that ultimately the market would adjust to increased risks of liabilities associated with poor environmental management practices. He knew about the green chill in banking and insurance circles.

He was fascinated by the eco-balance sheet that would provide an environmental footprint. He could see the links between such a footprint and corporate accountability for environmental stewardship. Once the footprint was in the public domain, there would be increased incentives to invest in the environment. However, he saw this approach as running parallel to his efforts to account for the sustainable management of the forest. While he recognized the importance of disclosure, he recognized that "good disclosure never made up for bad numbers."

Walker believed accountants could overcome the limitations in traditional accounting. Accounting could measure the economic and natural capital consumed in manufacturing goods and services. He saw no reason why the traditional definitions of assets and liabilities promulgated by the Financial Accounting Standards Board could not either be interpreted differently or redefined so as to account for the costs of natural capital. Walker experimented with the following working definitions (alterations and additions in **bold**):

- *Assets.* **"Assets include both the natural capital upon which a reporting entity is economically dependent** and probable future economic benefits obtained or controlled by a particular entity as a result of past transactions or events."

- *Liabilities.* "Liabilities are probable future sacrifices or economic benefits arising from present obligations or a particular entity to transfer assets or provide services to other entities in the future as a result of past transactions or events **and the risk of the consumption of natural capital.**"

- *Expenses.* "Expenses are outflows or other using up of assets, **including the consumption of natural capital,** or incurrences of liabilities (or a combination of both) from delivering or producing goods, rendering services, or carrying out other activities that constitute the entity's ongoing major or central operations **(including the preventive maintenance of the natural capital essential to maintain a going concern).**"

Following these new conventions and definitions would result in a different view of wealth, one that Walker believed would more compatible with a new concept he was now hearing about from all sides—sustainable development. The concept provided a new model for doing business that recognized an explicit connection between business and natural capital, a connection that would require the new definitions he had just worked out. In Walker's view, accounting for sustainable development provided a convenient ideology within which to fix long-standing problems in accounting.

Walker was now committed to developing the nontraditional accounting systems that would be needed by a sustainable corporation, one that practiced enlightened self-interest. Such a company would need to know full costs because it would recognize that if there were a significant gap between an "owner's cost" and a looming social cost they would need to have the cash ready to invest at a propitious time. Such a company would also be interested in any inherent limits to economic activity; no prudent company would want to run its asset base into the ground. Walker knew that what was measured was what was managed, and such a company would need measurement of depletion of essential assets. A sustainable company would recognize that it did not operate in isolation but rather in the context of "free" resources that it used but ultimately shared with others with different values and views about their use.

Last of all, an enlightened company would accept that before "owner's profit" was recognized there would have to be an accounting for the low-occurrence–high-magnitude risks to natural capital that result in extraordinary adjustments of profits in their year of occurrence.

Walker was now ready to delve into the content of the Bundtland Commission report in its entirety.

NOTE

1. Daniel B. Rubenstein, "Lessons of Love," *CA Magazine* (March 1991): 33.

Chapter 4

Origins of the Concept
of Sustainable Development

THE ROAD TO THE EARTH SUMMIT

Walker had heard a great deal about sustainable development. It sounded like a useful concept, but he really had no idea what it meant for his company. To better understand the concept he wanted to learn something about its origins — who popularized the term and why. He contacted a college classmate at the Institute for Research on Public Policy in Ottawa who explained the road to the Earth Summit at Rio. The 1972 United Nations Conference on the Human Environment (the Stockholm Conference) marked the debut of the environment as an issue on the international agenda. This initial conference led to the creation of the United Nations Environmental Program (UNEP). Henceforth, the environment became a stable item on the international agenda, where it bubbled on the back burner, competing with other global issues such as human settlement and population growth.

When the environmental program came to commemorate the tenth anniversary of the Stockholm Conference, it was becoming increasingly clear that the global environment had continued to deteriorate at an alarming rate despite the achievements made to date. The most disturbing trend from the debates at the tenth anniversary session of the environmental program's governing council was that environment and development were still being viewed as opposing concepts. Geoffrey Bruce, Canada's permanent representative to the environmental program, therefore proposed the creation of a global commission to examine the state of the world's environment and the relationship between environment and development. The commission's mandate was clear — to bridge the conceptual gap between the two solitudes of the natural world, the environment and the world of economic development, including the realm of business.

The World Commission of Environment and Development (the Brundtland Commission) worked for three years to produce a four-hundred-page report documenting in stark terms the accumulating evidence of planetary decline. *Our Common Future* reported the annual loss to desertification of an area the size of Saudi Arabia; the loss of over seventeen million hectares of tropical forest per year; the destruction of the earth's ozone shield by CFCs and halons; and the possibility of a warming of the earth's climate over the next 50 years that exceeded the warming over the past 10,000 years.

But this was merely the preamble. The commission reminded readers that the unprecedented growth in human numbers was being accompanied by an equally unprecedented increase in industrial production. The commission predicted that a five to tenfold expansion in world economies would be required to meet the minimum needs and aspirations of the ten to eleven billion people who would be on the planet by the middle of the next century.

When the commission's report was published in 1987, scientific evidence was again building that the deterioration of the earth's ozone shield was even greater than previously thought. The commission proposed to bridge the gap between a deteriorating environment and the imperative to feed, clothe, house, and provide for the education and sanitation needs of ten billion souls. The concept intended to bridge these two overriding concerns was the concept of sustainable development. Walker was now ready to wade through the commission's blueprint for a new century, *Our Common Future.*

OUR COMMON FUTURE

This unusual document allows both environmental activists and conservative CEOs, each with widely different views on the role of business, to find their own missions in the same book. Walker wondered whether this was both the genius of the work of the World Commission on Environment and Development and perhaps its principal vulnerability.

Our Common Future spoke of "development that meets the needs of the present without compromising the ability of future generations to meet their own needs." Two key concepts were the cornerstone of sustainable development:

1. The concept of 'needs,' in particular the essential needs of the world's poor, to which overriding priority should be given; and
2. The idea of limitations imposed by the state of technology and social organization on the environment's ability to meet present and future needs.[1]

From One Earth to One World

According to the commission,

In the middle of the 20th century, we saw our planet from space for the first time. Historians may eventually find that this vision had a greater impact on thought than did the Copernican revolution of the 16th century, which upset the human self image by revealing that the Earth is not the centre of the universe. From space, we see a small and fragile marble dominated not by human activity and edifice but by a pattern of clouds, oceans, greenery and soils. Humanity's inability to fit its doings into that pattern is changing planetary systems, fundamentally. Many such things are accompanied by life threatening hazards. This new reality, from which there is no escape, must be recognized—and managed.[2]

The commission spoke of interlocking crises.

Until recently, the planet was a large world in which human activities and their affects were neatly compartmentalized within nations, within sectors (energy, agriculture, trade), and within broad areas of concern (environmental, economic, social). These compartments have begun to dissolve. This applies in particular to the various global "crises" that have seized public concern, particularly over the past decade. These are not separate crises: an environmental crisis, a development crisis, an energy crisis. They are all one.[3]

Our Common Future goes on to say that humanity has the ability to make development sustainable. It notes that "the concept of sustainable development does imply limits—not absolute limits but limitations imposed by the present state of technology and social organization on environmental resources and by the ability of the biosphere to absorb the affects of human activities."[4]

Walker mused that a classical Marxist, if any still exist, would be likely to agree with the report where it says, "Poverty is not only an evil in itself, but sustainable development requires meeting the basic needs of *all* and extending to *all* the opportunity to fulfill their aspirations for a better life."[5] Meeting essential needs requires not only a "new era of economic growth for nations in which the majority are poor, but an assurance that those poor get their fair share of the resources required to sustain that growth."[6] In other words, the commission is talking about equity.

Sustainable development is seen not as a fixed state of harmony but rather as a process of change in which the exploitation of resources is made consistent with future, as well as present, needs. *Our Common Future* acknowledges that the process will not be easy or straightforward and that painful choices will need to be made.

Our Common Future recognizes that economic growth and development obviously involve changes in the physical ecosystem. It recognizes that every ecosystem everywhere cannot be preserved intact. A forest may be depleted in one part of a watershed and extended elsewhere, which is not a bad thing if the exploitation has been planned and the effects on the soil erosion rates, water regimes, and genetic losses have been taken into account. The study notes that, in general, renewable resources like forests and fish stocks need not be depleted, provided the rate of use is within the limits of regeneration and natural growth. However, *Our Common Future* notes that most renewable resources are part of a complex and interlinked ecosystem, and maximum sustainable yield must be defined after taking into account system-wide effects of exploitation.

Obviously, sustainable development of a renewable resource is going to be much easier than exploitation of a nonrenewable resource. As for nonrenewable resources like fossil fuels and minerals, *Our Common Future* notes that their use reduces the stock available for future generations. But this does not mean that such resources should not be used. In general, the rate of depletion should take into account the critical nature of that resource, the availability of technologies for minimizing depletion, and the likelihood of substitutes being available. Here sustainable development would require that the rate of depletion of such nonrenewable resources such as ore or fossil fuels should foreclose as few future options as possible.[7]

In Walker's view, *Our Common Future* depicted an uneasy marriage between the genius of capitalism (the ability to harness greed and self-interest to produce goods and services in sufficient quantities and at prices unmatched by that of any other system) and a way to deal with its greatest single flaw. The paradox of capitalism is that the very forces that make it an unparalleled engine to create economic wealth constrain it from distributing this wealth in an equitable fashion. The ideal articulated in *Our Common Future* suggested that society must run the engine of capitalism as fast as it can, without burning out the bearings, and focus on fair distribution of output.

Walker visualized the concept as having three components, as illustrated in Figure 4.1. The triad consisted of a moving, dynamic balance between economic sustainability, equity of distribution, and ecological sustainability. The obvious question for Jack and Walker was "What is a sustainable corporation?"

WHAT IS A SUSTAINABLE CORPORATION?

One of the serious omissions of *Our Common Future* is that nowhere does it explicitly define a sustainable corporation. However, buried in Annexe 1 is the closest thing to such a definition if the reader substitutes the word *corporation* for the word *states*. A quality-of-growth corporation is one that respects people's fundamental human right to an environment adequate for their health and well-being. The second attribute is that such a corporation conserves and uses the environment and natural resources for the benefit of present and future generations.

Attribute three requires that an organization "shall maintain ecosystems and ecological processes essential for the functioning of the biosphere, shall preserve biological diversity, and shall observe the principle of optimum sustainable yield in the use of living natural resources and ecosystems." Attribute four requires an organization to establish adequate environmental protection standards and monitor changes in and publish relevant data on

Figure 4.1
The Three Es of Sustainable Development

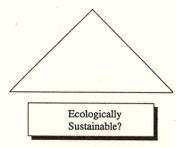

Economically Sustainable?

- Costs competitive?
- Demand sustainable?
- Innovation sustainable?
- Profit margin sustainable?

Equity of Demand and Distribution?

- Equitable distribution of product?
- Equitable transfer of wealth?
- Sustainable return on investment?

Ecologically Sustainable?

- Natural capital sustainable?
- Stress load sustainable?
- Web of life sustainable?

environmental quality and resource use. The last two attributes require an organization to conduct environmental assessments and inform in a timely manner all persons likely to be significantly effected by a planned economic activity.

At the close of its proceedings, the World Commission on Environment and Development issued the "Tokyo Declaration," which provided principles intended to guide policy actions. While not specifically addressed to corporations, the relevance of these principles to the corporate sector should be immediately obvious.

Because poverty is a major source of environmental degradation, industrialized countries can and must contribute to reviving world economic growth. However, they must also change the quality of growth. "Revived growth must be of a new kind in which sustainability, equity, and social justice, and security are firmly embedded as major social goals." At the same time, "Sustainability requires the conservation of environmental resources such as clean air, water, forests, and soils; maintaining genetic diversity; and using energy, water, and raw materials efficiently." The declaration called for the promotion of low-waste technologies and anticipating the impact of new products, technologies, and wastes.

The declaration noted that technology creates risks, but it also offered the means to manage them. Liability for damages from unintended consequences must be strengthened and enforced. And most important, environmental and economic goals can and must be mutually reinforcing.

A truly sustainable corporation, then, balances business limits, biological limits, and equity of distribution of wealth so as to achieve both intergenerational and intragenerational equity. While intergenerational equity means preserving natural capital for the next generation, intragenerational equity means sharing the wealth today between the developed and the developing nations. Quality growth involves better income distribution, reduced vulnerability to technological risks, improved health, and preservation of cultural heritage.

In 1987, at the conclusion of its work, the commission recommended that a world conference be held five years after the release of its report to assess the progress of the implementation of its recommendations for more sustainable paths to development. The proposed conference became known as the Rio Conference or the Earth Summit. The principal output of the Earth Summit was Agenda 21, the summit's central action plan. Chapter 8 of Agenda 21 called for "integrating environment and development at the policy, planning and management levels." The preamble to Chapter 8 noted that "prevailing systems for decision-making tend to separate economic, social and environmental factors at the policy, planning and management levels." To remedy this situation Chapter 8 called for all players in the economy to meet three fundamental objectives:

(a) To incorporate environmental costs in the decisions of producers and consumers, to reverse the tendency to treat the environment as a "free good" and to pass these costs on to other parts of society, other countries or to future generations;

(b) To move more fully toward the integration of social and environmental costs into economic activities, so that prices will appropriately reflect the relative scarcity and total value of resources and contribute towards the prevention of environmental degradation; and,

(c) To include, wherever appropriate, the use of market principles in the framing of economic instruments and policies to pursue sustainable development.[8]

To make these concepts a living reality, the United Nations funded research work to develop prototype accounts that could be used to support this new era of marrying business concerns with environmental concerns.[9] Walker obtained a copy of the case study that resulted from the research. He wanted to develop the concepts further, tailoring them to the unique circumstances of his company. He knew from personal experience why a company would be interested in integrating environmental and business information.

SUSTAINABLE DEVELOPMENT AT THE ENTITY LEVEL

Businesses Need Information to Chart
an Environmental Investment Strategy

North American businesses face investments in the billions of dollars in the next five years. In Canada alone, companies are likely to spend $6 to $8 billion annually in pollution abatement or prevention technology. In fact, the environmental sector is the fastest growing sector in the United States and Canadian economies. An environmental science and engineering magazine article Walker had read estimated the global environmental market to be $255 billion in 1990, growing to $454 billion by 2000. The North American price tag was estimated at $125 billion in 1990 and $185 billion by the turn of the century.[10]

It did not take a great leap of imagination for Walker to appreciate that many capital-intensive businesses, large or small, from local dry cleaning establishments to large pulp mills would be facing significant capital investments in environmental technology. The critical investment decisions for any business in this position would be "What level of technology should I buy into and when?" In addressing these questions, a company would need to develop an approach to managing long-term issues and to decide at what point in the evolution of these issues to become engaged. The biggest challenge would be to counterbalance short-term costs against possible long-term benefits that might not be well defined.

Businesses facing these billion-dollar investments would need information to develop the long-term environmental investment strategies that would shape future expenditures. Given the limitations of traditional approaches, Walker believed that conventional tools such as cost accounting, return on investment analysis, and payback analysis would not provide senior corporate management and the board with the information they need to make the strategic decisions that will shape long-term profitability. This initial view was reinforced by research conducted by the Tellus Institute on behalf of the Environmental Protection Agency. The study talked about the "economic/financial barriers linked to methods of capital allocation and budgeting once a pollution prevention project . . . competes with other projects for limited capital resources." According to the research study, there was a need to rethink cost-savings elements, use longer time horizons, and consider multiple profitability indexes to remove the biases inherent in conventional analytical methods.[11]

As Walker read this report, he had a sense of déjà vu. When the total quality movement was in vogue, there were endless debates as to whether total quality costs were a cost or a benefit. While he, as an accountant, could fairly readily identify the costs, trying to nail down the benefits in terms of quality and customers retained had proved more illusive. He sensed that when it came to identifying the benefits of investments in the environment, he would have to deal again with equally imprecise and illusive numbers.

To make these strategic decisions, senior management would need information on full costs, including the potential costs of natural resources consumed in production. In addition, businesses would need information on the ability of the ecosystems upon which they are economically dependent to absorb the toxins produced; to withstand the stress on wetlands, rivers, and forest systems. But perhaps most important, businesses would need information on the potential downstream costs of pursuing a business-as-usual approach toward the environment rather than making capital investments that help preserve natural resources and natural habitat for future generations. To do this, businesses would need future-oriented information that projected current rates of consumption of natural resources one (or even two) generations into the future. In Walker's mind, the basic issue was preparedness, anticipating the future rather than waiting for the regulators to define a business's options.

This information would be needed to ration scarce investment capital among competing environmental projects. Projects that would pay for themselves over a relatively short time (using conventional payback analysis of savings through closed loop recycling of materials or through energy savings) would not be the problem. They would probably be made under existing analytical methods. The problem was with those projects in the "grey zone" where payback periods were below corporate targets, where return on investment was lower than the cost of capital. Without information on the potential risk costs of not making these "grey" investments, in terms of potential degradation of natural resources or natural habitat, decision makers would be making million-dollar decisions without full knowledge of all relevant costs. Walker reflected on businesses' strategic options when it came to formulating environmental investment strategies.

Formulating an Environmental Investment Strategy

Walker identified the "business-as-usual" option, the comprehensive environmental management option, and the managing-for-sustainable-development option. Under the business-as-usual option, business is in a reactive mode, fixing known problems, complying with existing regulations. Under this scenario businesses are at the mercy of regulators, for there is little anticipation of future regulations. Because there is no slack in the system, any significant toughening of effluent requirements will force immediate investments or risk of fines. Companies in this position have little flexibility as to the timing of investments. As a result, businesses could be forced to make significant capital investments to meet new pollution standards in the middle of a recession.

Comprehensive Environmental Management

Walker consulted a publication of the International Institute for Sustainable Development called *Business Strategy for Sustainable Development, Leadership and Accountability for the 1990s.*[12] This informative text defined comprehensive environmental management as a strategy where management seeks to gain a competitive advantage by taking an active stance on environmental issues. A company's focus is on processes and systems — simple compliance with legislation and regulations is not enough. In these companies, everyone is encouraged to become involved in environmental matters. The company makes a real attempt to integrate environmental concerns into the existing decision-making process in all aspects of corporate management. Environmental objectives are set for key operating activities rather than being left to the environmental services department. Under this option, corporate management takes a more proactive stance. These companies build to specifications well in excess of existing regulations. When the regulations get tougher, they have the relative luxury of choosing when to make a major upgrade, choosing a time that is more desirable in the business cycle or a time when interest rates are down. Building ahead of current regulations has bought them time.

Under a regime of comprehensive environmental management, a company will set corporate goals for effluent and develop corporate policies on the environment, appointing a senior vice president to champion the environment at the boardroom level. These forward-looking companies will invest in site monitoring of effluent, empower internal audit to conduct environmental reviews, and probably issue a state-of-the-environment report describing compliance with existing regulations. These reports may summarize the amount of money spent on environmental investments. (This is not to be confused with environmental accounting as used in this text — the amounts disclosed in such reports are not full costs that include the costs of natural resources.)

The Canadian Standard's Association provided additional guidance on what constitutes the essential elements of an environmental management system:

An environmental management system is a management system to achieve an organization's environmental policies and objectives. The model . . . is designed to respond proactively to changing regulations, social, economic and competitive pressures, and environmental risks. Corporate policies and a corporate culture that reflect sensitivity to an expanded accountability to stakeholders (both traditional and emerging) and a commitment to continuous improvement are key to successful implementation. . . . An effective environmental management system is characterized by the following key elements:

(a) Stakeholder analysis;

(b) guiding principles;

(c) environmental policy;

(d) management's role and responsibilities defined;

(e) planning (program conception and setting performance goals);

(f) implementation (procedures, training, performance measures, monitoring and corrective action follow-up);

(g) documentation and record keeping;

(h) reporting (internal and external); and,

(i) auditing.[13]

The starting point for companies adhering to such a regime are basic profitability goals that marry plant capacity to volume of production. The environmental "variables" are the degree of environmental impact of the various technologies employed. Economic sustainability is the primary goal. The company's objective is not necessarily to find an ideal equilibrium between these business limits and the underlying ecological limits as described in *Our Common Future.* Business is accountable for the stewardship of the harvest of natural resources but not necessarily for the habitat that is the home to these resources. In short, wildlife management may be outside the scope of comprehensive environmental management.

Walker struggled to understand what these concepts really meant, whether they were the same as sustainable development, a part of the concept, or something entirely different. He tried to put them into his own words: "Under the business-as-usual option, a company sets the thermostat at the level of existing regulations. Under the comprehensive environmental management option, a company sets the thermostat well ahead of existing regulations. The primary criterion for setting the level is the business's comfort zone. Perhaps the difference is that under sustainable development a company agrees to set the thermostat at a level perceived by stakeholders to be comfortable for the ecosystem, or ecosystems, upon which a company is economically dependent."

Managing for Sustainable Development

Managing for sustainable development, as described in global terms in *Our Common Future,* appeared to be predicated upon a much broader definition of environmental stewardship. A company would be accountable for the use of existing stocks of natural resources, and natural capital for at least two generations.

Figure 4.2 illustrates Walker's interpretation of both the similarities and significant differences between comprehensive environmental management and managing for sustainable development. In the former regime, the starting point would be existing regulations and legislation. These would be continuously monitored and analyzed. Changes would be anticipated well in advance. Under a regime of managing for sustainable development, the starting point would be the carrying capacity of the ecosystem, not plant capacity. While business would be the senior partner in the former regime, the environment is an equal partner in the latter regime. Here the operant philosophy is that the business and the ecosystem upon which it depends are seen as interdependent entities.

As illustrated in Figure 4.2, a company practicing environmental management will monitor compliance with its goals through on-site measurement of effluent, through environmental audits. If there is a variance between goals and actual effluent, corrective action will be taken—fixing the problem, developing a new strategy for an unforeseen situation, or conceivably reassessing the economic viability of the goal. If all is well, the board will get assurance that they do not risk fines or personal imprisonment. As depicted, it is a closed-loop regime of self-regulation.

In contrast, under a regime of sustainable development, the starting point is whether the goal is sustainable, and for how long. Implicit in sustainable development is the concept of fairness between generations or intergenerational equity. In short, the inherent carrying capacity of the ecological domain is the primary consideration. Business limits must then be intertwined with these environmental considerations that are largely driven by scientific knowledge on attributes of ecosystem health, the chemical and biological properties of toxins released, as well as the related social factors. As illustrated, under a regime of sustainable development there is a lot more uncertainty, a different philosophy towards the inherent risk of damage to the environment. The "correct thermostat setting" is an ambiguous, shifting value reflected from the mirror of public perceptions. A critical concern is the level of irreversible damage to fragile natural capital and the monitoring regime that must be in place to anticipate this point of no return before it is reached. The company sees itself as a global citizen, a citizen interdependent on local and global ecosystems.

It seemed to Walker that ideally under a regime of sustainable development every major business decision could be a complex juggling act between business limits, such as plant capacity, and the ecological limits of, for example, wildlife that share the habitat in which a company operates. Dealing with scientific ambiguity, rather than prescribed parts per billion could become the norm. As a result of this fundamental orientation, the time frames under consideration would need to be longer and the level of acceptable risk, given scientific uncertainties, lower. Companies adhering to the tenets of sustainable development would be accountable for more noncom-

Figure 4.2
Are the Goals Sustainable for Two Generations?

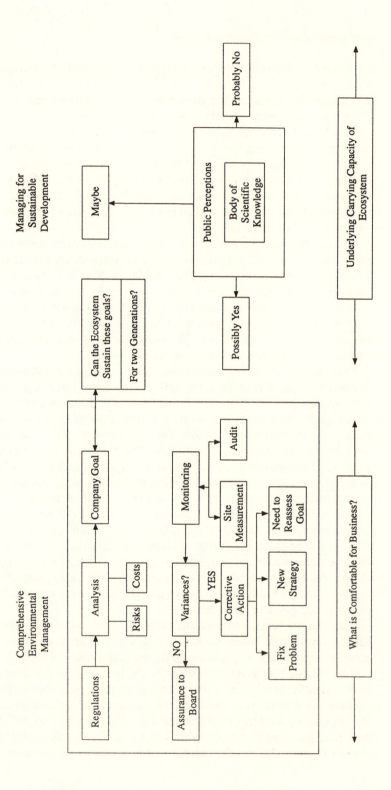

mercial aspects of the resource being harvested or extracted, such as wilderness or biodiversity.

Managing for sustainable development would mean entering a world where sustainable is in the eye of the beholder.

SUSTAINABLE IS IN THE EYE OF THE BEHOLDER

Walker wanted to know what the journey started two decades ago in Stockholm, codified in *Our Common Future,* and converted into an action plan in Agenda 21 would mean for the forestry sector. The CEO would be sure to ask, "What is sustainable development for my line of business?"

Walker's research revealed a wide range of definitions of sustainable development. Each represented a significantly different interpretation of the concept; each represented a significantly different level of investment in environmental protection, capitalization, and operating costs. It was obvious to Walker that any company intending to embrace sustainable development needed to know more precisely to what it was committing itself, how much this commitment would cost, and what the long-term benefits would be. Such a commitment would be no academic issue; it could cost a company hundreds of millions, even billions, of dollars over the next 20 years.

Walker reviewed the definition proposed by the International Institute for Sustainable Development (IISD) intended to be stated in terms familiar to business and government leaders so as to assist them in applying the concept at the enterprise level:

Sustainable development. For the business enterprise, sustainable development means adapting business strategies and activities that meet the needs of the enterprise and its stakeholders today while protecting, sustaining and enhancing the human and natural resources that will be needed in the future.[14]

According to the institute, this definition captures the spirit of the concept in *Our Common Future* and focuses attention on areas of specific interest and concern to business enterprises. To Walker, this was a "middle of the road" definition that represented a practical compromise between the two extremes of putting the environment first (i.e., environment first) and the status quo, business-as-usual option. The middle ground represents an ideal of a sustainable marriage between business and the environment, a relationship where both parties have to compromise to make an inherently fragile relationship work.

To the "right" of the institute definition is the definition proposed by Canada's pulp and paper industry. According to the environmental statement of the Pulp and Paper Industry of Canada, industry "shares with all Canadians important responsibilities to the environment in which we live and work. It supports the responsible stewardship of resources, including forests, fish and aquatic habitat, wildlife, air, land and water. Responsible stewardship makes possible sustained economic development. . . . Companies commit themselves to excellence in sustained yield forestry and environmental management."[15]

The policies of specific forest companies use similar words. "Noranda's Forest operations are committed to the principle of sustainable economic development."[16] Walker asked Jack for his definition. Jack responded, "We will protect, utilize and renew the forests in a manner that will provide the company's mills with a continuous and predictable supply of quality wood products [and] conduct forest activities at all times with the utmost consideration for the natural environment and other users of the forest." Walker knew this definition meant sustained economic yield.

The criterion Walker used to categorize the definitions was the underlying degree of risk of exceeding some notional biological threshold that would be an intrinsic part of the development strategy embodied in each definition. Walker was thoroughly familiar with the concept of risk. He viewed business risk as the flip side of opportunity. Risk was akin to taxes and death, an inevitable cost of getting through life. He knew that the level of risk would be a factor of the volume of production *and* the impact of the technology employed. A pulp mill pumping out large volumes of untreated effluent would run a higher risk of damage to the environment than a mill that was either running a reduced volume or both running a reduced volume and treating effluent before its release into a stream.

Walker served on the board of a First Nations community forestry project. He recognized that the Teme-akama an Anishnaba Band's definition of sustainable development was shaped by different underlying values, operating philosophies, and views on how to respond to the risks implicit in scientific uncertainty about the long-term outcomes of today's business behavior.

The Rule of Seven Generations

The Teme-akama an Anishnaba Band have long opposed the logging of ancient red and white pine forests stands. This view reflected their goal of following the "rule of seven generations" where decisions on the forest would have to take into account seven future generations, or at least the next 140 years. The Teme-akama an Anishnaba Band's definition of forest stewardship and sustainable development reflect this philosophy of favoring lower risk development.

Forest stewardship means: that the forest belongs to the life that lives within it, the future generations are dependent on the continuity of the forest. Human beings must respect forest life and use it only in ways that ensure forest continuity. The responsibilities of the managers and users of the forests are to recognize and respect the capacities and needs of the forested area. Forest stewardship goes beyond simple management, it is a commitment to care for the resources. It includes responsibilities to meet not a monetary end, but an end determined by the capacities and needs of the resource to be managed. Forest stewardship means being entrusted with administration of the forest in ways that will provide *sustained development* and ensure *sustained life.*

Sustained life means: the enduring cycle whereby currently living organisms must die, fall to the earth, become decomposed, be combined with elements from earth, air, and water to give continuing life to the forest, including all biological life forms within it.[17]

Walker recognized there would be no absolute, right definition of sustainable development but rather a continuum of subjective interpretations, each one in the eye of the beholder, each with a different set of capital and operating cost implications, each with a different level of impact on forest habitat. Each definition would establish a different tradeoff point between the two extremes of rapid, high-impact development and preserving nature. Each would represent a different type of relationship between business and wilderness, a different scale of development.

Walker summarized his preliminary research in a brief report to Jack. When they met to discuss it, Walker asked, "Are you sure you want me to go through with this? It's a lot more complex than I thought. We're going to have to assemble a multidisciplinary team with experts on silviculture, scientists, foresters, and lawyers. We are going to spend a lot of time spinning our wheels, generating draft after draft."

Jack cut him off, "Walker, I didn't hire you because you were ordinary. All I want to know is whether it is doable."

Walker reflected for a moment, "I believe it's technically feasible to compute fuller costs, costs that attempt to measure any natural capital consumed in pulp and paper operations. My concern is whether the benefit justifies the cost."

Jack laughed. "Listen, we're an industry on the defensive. Just read the bloody newspapers. Not only here but in London, Berlin. I'm sick of reading about the chain saw massacres in Canadian forests in those foreign papers. I'm willing to take the plunge into accounting for sustainable development, or whatever else you want to call it. I want to be able to chart that middle course and justify why I chose it to anybody who asks, inside or outside the company."

NOTES

1. World Commission on Environment and Development, *Our Common Future* (New York: Oxford University Press, 1987), p. 43.

2. Ibid., p. 1.

3. Ibid., p. 4.

4. Ibid., p. 45.

5. Ibid., p. 8.

6. Ibid.

7. Ibid., pp. 45–46.

8. Agenda 21, Chapter 8, "Integrating Environment and Development in Decision-Making," United Nations (New York, 1992).

9. Daniel B. Rubenstein, *Case Study in Accounting for Sustainable Forestry Management* (United Nations Conference on Trade and Development, June 1993).

10. Dr. James Higgins, "Global Environment Market Could Reach $US 454 Billion by Year 2000," *Environmental Science and Engineering,* March 1993.

11. Environmental Protection Agency, *Total Cost Assessment: Accelerating Industrial Pollution Prevention through Innovative Project Financial Analysis* (Washington, D.C.: Office of Pollution Prevention and Toxics, May 1992).

12. International Institute for Sustainable Development, *Business Strategy for Sustainable Development* (Winnipeg: The Institute, 1992).

13. Canadian Standards Association, *Draft Standards for Environmental Management Systems* (Toronto: The Association, 1992).

14. International Institute for Sustainable Development, *Business Strategy for Sustainable Development,* p. 11.

15. The Pulp and Paper Industry of Canada, *Environmental Statement* (Montreal, 1990).

16. Noranda Forest, *1990 Environmental Report* (Toronto, 1990), p. 1.

17. N. Daki Menan, *The Need for a Land Stewardship, Holistic Management Plan* (Lake Temagami, July 1989), p. 5.

Chapter 5

An Industry under Intense Public Scrutiny

A CYCLICAL COMMODITY MARKET

The Early 1990s Were Lean Years

The forest industry is a major engine of Canada's economy, and its survival and development affect all Canadians, particularly in communities that depend on forestry. Canada exports more manufactured forest products than any other nation. The United States is Canada's largest customer, purchasing 65 percent of its exports, followed by the European Economic Community (15 percent) and Japan (11 percent).[1]

An analyst said all this was in jeopardy. The Canadian forest industry lost $2.5 billion in 1991. Five plants closed. The pulp and paper industry was facing a multitude of troubles:

- Older, less efficient equipment compared to that used by the competition in the United States and overseas
- Higher wages than the competition
- Low demand for newsprint
- High debt-to-equity ratios
- Failure to modernize mills and install pollution abatement equipment when times were good
- Excessive reliance by the industry on the export of primary goods rather than value-added products
- Heightened competition from tough players in Europe and the United States and from new pulp producers like Brazil and Chile
- The growing demand for recycled newsprint[2]

Experts were saying the bust cycle in this recession had been the worst in the industry in 20 to 25 years. They predicted more mill closures and layoffs in the months to come. Investment in the new plants and equipment essential for survival, for economic viability, was way down. Surveys of the industry indicated that it expected to invest only $1.3 billion in 1991 and less than $700 million by 1994, compared with more than $4 billion in 1989 and $3.3 billion in 1990. The question for the Canadian forest industry was whether it could survive its worst battering since the Depression. Was it sustainable, in purely dollars and cents?

The price of softwood pulp, the industry's main pulp export, had fallen dramatically. In newsprint, North America had a tremendous overcapacity as the lingering recession dampened demand, forcing some prices down by as much as 40 percent. The push for more recycled content in newsprint had some firms considering the idea of building new mills far from Canada's northern forests. "Urban forests," near large cities, were being built where ample supplies of old paper existed. Hanging over the beleaguered industry was an estimated $5 billion bill for environmental cleanup mandated by new antipollution regulations.

By late 1993, some analysts were starting to believe that the spiralling losses in the pulp and paper sector over the past two years were coming to an end. They also realized there would be no roaring comeback as in the mid-1980s. Analysts were saying that the pulp and paper industry had hit the floor and were expecting the mid-1990s to be a "levelling out period." They felt the full-scale recovery, particularly for newsprint, which could not be expected until 1994 at the earliest, was dependent on the vigor of the U.S. economy.[3] Analysts saw lumber sales continuing to propel the forest sector. However, Jack, who had survived the years of transition, had more to worry about than recovery from the recession. He regularly had to face the hostile press coverage about the health of Canada's forests.

THE POLITICS OF PULP AND PAPER

The Uncertain State of Canada's Forests

Canada is, more than anything else, a forest nation, with nearly half the country — 453 million hectares — forested. About 10 percent of the world's forests are in Canada. But there are vastly different visions for the use of this forest.

Caramanah Valley, South Morseby, Clayquot Sound, Temagami — each locale had been the site of bitter, sometimes violent, confrontations between environmental activists, like Neil, and the loggers. While the arguments had been over specific sites, the opposing sides appear to have based their cases on quite different views of forests and forest management.

In recent years society, prodded by environmental activists, had come to recognize that forests are more than mere producers of fiber. Wilderness was now valued for its own sake. There was growing public awareness that forests support wildlife, hold water, and protect streams and lakes. Forests are the home of many native peoples. Forests provide recreation and aesthetic delights. Ecologists are investigating the importance of forests in maintaining the stability of the global ecosystem and in preserving biological diversity. All this was the precursor to the alleged "chain saw massacres" publicized by European environmental activists.

The Europeans joined in the British Columbia logging fight to save old-growth rain forests.[4] There was a *Time* magazine two-page spread called "Canada's Troubled Trees." The article talked about the "destruction" of British Columbia's temperate rain forests and the poisoning of rivers, lakes, and air by effluent from pulp mills. In response to these environmental campaigns, the Canadian Pulp and Paper Association established an office in Brussels to give its side of the story. What was troubling was the prospect of a generations of Europeans having a negative image of Canadian forestry practices.

Public hearings over the past four years on the future of Northern Ontario forests have cost at least an estimated $20 million and involved weeks of presentations. The public hearings were set up to give more than sixty groups, including logging companies, environmental activists, First Nations, tourist groups, and countless private citizens a chance to express their views about new rules meant to guide Ontario's forest industry into the next century.[5]

Groups like Forests for Tomorrow made submissions. They said that the future of 70 percent of Ontario "hangs in the balance." The Forests for Tomorrow submission included 76 pages of detailed recommendations concerning the planning process, public consultation, land use, and information requirements. The submission called for the maintenance of biological diversity, landscape planning and maintenance, wildlife species requiring special monitoring and management, old-growth forest ecosystems, access by the public, watercourse protection, and data collection. Forests for Tomorrow and other groups were serious about the control of Ontario's forests.[6] Ontario's forest industry saw things differently and believed that clearcut forestry practices, if properly applied, were not incompatible with maintaining other forest values such as biodiversity.

When reviewing the political debates in Canada about forestry practices, Walker noted that similar debates were raging in the United States. President Clinton prepared an array of suggested solutions to end a fractious debate over timber and endangered species in the Pacific Northwest, including one that would slash the amount of cutting on federal lands in the region by half or more. The administration's proposals would limit logging on public lands in this region to an average of 1.2 billion to 1.5 billion board feet annually over the next decade. In the late 1980s, at the peak of production, forestry operations produced more than 5 billion board feet annually.

Both timber-industry employees and executives and environmental activists attacked the administration's proposals.[7] In Oregon, groups burned coffins representing timber towns, while environmental activists spoke of loopholes so big that logging trucks could drive through them. It was a long hot summer on both sides of the border in the Pacific Northwest with active protests on Vancouver Island and disgruntled forestry companies on the Olympic Peninsula.

Faced with scientific uncertainty, public pressure about the health of Canada's forests and rivers, and tough economic times, Blackmore and Price recognized that business as usual was no longer an option. The company needed an environmental investment strategy that would keep the company consistently ahead of the regulators, generate consumer goodwill through perceived environmental leadership, reflect the scientific uncertainties, and most important, be affordable.

To develop this strategy, they would need information currently unavailable within the company on those with a perceived stake in the company's operations, the options for dealing with the persistent toxins that were an integral part of the chemical pulping process, and the full costs, including the costs of "free" natural resources, of current forestry and pulp operations. The company's goal was to develop a management information system that would integrate return-on-investment analysis with an analysis of ecological sustainability.

DEVELOPING NONTRADITIONAL ACCOUNTING SYSTEMS

Walker's starting point was the conceptual framework developed by the United Nations. Walker knew from prior experience that Jack was taking the project seriously and that the first step would be to develop a road map for implementation. The vice presidents of marketing, forestry, and environmental affairs sat down with the controller and brainstormed for two days. The result of their work is illustrated in Figure 5.1.

At the far left of the figure is the starting point of the exercise—the recognized need to establish an environmental investment strategy. Given the conditions of uncertainty and strife in the Canadian pulp and paper industry in the early 1990s, senior management knew that operating as they had during the heyday of pulp in the 1960s and 1970s was no longer an option. Their next key decision was to establish a project budget. After some considerable debate, management agreed to allocate up to two "person years" for development work, to be spread over two years, and up to $40,000 in travel and contract funds for a total budget not to exceed $250,000. This at first seemed high. However, given that the costs of a comprehensive environmental investment program could easily reach $250 million over the next decade, they felt that 1 percent of this capital cost was a not unreasonable initial expenditure.

Road Map for Developing Nontraditional Accounting Systems

Select Option

Environment is Equal

Enhanced Environmental Management

Business as Usual

Model Tradeoff Options

Fuller Costs

Risk Costs

Conversion Costs

State of Environment Report

How will it change the way the company does business?

Risk costs of doing nothing?

Intergenerational Liabilities

Ecological Limits

Level of investment in nontraditional accounting?

Terms of Reference

Standards for Sustainable Development

Corporate Account-ability

Need to establish environmental investment strategy

Multi-disciplinary team

Stakeholder Analysis

They now had a budget. The next step was to create terms of reference for the project. From past experience they knew these would have to strike a balance between what was achievable and the ideal. The terms of reference they drafted read as follows:

- *Project objectives:* To develop an analytical framework to compare the costs and environmental benefits, both real and perceived, of the environmental investment options currently faced by the company in its forest and pulp operations. As a minimum the project would address the following subobjectives:

  Generate information on the commercial value of the forests over time under different forest management scenarios.

  Develop an approach to dealing with "noncommercial values" such as wilderness or biodiversity.

  Identify the concerns and pressure points of major stakeholders who benefit from the forests managed by the company.

  Model the cost implications of different corporate goals, ranging from business as usual to comprehensive environmental management and sustainable development.

  Develop an approach to calculating fuller costs that would include the potential risk costs associated with potential environmental damage.

  Draft a corporate definition for sustainable development.

  Establish an approach to determining ecological limits under conditions of scientific uncertainty.

  Prepare a reporting strategy that would address the diverse needs of users for information, ranging from the board to environmental activists and consumers.

- *Desired outputs:* Project outputs would include a set of prototype accounts, supported by a methodology for determining full costs and nontraditional asset values.
- *Development timeframe:* The group developed a time-phased implementation plan:

  Year 1: Inventory existing databases and develop a conceptual framework.

  Year 2: Test the system on "live" investment decisions. Use the conceptual framework to publish a state-of-the-environment report.

  Year 3: If the first two steps proved successful, work on an on-line information system that could be used to support a regime of management for sustainable development.

  Year 4: Test the new system with live data, develop the software, market the system within the forest industry sector.

As illustrated in Figure 5.1 at the bottom left, the next step was to pick a multidisciplinary team that would include as a minimum a silviculture expert, an environmental policy analyst or lawyer, an organic chemist, a forester, a senior manager, a public relations or marketing person, and a cost accountant. The team would contract out for the expertise provided by an environmental economist specializing in natural resources. The personalities of the players would be critical. They would have to be imaginative and willing to get out of the ruts of conventional professional and organizational thinking. An intended benefit was a team that could view corporate problems from a holistic perspective rather than from the confines of a particular discipline or organizational perspective. Good interpersonal skills would also be an asset. Motivation would not be a problem because all knew that the CEO was solidly behind the project and eager to see the finished product as soon as a prototype was available.

The first task would be an analysis of stakeholders. This reflected the role of accounting information in society—to support informed decisions. Society's economic decisions about the forest would shape the format of the reports the team was intent on developing. This would not only pull together information already available on opinion surveys of consumer and local community views on clear-cut logging and effluent from pulp mills but also draw from the continuous monitoring of the media. In addition to these activities, the group would interview selected environmental activists, shareholders, and employees to more accurately map sensitive issues. The rationale for starting with an analysis of stakeholders was that the team needed to chart public expectations about the scope and breadth of environmental accountability to be assumed by the company. The team also needed to map the kind of information informed, and responsible stakeholders needed to make decisions on the business and the biosphere. This analysis would help the team define the limits of corporate accountability relative to public expectations about environmental stewardship.

This would be the starting point for the daunting task of developing a corporate definition of sustainable development. This definition would then be translated into tangible, measurable standards that could be costed in terms of their incremental costs relative to business as usual. These standards would define the size of clear-cuts, the technologies and practices to be employed relative to different site conditions and sensitive terrain such as spawning areas. These standards would also include a vision of a sustainable pulp mill that would preserve river systems, including aquatic life, for future generations. These benchmarks for forestry and pulp operations would have to be based on existing scientific knowledge about forest and river system health and carrying capacities.

Once the team had defined sustainable development in tangible, measurable terms, it would be in a position to compute the cost to convert existing practices to those compatible with the newly drafted standards. For example, changes in harvesting techniques, such as the size of clear-cuts, would result in increased road costs; reduction in the use of herbicides would result in increased labor costs for manual thinning of forests. These conversion factors would allow the company to begin to estimate the fuller costs of natural resources consumed. The company would also have to develop risk costs, or the costs of doing nothing. Here they would require the services of the environmental economist. If the company failed to respond to emerging practices, there was always the risk of loss of business because consumers wanted chlorine-free paper, or in the worst case situation because the public put pressure on the politicians not to renew the company's right to cut timber from public lands.

With this information in place, the company would be in a position to simulate different tradeoff options, each striking a different balance between a healthy bottom line and a healthy forest.

Now the team was assembled and ready to get on with the project. Step one was an analysis of stakeholders' perceptions of the company, and their information needs. The key question was then, "Who are the stakeholders and what information do they need to make the decisions necessary to protect their perceived stake in the forest?" As Walker reflected on this question, he realized how sick he was of the word *stakeholder*. He wished he could think of some alternative term.

NOTES

1. Forestry Canada, *The State of Forestry in Canada* (Ottawa, 1990), p. 43.

2. Bertrand Marotte, "Firms Issue Call for Lower Dollar," *The Citizen* (Ottawa), January 31, 1992.

3. Francois Shalom, "Turning the Corner," *The Citizen* (Ottawa), November 1, 1992.

4. "Europeans Join B.C. Logging Fight," *Globe and Mail* (Toronto), July 8, 1991.

5. Wendy Cox, "Forestry Management Mapping Industry's Future," *The Citizen* (Ottawa), December 9, 1991.

6. Ibid.

7. Keith Schneider, "In Peace Plan for Northwest Timber Dispute, Options May Anger Both Sides," *The New York Times,* June 19, 1993.

Chapter 6

Negotiating with
Today's Stakeholders

VISIBLE STAKEHOLDERS DEMAND A GREATER SAY

Stakeholders in the 1990s

Figure 6.1 illustrates two classes of shareholders — *visible* and *invisible*. Visible stakeholders are those with "everyday" economic transactions with the reporting entity such as buys, sells, loans, or other investments such as shares. Invisible stakeholders are those with a perceived interest in a shared resource such as spokespeople for future generations or other species.

The left of the figure focuses on the most traditional class of visible stakeholders. In the left box are the bondholders, shareholders, management, and the board of directors. These are the groups with a direct financial or contractual interest in the reporting entity. Moving to the right are the *interdependent* stakeholders. These are stakeholders that have shared transactions with the reporting entity, buys and sells, but usually have no direct financial investment. For example, suppliers are economically dependent on the entity. If it goes bankrupt, they lose business. Employees have a direct economic interest in the entity. They could lose their jobs. The government has a direct interest in terms of the taxes it receives. The local community and the region have a direct interest in terms of jobs and indirect economic spinoffs. While, for example, suppliers may also have accounts receivable from a company, their primary interest is the ongoing business. In short, interdependent stakeholders have shared, mutual economic dependence with a reporting entity.

To the right of the figure is the category of *invisible* stakeholders. These are largely the groups whose "interest" has developed in the postwar period as society's concepts of corporate accountability have changed. This group

Figure 6.1
The Stakeholders of the 1990s

Visible		Invisible	
Economic Interest		**Survival Interest**	
Contractual	**Interdependent**	**Current Generation**	**Future Generation**
Bondholders	Customers	Impact Zone	Spokespeople for
Shareholders	Suppliers	Other Users of Shared Resources	— Equity — Biosphere
Management	Employees		
Board of Directors	Government		
	Local Community and Region		

Traditional Stakeholders

can be divided into two categories—current and future generations. Invisible stakeholders include those in the direct impact zone of industrial activity. They are the human beings and other species that breathe the air and drink the downstream water. They have a survival interest today, their health is at stake. Then there are the other users of shared resources. In the forest this might involve trappers or tour guide operators.

Moving to the far right are the future generations. Obviously the unborn don't speak, but there are spokespeople who speak on their behalf. These spokespeople talk of equity in terms of preservation of the biosphere and diversity of plant and animal life.

FOR INVISIBLE STAKEHOLDERS THE ISSUE IS LAND USE

Blackmore and Price Forest Products Ltd. knew it had to deal with both the *visible* and *invisible* stakeholders concerned about the forest it harvested. Visible stakeholders in the forestry industry want the information they need to make money. Those with a direct contractual monetary investment— shareholders (especially the large institutional investors) and bondholders— want previews of coming attractions. Figure 6.2 illustrates in general terms the information they need.

Of the visible stakeholders, institutional investors such as public and private pension funds, insurance companies, banks, bank trusts, foundations,

Figure 6.2
Visible Stakeholders Demand a Greater Say

	The range of stakeholders					
	Shareholder	Community	Board of directors	Employees	Regulatory and Government	Customer and Creditors
Type	Equity	Interdependent	Equity Interdependent	Interdependent	Interdependent	Interdependent
Primary economic interest	Capital appreciation Dividends	Contribution to tax base	Protection of capital, profits	Jobs, security	Compliance, tax revenue	Service viability
Reporting interest	Earnings, dividend market Performance, data on risks	Early warning of failure	Earnings, return on investment	Earnings, early warning of failure	Taxable profit Key indicators	Early warning of failure
Key decisions	Invest, sell, hold	Decisions on economic development	Risk management	What to bargain for	To intervene or not to intervene	To deal or not to deal

Source: Reprinted from David M. Barnes and Daniel B. Rubenstein, "Revving up Our Standards Equipment," *CA Magazine* (November 1988), published by Canadian Institute of Chartered Accountants, Toronto.

churches, and university endowments are one of the most powerful groups. According to a joint study conducted by the Investor Responsibility Research Center and the Global Environmental Management Initiative, between 1981 and 1991 institutional holdings grew from 38 percent of total U.S. equities to 53 percent of total U.S. equities. Another study by the Columbia University Center for Law and Economic Studies reported that institutional investors held 49.5 percent of the equity securities of the 1,000 largest U.S. corporations in 1990.

Institutional investors reported that when it comes to corporate environmental information their highest priority item was information on environmental liabilities. Information on environmental penalties and capital spending were also important.[1] In short, these powerful institutional investors wanted the information necessary to assess a corporation's environmental stewardship. They would also need information to assess the company's future viability as a robust going concern.

Investors in the forestry sector would need at least the following information to assess economic sustainability:

- *Security of Supply.* Information about the continuity of the supply of logs would give an early warning about potential future operating problems.
- *Obsolescence of plant and equipment.* Detailed information on the extent to which a forest company was economically dependent on plants built almost 70 years ago would be most useful in assessing future profitability.
- *Competitiveness of labor costs.* Comparison of Canadian labor costs with those across the border would provide another early warning of potential vulnerabilities.
- *Sustainability of demand.* Is demand sustainable? Does the company have a secure market niche? How vulnerable is it to overcapacity in the industry and to shifting consumer tastes?

Walker knew from years of experience preparing financial statements that this was the very information a company would be loath to disclose. He continued his research, focusing his attention on the others with a perceived stake in the northern boreal forest under the stewardship of Blackmore and Price.

In Walker's view, stakeholders were all those who benefited from the forest. They included employees, the local community, customers, suppliers, contractors, and other companies they buy wood from. Environmental groups included Canadian Wildlife, Pollution Probe, World Wildlife Federation, Greenpeace, and the Federation of Ontario Naturalists to name a few. Recreational groups included anglers, hunters, canoeists, and snowmobilists. There were also tourist outfitters, as well as First Nations concerned about traditional land use, compliance with treaties, and heritage sites. There were also the province and the Ministry of Natural Resources. And then, of course, there was the forest industry that is primarily concerned about security of wood supply and a secure land tenure arrangement.

Figure 6.3
Stakeholders' Information Needs

Class of Stakeholder	Decisions To Be Taken	Information Need
Board of Directors	Environmental investments	Financial analysis of options
	Strategic directions	Risks of do nothing option
		Market analysis
	Assessment of corporate stewardship	Growth in wealth: — Forest wealth (natural resources) — Productivity — Innovation
Customers	Buy or not to buy	Resource managed renewably
	Pay premium	Production in sustainable way
		Full costs
Shareholders	Buy, sell, hold shares	Sustainable rate of return
Employees	How to protect jobs, health	Sustainable jobs
Environmental activists other forest users	Lobby or not to lobby	Environmental impact
		Costs of conversion

From an industry perspective, the agenda of each stakeholder group varied, but some common themes keep recurring: endangered species, endangered spaces, land control, chlorine-free products, and wilderness values. From a company perspective, overall land tenure was the pivotal issue. A fundamental question facing the forestry industry was how to respond to all these people who benefit from the forest.

Figure 6.3 summarizes the results of the initial interviews and review of the information needs of the stakeholders with an interest in Blackmore and Price's forestry management and business practices. The project team identified five major classes of stakeholders — the board of directors, customers, shareholders, employees, and environmental activists and other forest users such as canoeists or trappers.

As illustrated in Figure 6.3, the board of directors, being charged with making strategic decisions on the level of environmental investment, needed a financial analysis of the options, supplemented by information on the risks of minimal investments in environmental protection over the coming years. They needed information on the market such as the environmental elasticity of demand for products deemed to be environmentally friendlier.

Most important, they needed information to evaluate corporate steward-ship. This information need would require information on the growth of corporate assets or wealth from the forests, new products, or technological innovation.

The next stakeholder group, customers, needed a way to make informed purchasing decisions. Environmentally sensitive customers would want to know how well a renewable resource such as the forest resource was being managed with regard to what would be passed along to future generations. Concerned consumers would also want to know the full cost, including the costs of any natural resources consumed in harvesting and production of lumber and paper products.

The third group, shareholders, intent on buying, selling, or holding shares needed information on the projected sustainable rate of return over the next five years, after projected environmental investments. Shareholders con-cerned about forest and river health would also want to know whether the company was practicing sustainable development; and if it was still far away from this goal, how much it would cost to attain this ideal. Employees were concerned about the sustainability of their jobs. They needed informa-tion on the timing of planned modernizations and the downsizing that invariably accompanied heavy capital investments. They could then begin to plan their lives, to think about retraining or relocation. This information would also be the basis of a discussion on who would help finance this restructuring.

Environmental activists and other forest users such as hikers, trappers, or lodge operators would want information to access corporate environmental stewardship. This information would include the company's general defini-tion of sustainable development, augmented by detailed standards of sus-tainability that would define the size and use of clear-cuts, the harvesting of old-growth stands of red and white pine, the use of herbicides, and the costs associated with implementing standards in excess of current regulations.

In the light of these diverse information needs, the question for Blackmore and Price was how much of this information to provide. However, a more fundamental question for the company was, "What kind of a relationship does the company want to build with the potentially adversarial stakeholders?"

Creating a Working Partnership

One approach would be to deny that there is a problem with vocal envi-ronmental activists. If a company believes it has an exclusive right to a resource, then the natural inclination is to deny the legitimacy of the rights of other stakeholders. An alternative approach is to confront. This means getting industry-sponsored experts to testify at public hearings, to feed the press with an "industry" perspective. This is an approach that could have worked in the fifties and maybe the sixties where industry held most of the aces. It is an approach that progressive forestry companies do not follow in the 1990s. When the company that manufactures Tylenol faced a crisis with its most important stakeholders—its customers—it could have denied the problem and hired experts. It chose total recall as the only credible option in the 1990s.

The goal Blackmore and Price set for itself was "environmental transparency." Walker noted that on the financial side a company's operations were relatively transparent, but on the environmental side the company had no statutory requirement to report on its stewardship. In the United States regulators had put the gun to the head of business, but companies in Canada benefited from a "voluntary compliance" culture where enforcement was seen as a last resort rather than an opening position. Walker knew from discussions with his counterparts in the United States that for many of them their kneejerk reaction to the concept of environmental transparency would be "talk to our lawyers." However, according to Blackmore and Price's CEO, "Transparency pays because it builds credibility, and credibility buys image and image buys us an advantage at the cash registers."

To implement this concept of transparency, progressive forestry companies were trying to build working partnerships with visible and invisible stakeholders. They recognized that corporate power was greatly diminished, compared to that of the lumber barons of 100 years ago. One industry response has been to form outside advisory groups to make recommendations on a company's forestry management policies. These advisory groups contain a wide cross-section of stakeholders—university professors, trappers, local mayors, environmental activists, wildlife experts, biologists, and others. Their role is to discuss company policy and forestry management options and make nonbinding recommendations. The glue of this working partnership is information.

The project team recognized that it was easy to say stakeholders should have information. But how much access should they have to potentially sensitive information on profitability, rates of return, and the like? There was a need to develop protocols for access to sensitive corporate information.

THE DILEMMA OF ACCESS TO INFORMATION

In times of economic uncertainty, traditional investors with a tangible economic stake in a company would like information on costs, profitability, and breakeven points. Such information would allow industry analysts to assess a company's vulnerability to economic ups and downs, to the booms and busts. But this is exactly the information business is most reluctant to disclose.

The question that had to be confronted by the project team was "What *right* to access to information would each stakeholder group have, based on their explicit and implicit 'contracts' with the reporting entity?" The basic protocols developed were

- *Visible stakeholders with a contractual stake* have a right to access information necessary to assess whether their financial interest is changing in value. They need information to assess whether the company is creating, maintaining, or depleting corporate wealth.
- *Visible stakeholders with an interdependent interest* have a right to access to information that would, if closely scrutinized, provide an early warning of potential business interruptions that would affect their jobs, contracts, and the like.
- *Invisible stakeholders* in the "impact zone" have a right to immediate access to information on threats to their physical well-being (health).
- *Other users of shared resources in the current generation and spokespeople for future generations* have a right to access to the information that would support an informed debate of the various tradeoff options between business and ecological limits.

Traditional stakeholders could be provided with information on profitability and data on customer demand that would allow them to simulate different corporate survival scenarios, based on their own reading of the future (no one can predict the future, but we can all simulate it). Traditional stakeholders with a financial interest in a company could be provided with a preview of rates of return and prices under different environmental investment scenarios.

Walker and the rest of the project team summarized the results of their research with stakeholders. He wondered how Jack would respond to their analysis of information needs. Jack had talked so convincingly about the need for transparency.

"Walker, I didn't mean that transparent. What you are proposing to disclose is not transparent, Walker, it's naked. What you have for the board and head office is about right. That's got to be the focus of this project. We have to walk before we can run. Once I feel comfortable with this type of thing, then we can think about going outside with the numbers. Our challenge right now is to come up with some ways to quantify the intangible benefits of investing in tomorrow so we can get our request through the Capital Budget Committee at head office. Now we won't meet the company's return on investment criteria, and we won't get the money we are asking for."

Walker was amused, certainly not surprised. He and Jack had lived through similar conversations over the years when it came to the note disclosure in the financial statements, the final number on the bottom line. Jack always had a number in mind. Walker, a survivor, knew that some diplomacy was required. "You know Jack, it's a shame after we have generated all this useful information, that it sits in some accountant's files. It might be useful in your discussions with the ministry, the environmental activists."

"You might have a point there. But I've got something else in mind for them. Let me explain it to you."

Simulation Is the Key for Invisible Stakeholders

Jack went on to explain his idea of a partnership. "The objective of progressive forest companies like ours is a working partnership with environmental activists and with others who benefit from the forest. Let's put them all in the same room — the activists and the union and the mayor concerned about jobs. It would be an interesting dialogue. Perhaps it would lead to a greater mutual understanding of the limits of both business and the environment." Jack went on to explain that these interests would meet with business and review, on an on-line basis, different scenarios for the future. Each scenario would show the benefits for the environment and the costs for business. As there are a wide range of options, these would be simulated on a real-time basis. To stimulate this debate, business would produce an initial document outlining the broad options. Stakeholders would review these and make their views on the different options known to their representatives. Critical to this process is a shared view of the "contract" between the forest company and those who benefit from the forest.

Walker saw the job of the accountant to be creating models to describe the interplay of different limits — economic limits *and* ecological limits. He used an analogy from the aircraft industry to help explain his vision of the accountant's role. A Boeing 747 has predefined limits of operation, a range of speeds within which it can still generate sufficient lift. If it falls below a certain air speed, it drops like a rock. In contrast, a commuter aircraft can operate at a different range of speeds and take off from a shorter runway. In terms of the economics, a commuter aircraft has a far different break-even point. That is, the flight of a small commuter aircraft can cover variable costs such as the pilot's wages and jet fuel with far fewer passengers than a 747. The accountant for sustainable development tries to describe a set of economic options that could fit a certain situation, a type of aircraft that could work a particular route, given the constraints of *both* business and aerodynamic lift necessary to clear a given stand of trees at the end of the runway.

Walker, impatient to get on with the actual accounting, reflected about how far they had come in the process of creating a nontraditional accounting system. A multidisciplinary project team has been formed. It has completed the stakeholder analysis. In doing so it has addressed the first of five fundamental questions that would have to be answered:

1. *Who are the stakeholders?* To whom must a company account for sustaining the business *and* the biosphere? Who benefits from the forest, and what is a corporation's accountability to these stakeholders for sustaining the business *and* the forest.

2. *What is a company's accountability contract?* What is the company's accountability for maintaining the diversity of natural capital, habitat, preservation, flora, fauna, the jobs of loggers, and the return to shareholders?

3. *What are the limits?* What are the social and ecological limits that define business tradeoff options about the scale and technology of development?

4. *What are the business options?* What kind of tradeoff options does a company have when it comes to balancing business limits and biological limits? How much will they cost and who will pay for them?

5. *What are the costs of doing nothing?* What are the potential costs of proceeding with a business-as-usual strategy?

The team had addressed the first question, "To whom must the company account for sustaining the business *and* the biosphere?" Walker was now ready to address the second question, "What is the company's social contract for maintaining the diversity of natural capital, habitat, floral, fauna, and ways of life?" To answer this question he realized he would have to develop a conceptual framework that would cover such key concepts such as intergenerational equity and the natural capital of a boreal forest. His starting point for developing the conceptual framework would be the boreal forest itself.

NOTE

1. Investor Responsibility Research Center and the Global Environmental Management Initiative Stakeholder Communication Workshop, *Institutional Investor Needs for Corporate Environmental Information*, Washington, D.C.: September 1992.

Chapter 7

Introduction to the Basic Concepts of Natural Forest Capital, Intergenerational Equity, and Waste Minimization

A BOREAL FOREST AS A RENEWABLE RESOURCE

A Boreal Forest in Context

Canada's landscape is enormously diversified, encompassing tundra, boreal forest, deciduous forest, prairie, cordillera, three major oceanic systems, the Great Lakes, inland waters, and other ecosystems. Each of these ecozones is defined by its geography, vegetation, soils or surface materials, and climate.

Boreal forests, also known as taiga, are mostly coniferous, evergreen, and deciduous, plus some deciduous broad-leafed forests. The name comes from Boreas, Greek mythology's personification of the north wind. Globally, boreal forests are estimated to cover 11.1 million square kilometers, an area larger than all of Canada. In contrast, tropical rain forests amount to two-thirds as large an expanse. While there may be as many as 50,000 tree species in tropical rain forests, boreal forests are dominated by a handful of species such as pine, fir, spruce, larch, birch, aspen, alder, and willow. Boreal forests stretch in a broad band right across the northern hemisphere. Some 70 percent of the forests are in Siberia, 22 percent are in Canada and Alaska, and the rest are in Scandinavia. Siberia's sector is three times as large as the Brazilian Amazonia. The Siberian boreal forests contain half the world's coniferous forests, one-fifth of all trees, and one-quarter of the world's wood. Because of the size of the global boreal forests, Dr. Anthony Scott of the Pacific Energy and Resources Centre has estimated that boreal forests store at least 30 billion tons of carbon. An equivalent amount of carbon would be emitted by burning 37.5 billion tons of "dirty" coal in coal-fired power plants or extending present U.S. coal consumption over 46 years. Others have estimated that global boreal forests store one-sixth of the earth's terrestrial carbon above ground and one-fifth of the below-ground stock, making a total of more than 400 billion tons.[1]

In a boreal forest, unlike a tropical rain forest, two-thirds of the carbon is stored in forest litter and soil. In the tropical forest, the essential nutrients are in the forest canopy. The fast decomposition of organic matter and the leaching of the soil do not allow organic matter to accumulate. In the boreal forest, nutrients accumulate in the soil and organic material on top of the soil and in the canopy. However, on nutrient-deficient sites in a boreal forest, most of the available nutrients can be in the canopy.

In a living boreal forest, the sources of natural replenishment of nitrogen, for example, are precipitation and nitrogen fixation. There is a natural balance between removal and replenishment. Rock weathering is a source of calcium, for instance. Of the essential minerals, nitrogen is key in the short run. In the longer term, other essential plant minerals include phosphorus, potassium, calcium, magnesium, boron, iron, and sulfur, to name a few.

The forests comprise a diverse mosaic of vegetational and soil/site ecosystem conditions. For example, pure, even-aged jack pine stands occur widely on well-drained, coarse-textured soils. Stands occur often with poorly developed understorey vegetation across a range of soil and site conditions — from thin mineral soils overlaying bedrock to poorly drained organic wetlands. Extensive and repeated forest fires, cyclical insect infestations, disease, and other factors have an ongoing and pervasive effect on the ecology of boreal forests.[2]

Diversity of Natural Capital

Forest ecosystems are more than the trees in the main canopy. Climate, understorey vegetation, soil, and other physical site features play important roles in determining how the forest will evolve and develop. The forest resource manager must consider more than just forest cover. The boreal forest region is characterized by extensive black spruce, jack pine, and balsam fir forests, as well as mixed stands of conifer and northern deciduous species such as trembling aspen and white birch.

The Ontario Ministry of Natural Resources is concerned with managing a diversity of wildlife but treats the management of trees as the priority when ranking different uses of the forest. Wildlife management considers moose, deer, black bear, waterfowl, small game, caribou, birds, bats, and other fauna. Wildlife management is seen as a constraint to timber management; specific management for wildlife occurs only in a relatively small part of the area managed. The focus of the ministry's wildlife efforts is on moose and deer. Managers may make local decisions about which species warrant special forest prescriptions. The theory is that legitimate concerns for wildlife other than moose or deer will often be accommodated to a large degree in the prescriptions for the preservation of the "key species" (i.e., moose or deer).

The ministry's overall philosophy for moose habitat management is to achieve a proper combination of moose population management, control of hunters, and careful habitat manipulation. For the boreal forest region, the plan recognizes that new access creates a potential for local overharvesting of moose. It recognizes that road access should avoid mineral licks, aquatic feeding areas, and calving sites to protect those important habitat features and to minimize disturbance and accidents to moose using these areas.[3]

A boreal forest is a *renewable resource.* The predominant conifer species, black and white spruce and jack pine, can regenerate themselves, every 70 to 300 years *if* the land retains its productivity. Walker knew this *if* would be critical in accounting for natural capital, the natural resource base that supports the economic development of the forest. Accounting for any potential risks of a loss in this forest productivity would be akin to accounting for the Exxon expectation, a high-magnitude event with a low probability of occurrence.

Walker knew that in a natural setting, jack pine regenerates itself by producing cones that open in response to the heat of forest fires. Before the advent of fire control, fires recurred on average every 50 to 100 years. Retaining biomass (i.e., cone-bearing branches on living trees) is a necessary but perhaps not sufficient condition for natural jack pine regeneration; fire is also needed, or eventually other species will replace jack pine. Lopping and scattering branches following a harvesting operation sometimes provides adequate regeneration as some cones shed their seeds in the warmth of the clear-cut. Slash burning creates excessively high temperatures that consume the seed. Helicopter seeding is becoming increasingly popular as a regeneration technique. These limits to the forest would have to be respected in the conceptual framework Walker wanted to create for accounting for natural capital such as a living forest.

NATURAL CAPITAL AND ECONOMIC ASSETS

Accounting for Natural Capital

Figure 7.1 illustrates the framework Walker developed. The traditional focus of business and accounting is on the outputs at the far right of Figure 7.1 — economic assets such as lumber and pulp that form the basis of economic transactions. When a company buys lumber, it debits inventory and credits cash. This is the grist of accounting, the focus of recorded transactions. But this is only the beginning of the story.

Figure 7.1
Accounting for Natural Forest Capital

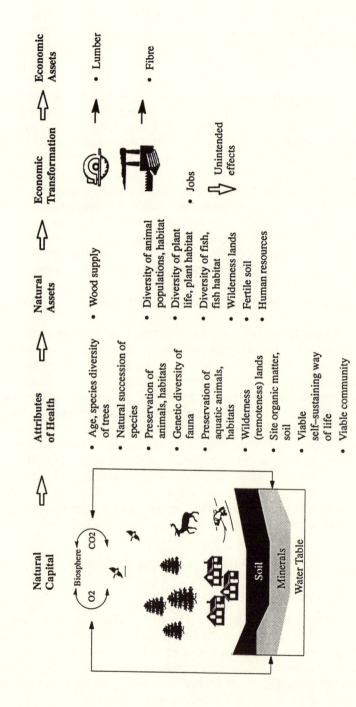

In an industrial world, a world dependent on the age of chemistry and realignment of atomic structures, most economic action seems to have intended and unintended effects. This appears to be a fact of life, the reality of synergistic, complex systems. Walker wondered whether perhaps unintended effects follow from a law similar to the conservation of matter. A natural resource is distilled and converted into something else, but the remainder of the resource must go somewhere. These are the unintended by-products.

Moving to the left of Figure 7.1, accountants move from economic assets such as milled lumber to natural assets such as the wood. A forestry company sees the wood supply as its primary asset. When asked to account for natural resources, its initial and primary focus is on wood supply over the next 70 years, comparing regeneration to harvest. While the company sees the wood supply as an asset, in reality the wood supply is merely the interest on the principal. The key question is then, "What is the principal?" This asset would then be the basis of accounting for sustainable development.

As illustrated in Figure 7.1, wood supply is only one of a multiplicity of assets. There is the diversity of animal populations and habitats; a diversity of plant life and plant habitats; a diversity of fish and fish habitats; and wilderness. The natural focus of the company is on a narrow band of the spectrum of natural assets, the wood supply. This reflects how it sees its primary mission in life, that of developing, transforming, and creating human economic wealth rather than preserving natural capital. The focus of the community is on sustainable jobs.

But moving to the far left, the objective of the exercise is to try to account for *natural capital* that spans an incredibly complex interconnected northern boreal forest. This involves accounting for the underlying natural wealth that supports the forest and leads to continuous wood supply. Other forest functions include the processing of carbon dioxide. There are the flora, the fauna. There are the river, the watershed, the aquatic populations. There are the human communities. There are the soil itself, minerals in the soil, inorganic and organic matter. There is the water table.

The objective of accounting for the sustainable corporation would be to account for this integral link between economic assets and natural capital. The purpose of this accounting would be to report whether the company was living on principal or interest. If it is living on principal, the obvious question is, "How much is being consumed?"

THE CONCEPT OF AN ECOLOGICAL ENTITY

The Concept of a Board of Resource Stewardship — at the Ecoregion Level. An *accounting entity* is the organization on which accountants report. Normally it is a corporation, an individual business, or a consolidated corporate empire. However, an accounting entity could be anything

Figure 7.2
Ecologically Based Accounting Entities

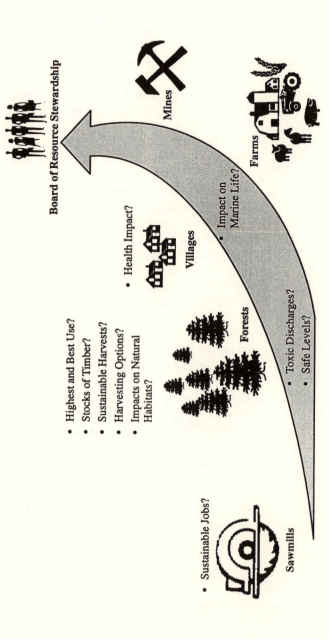

Board of Resource Stewardship

Mines

Farms

- Health Impact?

Villages

- Impact on Marine Life?

- Highest and Best Use?
- Stocks of Timber?
- Sustainable Harvests?
- Harvesting Options?
- Impacts on Natural Habitats?

Forests

- Toxic Discharges?
- Safe Levels?

- Sustainable Jobs?

Sawmills

an accountant defines. In national income accounting, the entity is a country. Accountants could also account for the economic activity of a province, a state, or a region. In other words, the definition of the accounting entity is up to the accountant and the stakeholders. The problem with the traditional accounting entity concept is that it focuses totally on the company and excludes information on the relationship between the company and the *ecoregion* of which is an integral part.

An *ecoregion* is a territory with a boundary defined not on an economic or political basis but on an ecological basis. An ecoregion encompasses the natural capital of a particular region, including habitat, flora, fauna, and river systems. A few communities are experimenting with the concept of a community-based board of resource stewardship that monitors the health of a given ecoregion. Such a board would be the ultimate recipient of the prototype accounts on sustainable development. This board would have an oversight role for the ecoregion and try to arbitrate between competing uses of scarce resources. The board would lobby state and local governments. This concept is currently in use in some remote communities in the Yukon in Canada's North.

To protect themselves from the strict application of joint and several liability, companies in a given region could self-regulate on a regional basis. They would demand an accounting from their codevelopers of a given resource base. Self-regulation by a board of resource stewardship of the use of wetlands and other sensitive areas would be a natural part of enlightened self-interest. In Walker's view, the current approach to assigning liability for cleanup was modeled on the game of "the last one at the bar picks up the tab." The sustainable corporation with the deepest pocket would be the most likely to get stuck picking up the tab. In Walker's view, if all companies had to account for their stewardship along the lines of the model he was developing and had to share this information with a board of resource stewardship, the responsible corporations might be better able to cut off the heavy drinkers before the tab got out of hand.

Ecologically Based Accounting

Figure 7.2 describes an accounting regime appropriate to this accountability framework. The corporation and the stewardship board would both be accountable for natural resource management. In addition to traditional financial statements, companies would prepare satellite environmental accounts that provided information that could be aggregated to present an overall accounting of the ecosystem managed. The proposed stewardship accounts would provide information on changes during the year to physical stocks of national resources such as timber, as well as the asset values of the timber over the forest's growing cycle. These stewardship accounts would provide information on environmental obligations (cleanup or reforestation costs) as well as information on emission and effluent levels. The objective would be to make the future explicit—today, to sort out the intergenerational accounts. Walker had no trouble with the concept of intergenerational liabilities—they were obligations that would extend at least a generation into the future and would probably reflect those high-magnitude–low-probability accounting situations. His problem was with how a company would ever compute these liabilities.

INTERGENERATIONAL EQUITY

Accounting for Unrecorded Intergenerational Costs

Intergenerational costs arise when natural capital is impaired by one generation. Man the extractor, the creature in quest of fiber and lumber, has a number of choices. He can leave the forest alone, he can harvest it sustainably, or he can harvest it nonsustainably. Whenever there is an intervention, there may be the need to mitigate the consequences of this intervention. The more extensive the volume of cut, the higher the impact of the technology employed, the greater the risk of the need for remediation. Society can account for these costs either now or later, but society will end up accounting for them. As illustrated in the case of the *Exxon Valdez,* business could account for the risk costs of shipping thousands of gallons of oil now when it purchases double hulled oil tankers or when there is a spill. Good accounting requires a recognition of these costs now.

For example, in a tree, the highest percentage of nutrients is in the needles or leaves. Under existing logging practices in the boreal forest, this biomass is generally removed from the site. The tree is "de-limbed" by the side of the road. The biomass and nutrients do not return to the soil. Over years, this loss of organic matter and nutrients can lead to a degradation of the fertility of the soil on sites where the natural replacement of nutrients, from the atmosphere and mineralization of the soil, is less than the amount depleted. It can lead to deferred maintenance costs. Some of this negative impact can be offset by the use of fertilizers (either organic or inorganic). However, there is a cost of remediation that should be recognized the day the tree is cut. This is an intergenerational cost. Walker knew that the concept underlying the calculation of such costs was a variation of a well-established concept, the preventive maintenance concept.

DEFERRED MAINTENANCE HAS A COST

Preventive maintenance is a well-established industrial concept. Millions of airline passengers expect a well-established preventive maintenance program to be in place. Catastrophic engine failure at thirty thousand feet is

fatal. Generally, there is an inverse relationship between preventive maintenance and breakdown maintenance.

If corporations service the corporate jet at regular intervals, have its parts
serviced and replaced according to parts specifications based on usage,
there is a lower probability of an unanticipated breakdown or "catastrophic
failure" of the electrical system during flight.

The concept of preventive maintenance also applies to real estate. A roof
should be changed after 20 years. If it is not, a company is going to pay,
either through the costs of repairing leaks, the cost of lost shingles, or the
cost of replacing the roof. That is, for fixed assets there is an expected maintenance program.

When homeowners do not replace a roof after 20 years, they are practicing deferred maintenance. Prospective buyers of a rental property that
showed a steady stream of reported profits would like to know whether the
roof had been replaced and whether other routine maintenance had been
performed on schedule. If there is deferred maintenance, the income reported
may not be sustainable. Prospective buyers, users of the financial statements of this rental property, need to know about the state of the roof, the
state of the fixed asset, the existence of deferred and backlog maintenace
that has started to accrue like a liability.

But what happens when deferred maintenance becomes backlog maintenance? Sooner or later something will break down. The probability of that
breakdown increases as maintenance decreases. One way to deal with this,
from an accounting perspective, is to set up reserves for future expenses
(i.e., self-insurance). Another way is to buy an extended warranty. Airline
companies deal with this problem in two ways—they spend on preventive
maintenance and they pay for insurance. Both expenses are consistent with
the matching concept in accounting. The insurance premium is a critical element in matching the potential cost of catastrophic failure with current activities, as the risks are experienced every passenger mile flown.

While there are similarities between accounting for natural capital and accounting for a fixed asset (i.e., for the corporate jet), there is a fundamental
difference. If there is a catastrophic failure of a jet, owners buy a new one.
If there is catastrophic failure of a northern boreal forest, society might
have to wait 10,000 years for a new one. This suggests the need for reserves
in kind rather than monetary reserves. Given the irreplaceable nature of a
10,000-year-old forest, accounting in dollar terms may not be enough. A set
percentage of the forest could be set aside as wilderness lands.

For example, a jack pine forest has a growing cycle of 60 to 100 years.
Given the uncertainty of the biological threshold or limit, a company could
set aside wilderness reserves. The company could monitor the health of the
portion of the forest that had been cut. After 30 years of monitoring, looking for early warning signals of impairment of forest health, the company

could then assess the advisability of harvesting the balance of the logging limit that had been set aside. This reserve is physical insurance, a physical heritage passed on from one generation to the next.

Walker was now ready to integrate what he had learned so far into an overall conceptual framework. He hoped that the concept of a product life cycle might be helpful. The model he had in mind would identify the risks associated with each phase of production. This model would be particularly relevant for dealing with risks associated with toxic discharge from the company's pulp operations.

THE UNIVERSAL LIFE CYCLE

Walker was familiar with the generally accepted life cycle for describing business activity. The life cycle starts with human need; moves through the harvesting and extraction phase, the regeneration phase, the manufacturing phase, the distribution phase, and the in-service phase; and ends with the disposal and recycling phase of business activity. This life cycle is a convenient way to organize economic activity.

The first phase in the life cycle is grounded in the human need for paper products, for lumber, with a corresponding risk that demand may lead to excess harvest. In the next phase, there is the harvest of the resource, with the corresponding risk of impairment to natural capital. In the next phase, there is regeneration or replanting. A failure to plant enough trees will impair the commercial value of the forest. In the manufacturing phase, there is a risk of the release of persistent toxins that will not break down naturally. In the case of pulp production, it would be chlorine compounds. There is also the risk of the nonsustainable use of energy. In the ideal world, pulp production and lumber production should not be net users of energy. In the distribution phase, the lumber has been milled and has to be transported to market. There are ecological costs, the burning of fossil fuels.

The penultimate phase is the in-service phase that deals with the use of the product itself. In the case of lumber, lumber stores CO_2, has a positive in-service ecological value. The use of automobiles would not be so benign but would result in increases in CO_2. While lumber is a carbon sink, cars are a carbon leak. Each product will have a different ecological impact during the in-service or use phase.

The last phase is the disposal and recycling phase. The failure to recycle results in landfill, toxic discharge, and waste of scarce resources such as ores or minerals. Ways to make a nonrenewable resource last longer are to limit demand, to make the manufacturing phase as efficient as possible, and to ensure maximum recycling.

Walker had been reading a great deal about life cycle costing in the accounting journals he was reviewing. He tried to get clear in his own mind the differences between this new approach and traditional managerial cost accounting. In his mind, managerial accounting was the process of collecting, preparing, and analyzing information principally for internal decision making. This represented the cost accounting he had been doing most of his professional life. Full cost accounting was a method of managerial cost accounting that tries to allocate environmental costs (direct and indirect) to a product, product line, process, service, or activity. Walker's research indicated that different people used the term *full cost accounting* in different ways. Some include only a firm's legal costs (i.e., those costs that would be assessed under Superfund legislation). Others include a much fuller range of costs throughout the life cycle of the product — from raw material extraction to product disposal. Many of these costs to society, such as landfill costs to a municipality, would never directly or indirectly show up on a firm's bottom line.

The current debate among environmental accountants is whether full cost accounting means accounting for all the risks conceivable. In Walker's view, the issue was one of accountability for the payment of the costs of disposal or recycling. Clearly disposal or recycling costs are a shared responsibility among producers, consumers, and governments. However, business must bear a portion of the cost of potential environmental waste that is not avoided in the product design phase (including the design of the factory used in its production). Walker decided that for the exercise he was undertaking full costs would not include the in-service and disposal and recycling phases. However, his working definition of full costs would include the environmental costs associated with the pulp operation. To complete his conceptual framework, he felt he had to learn more about the difference between waste avoidance and waste reduction (in the former case, the waste is not produced at all; in the latter case, it is minimized).

WASTE AVOIDANCE AND WASTE MINIMIZATION

Walker read that increasingly, progressive companies are placing greater emphasis on policies and technologies for waste reduction prior to generation, a concept included within the broader context of waste minimization. The key incentives for waste reduction are

- From an environmental standpoint, it is almost always the ecologically superior alternative.
- The costs of future corrective action and liability can be very high.
- Costs for land, disposal, incineration, and other waste-treatment alternatives are high and rising rapidly.
- Increasingly stringent regulatory requirements are encouraging the phasing out of land disposal of hazardous wastes.
- Evidence suggests that waste-reduction programs present industry with opportunities to lower manufacturing costs while making a safer workplace.

According to a comprehensive manual prepared by General Electric Company, waste reduction can be thought of as any method that will reduce or eliminate the amount of hazardous waste *before* it is generated within a given manufacturing process. Waste minimization is a regulatory term referring to treatment, recycling, and other process alterations that result in less waste requiring ultimate disposal.

Waste minimization generally applies in a regulatory context to include reduction or elimination of the *amount* of waste requiring ultimate disposal through treatment steps, recycling steps, or waste source reduction as defined above.

According to GE, the treatment of a hazardous waste shifts the burden of disposal from one environmental medium to another (e.g., from ground water to the atmosphere and surface water). Continued corporate exposure to rising treatment costs and unpredictable financial liability penalties requires waste reduction at the source. Special priority is assigned to waste reduction as the waste minimization method of preference at progressive companies.

In the context of these definitions, the GE manual notes that *amount* of waste can be defined in two ways. One relates to a reduction in the total volume of a waste stream defined as hazardous; the other relates to a reduction in the amount of specific chemical constituents in the waste that cause it to be hazardous. The former is considered volume reduction; the latter hazard reduction. The following examples illustrate the distinction between the two definitions:

1. *Volume reduction.* When sludge is "dewatered" by the company generating it, the company usually pays a smaller disposal fee simply because a smaller volume of waste is shipped off site for disposal.

2. *Hazard reduction.* Hazard reduction uses methods that either reduce or remove the hazardous constituents from the waste stream and thus render the waste less hazardous, preferably to the legally nonhazardous level.

The distinction between these two definitions is important. The total potential toxic burden on the environment is determined more by the quantity of specific hazardous constituents in a waste than by the volume of waste. However, the cost of waste management is governed by both the concentration of hazardous constituents and the quantity of waste.

Waste minimization also encompasses various techniques for reducing wastes after they are generated. These other waste minimization techniques (e.g., treatment, reclamation, waste exchange) can be reasonable and appropriate when considered as short-term alternatives to less desirable practices like underground injection or landfilling. The following examples illustrate some of these waste management techniques:

1. *On-Site Recycling*. This simply involves using wastes as the material input to some productive process at the plant which will enable the waste stream to be cycled back into the product line.

2. *On-Site Treatment*. This method reduces the output of hazardous waste to off-site facilities. Examples of such treatments are dewatering, which reduces the volume of hazardous waste requiring disposal, and incineration, which can destroy hazardous constituents in the waste.

3. *Source segregation*. This is a simple method which prevents contamination of large volumes of nonhazardous waste by isolating those streams containing hazardous constituents.[4]

Overview of Waste-Reduction Processes. The goal of a waste-reduction program, according to GE, should be to modify current operations and to design those for use in the future to reduce the quantity and hazard of the wastes generated. Hazard-reduction opportunities lie both in changing amounts of hazardous raw material input and in changing technical aspects of production processes. In developing a waste-reduction strategy, progressive companies examine the following range of techniques:

1. *Product innovation*. When developing new products, companies consider their pollution potential. As part of a waste minimization program, a facility may choose to substitute one product for another based on the potential for decreased waste or waste toxicity. This is an area in which research and development efforts play a major role. It is most useful to industries that experience rapid product innovation.

2. *Chemical substitution*. This method, also know as product reformulation, involves substituting raw materials used in a manufacturing process. It is applicable to existing product lines. For example, the paint industry has developed substitutes for once-popular lead-based paints. The adhesives industry has substituted water-based adhesives for those containing solvents. Other examples include solvent substitution, catalyst substitution, and the use of higher-purity raw materials.

3. *Process modification*. Most industrial processes generate hazardous by-products or wastes. Changing the process to increase production efficiency can reduce hazardous waste streams. For example, operating an electroplating process at a higher temperature to enhance drainage of the plating solution from parts before rinsing can potentially reduce both the hazard and the volume of the waste. Other methods include equipment modification or replacement, direct waste recycling, and better housekeeping.

ACCOUNTING FOR EXTERNAL COSTS

Definition of Internal and External Costs

Based on his experience with pulp operations, Walker could easily relate to the GE method. It made good business sense to account for all related production costs, including waste handling, and factor them into decisions. But Walker, a relative newcomer to fuller cost accounting, wondered if this would be going far enough into the uncharted realm of nontraditional accounting. In addressing these doubts, Walker's research led him into the domain of environmental economics. What he discovered was that economists had been researching social costs, or externalities, for decades and that there was a growing body of research upon which he could draw.

Externalities are impacts created by production or use of a good or service that directly or indirectly affects other entities and for which the party responsible does not incur costs equal to the damage caused by the impacts. The externalities are not reflected in the price. By convention, externalities are considered to be negative (i.e., damages), but they could also be positive (i.e., benefits). Examples of externalities included residents disturbed by highway noise and the noise caused by jet planes in their final approach to urban airports. If the responsible party incurs costs equal to the damage caused, the costs are then *internalized*. These impacts may continue, but they are no longer externalities. Walker noted that the GE method was focusing on these internalized costs.

Economists are concerned about these externalities because they represent real costs to society in the form of damage to human health, agriculture, and natural ecosystems as well as leading to an inefficient use of resources. This is caused when demand for products exceeds an "optimal level" (i.e., demand that would fall if prices reflected the full cost, including the damage to health and the ecology). These unrecorded externalities also put more benign products at an economic disadvantage.

As indicated by the precedent-setting case of the *Exxon Valdez,* the frontier between internalized (or internal) costs and externalized (or external) costs was neither obvious nor static. What may be external today may be internal tomorrow. This shifting reflects an enlargement of corporate accountability and stewardship. Walker realized that conceptually holding a corporation responsible for cradle-to-grave impacts would mean the breakdown of the traditional internal–external cost boundaries.

Abatement versus Damage Costing

Walker's review of the literature suggested that across North America there was relatively little experience in tracking and allocating internal environmental costs and in accounting for environmental externalities. However, electric utilities were doing more research in full cost accounting, relative to other sectors. In accounting for the external costs of electric utilities there were two main approaches—the abatement cost approach and the damage costing approach.

The *abatement cost approach* uses the cost to fix a given pollution problem as a proxy cost for the real external cost. Walker found this easy to grasp. Under this approach the external cost of the waterborne effluent from the pulp mill would be the cost of building a low-impact pulp mill that virtually eliminated the release of persistent toxins. The advantage of this approach would be that the costs would be relatively easy to estimate, compared to calculating the downstream effects of mill effluent. These abatement costs would represent the costs of fixing the problem, moving way ahead of the regulators. These would be costs that senior management could easily understand. The disadvantages of this approach were that they would bear no relationship to the damage actually caused.

In contrast, the *damage costing approach* would integrate the science, the economics, and the accounting in a five-step process:

1. Identify and estimate emissions and potential impacts.
2. Model the dispersion of the air and waterborne emissions in the immediate and wider impact zone.
3. Quantify the physical impacts on human health, agriculture, and natural ecosystems, based on established scientific "dose-response functions."
4. Monetize the physical impacts, based on the principles developed by environmental economists.
5. Account for the estimated costs (or most likely a range of costs) of these externalities as environmental costs, "booking" the related environmental liabilities in both the internal corporate management information systems and, eventually, in a corporation's published annual report.

Walker sensed that the damage costing approach would lead into uncharted waters, and he was hesitant to put all his energies into an approach that might not bear fruit for some years. Rather, he decided on a time-phased strategy. Initially, the team would focus on the abatement cost approach, trying to estimate the costs of changing course to more sustainable ways of doing business. Later in the project, the team would hire an environmental economist to help develop an approach to determining the damage costs associated with not fixing existing problems.

Walker now felt he had begun to put together a rough conceptual framework for accounting for full costs. On the forestry side, the project team would have to account for any costs of deferred maintenance, as a minimum. They would also have to figure out a way to account for the risk costs associated with current forestry management practices. How they would account for the Exxon expectation costs was yet to be determined. The concepts on waste minimization and waste reduction should help account for pulp operations.

Walker believed the concepts of biological limits and natural capital could be applied to forestry operations. He now believed he had the conceptual framework necessary to confront the first two of the five basic questions to be addressed in accounting for sustainable development. He had begun to consider the first two questions:

1. To whom must the company account for sustaining the business and the biosphere?
2. What is the company's social contract for maintaining the web of life, including the diversity of natural capital, flora, fauna, and ways of life?

Walker was now ready to move from the theory to the practice both to address the last three questions and to define the company's accountability for the forest:

3. What are the social and ecological limits that define business choices as to scale and technology used in development?
4. What are the best sustainable tradeoff positions between business limits and biological limits, and who will pay for the costs of conversion?
5. What are the potential costs of not changing course?

NOTES

1. "Disturbing the Ecological Balance: The Boreal Forests," *The Citizen* (Ottawa), July 18, 1993.

2. R. A. Sims, W. O. Towill, K. A. Baldwin, and G. M. Wickware, *Forest Ecosystem Classification for Northwest Ontario* (Ottawa: Forestry Canada).

3. Ministry of Natural Resources, *Timber Management Guidelines for the Provision of Moose Habitat* (Toronto: The Ministry, 1988).

4. General Electric Company, *Financial Analysis of Waste Management Programs* (Fairfield, Conn.: GE Corporate Environmental Programs, 1987), pp. 2–8.

Chapter 8

Transforming Natural Capital into Product

A REPRESENTATIVE FOREST COMPANY TODAY

Corporate Structure. Blackmore and Price is an integrated pulp and paper company. It is one small piece of a complex corporate giant with extensive holdings in brewing, real estate, and mining. It harvests large tracts of woodland in northern Ontario and manufactures pulp, paper, and lumber for distribution mainly in Canada and the eastern and midwestern regions of the United States. Blackmore and Price's principal facility includes a kraft pulp and paper mill at Kirkland Lake, Ontario. The company is one small piece of a much larger forestry company, Elgin Resources, with extensive operations in British Columbia, Georgia, and New Brunswick.

Blackmore and Price's operations have an annual capacity of 475,000 air dry short ton (ADST) of bleached softwood kraft pulp. The sawmill operations have a total capacity of 350 million board feet per annum of spruce and jack pine lumber. The majority is sold in Ontario. Blackmore and Price employs approximately 2,500 full-time and part-time workers. Blackmore and Price had sales of approximately $500 million. The net loss for 1991 was approximately $50 million, principally because of the recession and depressed prices for many pulp and paper products. The loss for 1992 was $20 million; in 1993, the company broke even.

Because of the aesthetic beauty and relatively pristine wilderness in which Blackmore and Price conducts much of its activity, there have been, not surprisingly, demands from nonlumber industry interests to ensure sound forestry management practices, as well as preservation of parts of the forest for noncommercial uses.

Blackmore and Price's cutting rights include an average annual allowable cut of approximately 690,000 cubic meters of softwood on Crown land held under long-term forest management agreements. Because this is not sufficient to fully satisfy the mill requirements, the company buys supplementary saw logs and wood ships from contract suppliers. However, this is an unpredictable source, and the main source of supply must come from the forests managed directly by the company. Blackmore and Price's cutting rights are for 20 years, renewable by the Ontario government every 5 years, based on compliance with forest management regulations. The royalty and stumpage fees paid to the Crown are treated as other operating expenses in the company's income statement but not reported as a separate line item.

Logging Methods Used in the Woods. Harvest operations continue year-round. In recent years, Blackmore and Price changed the focus of its woodlands operations to tree-length logging. The Company's pulp mill is serviced by chips from their sawmill and other area sawmills and by wood purchased from private contractors. The three major harvesting systems are

- A totally manual system in which trees are felled, delimbed, and topped by chainsaw, then skidded to roadside.
- A totally mechanized system using mechanical feller, grapple skidders, and mechanical delimbers.
- A combination of the two, where trees are felled manually, skidded to roadside, and then mechanically delimbed.

25,000 Homes a Year. The result of these efforts is the ability to supply one of the larger sawmills in Canada, a sawmill that produces enough finished lumber to build 25,000 homes a year. This modern complex has automated its production as much as possible, to derive maximum benefit and yield from each tree.

Chemical Pulping and Bleaching Process. The process used by the Blackmore and Price mill, which involves chemical pulping, is known as kraft pulp production. Chemical pulping is the process by which chemicals are used to dissolve the lignin from the wood and individual cellular fibers. A chlorine bleaching process is used.

The mill is in compliance with Ontario regulations on biochemical oxygen demand (BOD) discharges for Ontario. However, it will be required to install secondary treatment under provincial regulations (MISA). It will also have to reduce chlorine discharge to comply with pollution regulations in the Canadian Environmental Protection Act (CEPA) and levels mandated by the Ontario government. The mill's air emissions for particulate and odor are in compliance with regulations 90 percent of the time.

Corporate Goals of Blackmore and Price. Blackmore and Price's management is committed to achieving long-term environmental goals in excess of those required by regulations. The benefits of getting ahead of the regulations are recognized in terms of financial planning and improved competitiveness. Management has been influenced by other progressive medium-sized forest companies that have established themselves as forestry industry leaders. The Blackmore and Price goal is to approach a zero-impact (i.e., virtual elimination of persistent toxins that accumulate) mill by the year 2000.

Corporate Concerns. Blackmore and Price's goals are based on self-interest, albeit enlightened self-interest. When it comes to the forest operations, Blackmore and Price has two overriding concerns — security of supply and public perceptions about clear-cut logging, the predominant technology used.

Blackmore and Price desperately wants a secure forest base. The way the company sees it, there are ever more stringent demands from the Ministry of Natural Resources and from advocacy groups, demands that keep shrinking the forest base that they can harvest on a sustained-yield basis. Forest land is always taken out of production, never put back. The trend seems inevitable.

Blackmore and Price sees forestry as a farming operation. An important difference is that the forests take decades to regenerate, while a new crop of corn appears next spring. Blackmore and Price recognizes that the public doesn't see clear-cutting that way. Blackmore and Price also accepts that the public does not understand the business implications of different logging scenarios.

CAPACITY DEFINES THE BUSINESS LIMITS

Blackmore and Price recognizes it must address the question of the best sustainable tradeoff between business limits and biological limits. Management and the accountants are looking forward to a dialogue with stakeholders based on fact, hard numbers, and scientific evidence rather than rhetoric. To achieve this reporting goal, Blackmore and Price wanted to develop an accounting model with two components — the business-limits component (which the accountants could develop) and the biological-limits component (which the scientists, foresters, and ecologists had to develop).

Yesterday's Investment Decisions Define Today's Options. Walker had been a cost accountant with Blackmore and Price for almost 20 years. After high school he worked as a cook on the last of the river drives. Walker moved on from being a cook to working in the bush, eventually settling in cost accounting and working his way up the ladder at the head office. Walker knew the unit costs of every phase of the company's logging operations — the unit costs per mile of wood hauled, the unit costs for falling a tree, the unit costs for a meal in the bunk house.

Walker could break these costs out into fixed cost and variable costs. The fixed costs were related to major capital purchases of plant and equipment that had been made years ago. These were the sunk costs. There was nothing to do about them. The costs to manage were the variable costs — fuel, oil, costs that change with the volume of production.

Walker knew that it was Blackmore and Price's pulp and paper mill, with its annual capacity of 475,000 ADST of bleached softwood kraft pulp, that drove everything in the field. Walker was part of the decision 10 years earlier to build the pulp mill. The company invested $150 million. Walker knows that implicit in this decision was a projected continuity of wood supply. To run the Blackmore and Price mill at near capacity, the company needed to be able to cut an annual minimum volume of 700,000 cubic meters of forest. To do this, Blackmore and Price recognized that it would need to have a land tenure agreement covering upwards of 42 million cubic meters of timber.

The senior forester on the team, Mike Ashton, explained that the projection of the need for 42 million cubic meters of timber was very "optimistic." The projected harvest would be fine in the first years of operations. But as the uncut forest stands keep aging and their probability of destruction owing to fire or insects keeps increasing, could the company sustain the minimum volume of 700,000 cubic meters? The company could accelerate cutting, intensify pest and fire control programs, and concentrate its efforts on regenerating cut-over areas. Clearly, there was no margin for error, for natural catastrophes, or for pressures for increased land withdrawals in the company's scenario.

There was the option to supplement wood supply from outside purchases, from contractors who harvest beyond the Blackmore and Price wood supply. However, this was not the desired option. Implicit in Blackmore and Price's decision making was the lifespan of the prime species, jack pine. This species regenerates in 60 to 70 years. Blackmore and Price then needed a land mass large enough to support a continuous harvest over this life cycle.

Blackmore and Price had been getting increasingly nervous as the land that could be harvested continued to shrink. There were ever more stringent regulations from the Ministry of Natural Resources restricting sensitive areas around spawning streams for trout, nesting areas for herons, and calving areas for moose. Walker's concern was that if supply is lowered below a certain breakeven point, there would not be a sufficient supply to run the mill at near capacity. As the volume drops or throughput drops, unit costs rise because there is a lower volume to spread these fixed costs across.

There was a notional breakeven point where volume of production is close enough to capacity to give the desired return on investment, the return that was contemplated in the initial investment decision. Over the long haul, Blackmore and Price was looking for a rate of return of between 20 percent and 30 percent.

Walker was also aware of the unforgiving nature of a commodity market. For both its major products — lumber and pulp — Blackmore and Price faced a commodity price that fluctuates daily. Blackmore and Price had two options — either take the price or not sell its products. Walker knew that a 10 percent to 15 percent increase in costs to Blackmore and Price can be fatal, given that these costs cannot be passed along to the consumer. The commodity price is nonnegotiable. Blackmore and Price's pulp and wood products could be the most environmentally sustainable in North America, but the commodity price would not change in the short run. In the long run, there might be options for specialized products, for developing a unique market niche where consumers may pay a premium.

Walker had now worked out in his mind the elements that would make up the business limits and the cost variables. But before he could start determining the relevant costs, he had to sort out exactly what he was accounting for.

THE COMPANY'S DEFINITION OF
SUSTAINABLE DEVELOPMENT

Accounting for Sustainable Development Is a Black and White Issue for Management. Walker worked with Mike, who had also been with the company for over 20 years. When Mike started, they were using two-man hand saws. Walker and Mike soon found that the chief executive officer had strong views on sustainable development. Jack reminded the team that he wanted a way to tell his side of the story. According to Jack, the company was practicing sustainable development, and he wanted someway to prove it. Sustainable development meant replacing trees with the same or with an improved kind. Sometimes that would mean monoculture, sometimes that meant industrial working forests. In Jack's mind, sustainable development meant sustained economic yield from the forests.

The project team, using an accounting framework developed by the United Nations as a starting point, drafted the following definition of sustainable forestry management:

Sustainable Forestry Management. Sustainable forestry, from Blackmore and Price's perspective, means a dedicated land base, secure tenure, efficient timber utilization, immediate reforestation, and protection and tending of the forest, as well as recognition of other uses. Specifically, this means a sustainable volume of wood is to be harvested from a given area in a given length of time. This volume is the annual allowable cut. The company's objective is to harvest timber of a sustained quality, quantity, and economic value. This translates into a predictable, continuous supply of quality of raw material, which is fundamental to the company's economic sustainability. It is Blackmore and Price's belief that if a major productive forest area were withdrawn from timber management activities, the wood supply and socioeconomic environment of the province would be negatively affected.

Next they grappled with defining their company's accountability to stakeholders.

Stakeholders Include All Those Who
Benefit from the Forest

The team had already determined that stakeholders included Blackmore and Price, its shareholders, employees, consumers, the local community, suppliers, environmental activists, canoeists, trappers, aboriginal people, the Ministry of Natural Resources, and the federal government—to name a few groups. Blackmore and Price recognized that the forest belongs to the people of Ontario and that the forests have to serve a multitude of users. That was acceptable to the company as long as the main use was commercial forest production. But the big question that remained was the company's accountability for the forest. Were they accountable merely for the trees, or for everything else that made up the forest?

We Are Not Accountable for Everything. The CEO was adamant that the company did not have a responsibility to manage for all those other values, such as wilderness. The company was responsible for harvesting in a sustainable way, with those other values in mind. The Ministry of Natural Resources was accountable for the wildlife and the rest of the forest. The CEO said he was definitely not responsible for managing the moose population at a certain level per thousand hectares of forest.

Jack directed Walker to start working out the costs of those other forest values, such as preserving moose habitat. The CEO was concerned that there would be no long-term payback in terms of preserving wilderness, biodiversity, the host of the concerns voiced by environmental activists. According to him, the company was on site every day, seven days a week, 24 hours a day. A canoeist passes by for one day. In his view, a canoeist just would not have the same long-term perspective.

After some work, this was the team's statement on biodiversity, on other forest values:

Blackmore and Price recognizes that maintaining genetic and species diversity and diversity of ecosystems while meeting its wood fiber need will pose a real challenge. The company feels that it is essential to make the optimum use of available productive sites, using tree improvement programs to grow the best trees in the shortest rotations. The company recognizes that this is an expensive long-term strategy requiring dedication. It believes that sustainable forestry is attainable only through integrated management that balances forest use among timber, wildlife, and recreational interests. The company recognizes that its definition of sustainable development is narrower than that of Greenpeace or other environmental activists. Some indigenous peoples refer to "the rule of seven generations." These groups talk of "sustained life" as meeting the objective of protecting and maintaining the quality of the earth, air, and water that give life to the forest, which in turn protects and replenishes the earth, air, and water and creates an independent home for all biological life forms within it. The company's definition of sustainable development is more restrictive and limited.

It is essential that society determine the various components that need to be sustained to determine what it wants from its forests. From this determination follows the question of what has to be done to achieve these goals, how much money will be required to implement and sustain them, and where the money will come from. Blackmore and Price is committed to developing the required management practices, including timber harvesting and renewal techniques that are scientifically and socially acceptable for a boreal forest. To achieve this commitment, Blackmore and Price strives to communicate with a wide base of the public so that all parties can understand the complex, long-term nature of sustainable forestry. The company's objective is to build effective bridges to the users of the forest and to the nonusers in urban centers. Blackmore and Price sees this accounting of the forest's sustainability as a key bridge between the company and others who use and benefit from the forest.

Creating a Company Definition of Sustainable Development. Walker and the team now had a rough framework, but they were far from any accounting. Before they could start developing any numbers, they needed to confront the perplexing question of the biological limits of the forest. This would define the harvesting and production options. Each option would involve a different set of costs. They were still floundering because they had no benchmark to use in determining costs. It was at this point they worked closely with the corporate communications expert, Larry Martin, whose job was to monitor the different stakeholder groups, the political pressure generated, and the directions they might wish the company to pursue in terms of land use. Larry pointed out that each group would have a different definition of sustainable development.

This was the draft corporate position the team developed:

The theory of sustainable development is development within the limits of the ecological bounds of the area harvested. The difficulty is in determining those bounds. In the ideal world, there would be a definitive statement of limits. In reality, sustainability appears to be less well defined. That is, whether a forest is deemed sustainable depends on the user's definition of sustainable. Sustainable development is not a question of choice between growth and the environment, it is the establishment of a decision-making process which integrates the efficient conversion of resources with concern for long-term environmental consequences. Simply put, sustainable development is a question of balance. Accordingly, the company will model a range of different development options, each reflecting a different balance point.

Identifying these different balance points would require some mental gymnastics. Walker and the foresters had to put themselves in the shoes of the environmental activists, trying to articulate their view of forest development. The team had to suspend their own value system and try to accept a different system. During the post mortem of the project, they would say that this was one of the most useful parts of the exercise. They saw the opportunity to move from a defensive posture to a more proactive stance with activists. They could now say, "We are all environmentalists, we all care about the forest. The science is not definitive, but let's look at the costs of different options." This approach would allow all sides to save face, to avoid getting backed into the corner of scientific argument, with expert against expert, neither having the long-range scientific studies necessary to support their positions.

The team agreed that the next step was to try to get specific, tangible, measurable benchmarks for each option. Once they had these, they could begin to generate relevant costs. But to do that they had to confront clear-cutting from the perspective of both the company *and* the environmental activists.

The team knew what happens when the company takes a group of environmental activists up in the chopper and flies them over a clear-cut. With the whine of the chopper blades slicing through the air, the heavy vibration of the cabin, the wind sweeping through the window, they try to talk to the activists about jack pine forests. There might be a journalist with them. His camera would zoom in on the cut area, an area surrounded by thick green forests of pine and mixed hardwoods. Through their headphones the company people would talk about jack pine being shade sensitive, how it needs light and thrives in a clear-cut. But they knew these words would conflict with what their visitors were feeling in their guts. For most people will have a visceral reaction to clear-cutting outside of their own control.

The sight of massive harvesting machines moving through the thick bush, harvesting trees the way most people would cut weeds, leaving heavy tread marks is a disturbing sight. Then there is the scarification of the soil with bulldozers and trenchers, getting the soil ready for subsequent reforestation.

The team knew they had to confront clear-cutting, something as ingrained in their values and attitudes as ploughing and reseeding would be to a farmer. But they knew they had to get beyond the rhetoric and go back to the biology, the science of silviculture. First, they would need a definition of clear-cutting. They started with a definition of J. P. Kimmins, a noted academic who defines clear-cutting as the removal, in a single cut, of all trees from an area of forest land. In his view an ecologically based definition of clear-cutting is the removal of all trees of an area sufficiently large that the "forest influence, is lost in the majority of the harvested area." By forest influence he means the modified microclimate, the presence of living roots in the soil, the process of organic matter turnover and nutrient recycling that is a key part of a forest environment.[1]

Another definition of a clear-cut was removal of 50 percent of the commercial species. The forester on the team explained the complexities of defining a clear-cut. Under the Kimmins definition, the high grading of a conifer hardwood forest would not be treated as a clear-cut. He explained that the team had to consider the timing and the spacing of the cuts. For example, when the company made two cuts of 100 hectares each in two successive years, "Would you treat these as two 100 hectares clear-cuts or one 200 hectare clear-cut?" He continued to explain that if a company leaves standing timber between cuts, "How much is enough?" For example, if the company left a 30-meter strip between the two 100 hectare blocks, has the company created one or two clear-cuts?

According to the forester, present theory maintains that a diversity of cut sizes was needed for wildlife and ecology. Time between adjacent cuts should allow regeneration of the first cut area to a tree size sufficient to provide some ground cover in 5 to 20 years. Therefore, it is not just a matter of the size of the clear-cut. The timing between adjacent cuts and the size of the area between the adjacent cuts must also be considered. The forester stressed that this current theory could be important in accounting for the ecological effects of clear-cutting.

The team then took their definition of a clear-cut and Kimmins's taxonomy of forest functions and analyzed each for the implications of clear-cutting. Their objective was to determine if there was a potential impairment of natural capital that could have cost and intergenerational equity implications.

ACCOUNTING FOR THE ECOLOGICAL
IMPACTS OF CLEAR-CUTTING

The team quickly realized that their analysis of the current forestry practices would force them to confront the way forestry management would be different under a regime of managing for sustainable development. No longer would provincial regulations set the standards for forestry practices. Now, under a regime of sustainable development, their starting point would have to be the vulnerabilities and growth cycles of the forest itself, the components of the total forest ecosystem. To determine whether current practices would need to be modified, they used a model developed by Kimmins. In this model of a forest ecosystem, there were two broad areas of concern — the components of a living ecosystem such as plants, animals, or fungi in the soil and the functions of the ecosystem in the more global environment such as the transformation of carbon dioxide into oxygen. Both dimensions of the forest were deemed critical.

Components of the ecosystem included

- Climate and microclimate in the immediate area of a clear-cut.
- Soil, including soil nutrient and essential minerals.
- Vegetation, including trees, smaller growing plants, and ground cover.
- Microbial life, which included the microorganisms in the soil such as fungi.
- Invertebrate and vertebrate wildlife, including birds, animals, and soil animals.
- Fish and water quality.

From the corporate perspective, all these components represented "noncommercial" values of the forest being managed. However, to environmental activists, and the aboriginal foresters, these components of the forest represented forest principal — the annual growth of trees and fiber with a commercial value representing the annual interest on this principal or core natural capital upon which Blackmore and Price was economically dependent.

The Kimmins model also required the team to consider the impact of clear-cutting on other ecosystem functions. Environmental activists would say that the principal, this natural capital of a living, intact forest, would result in annual interest in two forms—commercial interest such as commercial timber and noncommercial interest such as the contribution of this forest to reductions in total global warming. Other functions of the forest ecosystem that contributed to global well-being included the storage of carbon, biodiversity, temporal diversity, genetic diversity, and aesthetics and recreation.

For each component of the ecosystem and each identifiable function of the ecosystem, the team researched scientific literature, interviewed prominent scientists at Forestry Canada and at universities, to gather the best available information on the potential impacts of current clear-cutting practices on the ecosystem. The team gathered data on the immediate impact and the longer-term impacts. The team's objective was to reach a tentative conclusion on the valuation of natural capital. The fundamental question to be answered was, "Is there persuasive scientific evidence that current clear-cutting practices are degrading the forest ecosystem? If so, how is the value of natural forest capital being impaired, and how should the accounting reflect this potential impairment in the form of fuller costs?"

IMPACT ON THE COMPONENTS OF THE ECOSYSTEM

Climate and Microclimate. For climate and microclimate, the team found very little to study. The forester on the team said that the scant literature available suggested there could be a long-term change in air and water temperature. Other articles suggested that clear-cutting had a dramatic initial effect on light intensity, air temperature, humidity, wind speed, and daily fluctuations of temperature. However, over the longer term, the microclimate in the immediate vicinity of the clear-cut would be restored as trees regrew. Sustainable development focused on the extent to which one generation was consuming principal, not living off the interest, and not passing along depleted natural capital to the next generation. The project team concluded there was no persuasive evidence of intergenerational damage to the local microclimate. This would mean that there was no need for intergenerational accounting to reflect this potential impairment.

Soil. Impact, in the short term, generally depended on the specifics of the site (i.e., slope, geographic orientation, elevation, soil type, vegetation type, soil condition prior to harvest, or climate). The team also noted that the impact varied according to the type of equipment used (i.e., does the equipment remove the tree limbs in the bush or by the side of the road), the skill of the equipment operator, or the time of year of the harvest. For example, a winter harvest would result in less soil compaction or compression of the soil under the tires of heavy equipment.

In the longer term, the literature suggested a risk of nutrient loss through the removal of the tree limbs with their nutrient-rich cones and needles. The project team concluded there was a potential remediation cost to be recognized for the loss of biomass. If this remediation was not performed during the tenure of the current generation, there could be intergenerational liabilities stemming from soil erosion from improper harvesting or loss of soil nutrients. The team's working principle was that "science, and physical evidence of impairment of the ecosystem would drive the accounting."

At this point in the process, the project team began to more fully appreciate the problems with uniform, legislated standards that could not factor in all the variables that would have to be considered to reach site- and terrain-specific standards. Under a regime of comprehensive environmental management, provincial standards would be the benchmark; under a regime of sustainable development, site- and terrain-specific standards would have to be the norm. These standards would reflect the fragility, strengths, resiliency, and carrying capacity of the sites being harvested.

Diversity of Vegetation. The team noted that the diversity of vegetation would inevitably be altered by a clear-cut. Large dominant trees would be removed, there would be a change of species composition. Plants that could not survive in a closed forest would invade a clear-cut, light-sensitive vegetation would die. The principal risk was that the diversity of plants could be reduced, depending on the size, shape, and extent of the clear-cutting practices. The literature suggested there were ways to reduce this, including the use of mixed species stands. The team concluded that the potential loss of diversity was a serious question from the perspective of intergenerational accounting. They would come back to it when addressing biodiversity. However, the fundamental question this raised in their minds was, "What if a practice alters, but does not impair or degrade, an ecosystem that will be passed on to future generations? Is there an intergenerational liability to be recognized?"

Microbial Life. Scientific evidence suggested there would be marked changes in the microbial populations (i.e., fungi and other microorganisms whose role in the chain of forest life was largely unknown) that inhabited tree roots resulting from the death of the live tree roots that supported fungi in the soil. The death of these fungi could result in the increase in bacterial populations and in the population of animals that feed on these bacteria. There would be a decline in the abundance of fungi and fungi-feeding soil animals. In the longer term, the reduced diversity of vegetation could result in the reduced microbial diversity. The obvious question for the team was, "So what?" The problem the team faced was that the implications of the changes in microbial life were largely unknown. The scientific literature was fairly sketchy.

The project team was initially skeptical when they read of the concerns expressed by the environmental activists. The team had considerable difficulty becoming concerned about organisms so small and apparently inconsequential in comparison to an immense red or white pine. During the research phase, however, one of the team members happened to talk to a neighbor who sold homemade honey. The neighbor related how a microscopic organism infiltrating his hive of bees required him to kill his whole hive. There was a risk of an epidemic in Ontario; if allowed to spread unchecked, it could have threatened the pollination of fruit next spring. This incident stressed the importance of infinitely small interconnected threads, the severance of any, however minute, could have unforeseen and irreparable consequences, some of which would eventually register in dollar terms.

As the team researched microbial life further, they attended a lecture by another ecologist who stressed the importance of microbial life in the forests and the delicate and largely unknown relationship between diverse and healthy populations of these minute organisms and forest health. He talked about squirrels feeding upon and spreading beneficial mycorrhizal fungi that protect tree roots against disease-causing fungi. The issue for the team was how to approach an area where science was largely silent. One of the team members loved to take apart old engines, to tinker. According to him, "an intelligent tinkerer," who doesn't exactly know how each part of an engine fits into the whole, should proceed carefully, preserving and labeling each part, so he could reassemble the engine in the future. The team developed the following operating philosophy. Given the interconnection of the components of a living northern boreal forest and conditions of scientific uncertainty, ambiguity, or silence, they would follow the "intelligent tinkerer" approach to intergenerational accounting. What they meant by this was that if company proceeded cautiously there would be a lower chance of unforeseen degradation of the forest through the unintended loss of forest or wildlife diversity. The concern was with unintended damage for which there would be no remediation, the high-magnitude loss with a low probability of occurrence. The reality was that there were potentially thousands of species of microbes, other critical elements in the web of forest life whose role was largely unknown.

The accounting issue the team faced was to come up with an approach to accounting for intergenerational equity under conditions of scientific uncertainty and ambiguity. The team discussed the options for implementing the intelligent tinkerer approach to dealing with the low-probability risk of irreparable damage to the web of forest life. In the view of the forester, the only way to insure against such an eventuality was to set up ecological reserves. Under the intelligent tinkerer approach, the only effective way to preserve the heritage of natural capital would be to set up forest reserves (i.e., land removed from productive use). In this reserve, existing elements of diversity of vegetation, microbial life, and the like would remain largely undisturbed. If monitoring the area harvested, over time, indicated unforeseen effects of changes in habitat through clear-cutting, perhaps the existence of reserves would help future generations "reconstruct" some of what was lost (i.e., mitigate irreversible damage). The accounting implications of the intelligent tinkerer approach would be that there would be tangible, measurable costs associated with removing stands from productive use. To the extent that these reserves and the requisite site-monitoring regime were not set up, there would have to be liabilities to be recognized. The accounting concept here would be that of deferred maintenance expenses. If a householder did not replace the roof of his house after 20 years, there would be a liability passed on to the next generation when they inherited the asset.

Other relevant costs could be the costs to modify current clear-cutting practices in terms of the size and timing of the clear-cut. This approach would involve trying to determine whether existing clear-cutting techniques could be modified so as to minimize the impact. The relevant costs would be the research costs to explore this option and the actual conversion costs to the new methods developed.

The team chose to pursue a combination of the ecological reserves and modified clear-cut options. This choice reflected the overall corporate philosophy about the level of risk of potential damage with which the company was prepared to live. Following the "rule of two generations," Blackmore and Price would proceed cautiously, monitoring attributes of forest health, but would not set up ecological reserves. Accordingly, Blackmore and Price would have to record a notional liability related to the low-probability-high-magnitude loss of forest wealth caused by unintended loss of forest diversity and forest health. Were any such adjustments to confirmed by external events, it would be likely to occur in 30 years—the approximate halfway point in the harvesting cycle. Thus, there was an unknown, but not unimaginable, probability that half the commercial value of the forest could be at risk in 30 years.

For every liability recorded by accountants, there is a corresponding cost. The cost here would represent an "insurance" cost, or risk cost of damage to the web of life. These costs represented a consequence of a business-as-usual approach—of not following the intelligent tinkerer approach. In short, they represented the cost that future generations might have to bear because a piece of the puzzle had been lost by this generation. These costs would have to be factored into any calculations of fuller cost and would be relevant in evaluating the company's projected return on investment under the business-as-usual mode of operations.

Wildlife. Relative to the impact on wildlife, the team identified an immediate change that would follow a clear-cut. Late successional animal species such as pine marten, woodland caribou, and some species of birds could be lost. The literature suggested that wildlife and soil animals are habitat specific and that they depend on the availability of appropriate shelter and food. Forest harvesting would change both these essential elements. Among harvesting techniques, clear-cutting had the most dramatic effect. The scientific literature suggested the longer-term impacts on forest wildlife species would be dependent on the size, shape, and orientation of the clear-cut, as well as the age and composition of the remaining adjacent forest. Other variables included postharvest site treatment (i.e., tilling of the soil with large metal blades, slash burning, and weed control).

All this suggested to the team that operating under a regime of sustainable development would mean looking at each clear-cut relative to unique site characteristics and tailoring the size, the machines, and the practices employed to the specific ecological carrying capacity of each square hectare logged. Clearly, this would have significant cost implications in terms of increased planning time, road costs, tree removal costs, labor costs in the bush, and so on. Failure to make these changes in practices would lead to recognition of deferred maintenance cost liabilities on the Green Balance Sheet. As with all asset maintenance, an owner has the choice of paying now or paying later. Not paying is not an option. Accounting for two generations would help make these costs more transparent.

Fish and Water Quality. The last ecological component examined was fish and water quality. There could be potential impacts of clear-cutting on stream flow, water temperature, fish abundance and productivity, stream bank stability, sedimentation in the stream, or changed nutrient inputs. Scientific evidence suggested that compliance with existing regulations that required the use of "riparian strips," or buffer zones between areas to be clear-cut and sensitive areas such as streams, could help minimize longer-term impacts. The scientific evidence seemed to suggest that fish habitat and stream water quality would eventually return to preharvest conditions. However, there appeared to be sufficient scientific ambiguity that the team could not rule out the remote possibility of long-term damage to aquatic habitat.

The project team concluded that there could be implications for the valuation of natural capital if the company failed to construct the required culverts, establish riparian strips appropriate to site conditions, construct dikes and other baffles to prevent sedimentation from interfering with fish spawning. In contrast to the much more difficult and ambiguous areas of microbial life or diversity of vegetation or wildlife, protection of this ecological component appeared to be more straightforward. There was a fairly consistent and visible trail between a body of scientific knowledge, the current regulations in place, and the tangible modifications of clear-cutting techniques that would lower the risks of potential damage to within acceptable ranges. In this setting, the accounting was relatively straightforward. The relevant costs would be the conversion costs of changing harvesting methods for particularly sensitive areas. These would be factored into fuller costs.

IMPACT ON THE NONCOMMERCIAL
FUNCTIONS OF THE ECOSYSTEM

Sustained Life. In broad terms, ecosystem functions referred to the capture and storage of solar energy by plant biomass, the transfer of this energy to the biomass of birds and other wildlife, and the dynamics of dead organic matter as it is decomposed by soil, animals, and microbes. The community forest group where Walker served as a board member referred to this function as "sustained life." When dealing with this function, the team noted that nutrient uptake by plants is reduced or terminated by clear-cutting and possibly by subsequent silvicultural treatments. The release of nutrients increased as decomposition of dead organic matter accelerated because of the microclimate and the microbial changes that accompany clear-cutting. In the longer term, the extent of the loss of life-sustaining materials appeared to be more a function of the proportion of tree biomass that is harvested and removed than a function of whether the harvest is a clear-cut.

In general, the loss of organic matter in a typical deciduous or coniferous forest should be temporary. However, for poorer sites this may not be true. The silviculturist explained that this area needs further study. In his view, Canada's boreal forest sites were on the average of low productivity because of poor soil. Any decrease in this productivity because of harvesting would have to be replaced during subsequent rotations of stands of trees. The problem was that this might not be possible in all sites. Some would require special care, and there would be costs associated with this special care. There could be the need for intergenerational adjustments for these costs. Implicit in the team's conclusion was a belief that sustainable development does not lead to an unchanged, pristine forest ecosystem but to a forest that continues to renew itself, generation after generation, and allows future generations to enjoy the same level of commercial wealth *and* noncommercial well-being.

Carbon Storage. The silviculturist on the project team pointed out that forests generally store carbon and mitigate the greenhouse effect. However, there is a concern about the release of carbon when old-growth forests are clear-cut and replaced by second growth. Drier inland forests, such as boreal forests, generally have much lower accumulations of woody debris on the forest floor. Lowland boreal sites can have massive peat-like organic carbon, but this is relatively stable unless the site is drained. The forester explained that the main difference between carbon storage in coastal and boreal forests is not in the soil but in the above-ground living biomass. The natural fire regime in boreal forests creates a mosaic of age classes not unlike the ideal for a well-managed forest, so carbon storage changes little under the management of man. In contrast, coastal rain forests are dominated by old growth, and carbon storage declines by 50 percent or more when they are converted to managed forests. Mike stressed that newly planted trees have high carbon intake during their early growth cycles and that as long as the company regenerated, the net carbon change could be successfully managed. The team concluded there was no persuasive evidence of the need for inter-generational adjustments for a boreal forest.

Of all the forest functions, the one that caused the foresters the most grief was that of biodiversity. "What does it mean? The environmental activists keep talking about biodiversity, but what is it? What do they want us to do?" This is how the team approached the issue.

Accounting for the Diversity of Natural Capital. The team recognized that no single ecological impact could be considered in isolation. They had already considered ecosystem functions like the storage of solar energy as plant biomass, carbon storage, and the greenhouse effect, and they were now ready to address the complex question of biodiversity. Here they tried to define biodiversity more precisely, identifying

Alpha species diversity. Refers to the number of species in a given ecosystem type; a measure of species diversity.

Beta species diversity. Refers to a measure of species diversity across the landscape; the differences in the species lists among the different ecosystem types in a particular landscape.

Landscape diversity. Variation in species lists across a geographical unit (like a province) as a result of reduced populations of many of the species resident.

Temporal diversity. Refers to the change over time in the species list and vegetation structure of a particular ecosystem type, from the time of a disturbance until the ecosystem has returned to its original condition.

Functional diversity. The variation in productivity, nutrient cycling, and successive processes in different ecosystems across the landscape.

Genetic diversity. Genetic mix indigenous to a given ecosystem, reflecting past evolution. (It is vitally important to conserve genetic diversity to maintain a species's resilience to disease and other assaults.)[2]

The team found few conclusive studies on the effects of harvesting or silviculture on these dimensions of biodiversity. In their view, the potential loss of genetic diversity was the most troubling. The value of such genetic diversity appeared to be infinite, and the literature identified no remediation option. One risk of an inappropriate harvesting technique was a potential reduction in genetic diversity as a result of a reduced population in the vast varieties of species resident in a boreal forest. In short, the risk would represent an impairment of the genetic pool.

With a reduction of genetic diversity, there could be a potential risk of irreversible damage to natural capital beyond what could be reclaimed. A review of the literature suggested this was an important area for further research. The accounting issue was one of potential intergenerational costs. This issue raised the time element, the question, "How long is long?"

The Time Dimension in Maintaining Natural Capital. The key question is how to maintain natural forest capital "forever." But how long is "forever"?

J. P. Kimmins states that the answer depends on which time scale the viewer is using to define forever. Evolutionary time scales for long-lived trees in forests cover thousands to millions of years. Ecological time scales, covering natural cycles of ecosystem disturbance and recovery, can extend up to thousands of years. Forest management time scales of the tree crop production in northern forests generally span from half a century to a century and a half. In contrast, "social" time scales span from a few years (the four to seven year political cycles) to the seven decades that adults hope to survive.[3] The team decided that for the purposes of their accounting, "long" would be two generations.

After analyzing the impact of clear-cutting on natural capital, the team was forced to revisit their initial definition of sustainable development. Their view of the forest had changed. They now visualized natural capital as all the countless critical components necessary to support and sustain a living forest ecosystem. They visualized some notional biological threshold beyond which the stress on the forest would be too high to be sustainable, where the risk of damage would be too high. They also realized that, given their previous analysis of clear-cutting, there was a high degree of uncertainty as to the limits of the carrying capacity of the boreal forest. This would require some form of recognition of the financial implications of damage to at least one or more components of the ecosystem. This strongly suggested the need for some form of intergenerational accrual. To ignore the potential risks they had identified, however imprecise, would be poor accounting in the same way that failure to recognize the Exxon expectation had been poor accounting. If the company did not, or could not, find steps to lower this notional risk below the level of "remote but conceivable" to "remote and inconceivable," then the matching principle in accounting would require the team to set up some form of accrual. The question this posed for the team was, "What are the options for lowering this fuzzy risk to the remote and inconceivable category?" They quickly realized that variables to control the stress on the ecoregion were volume of harvest and technology employed. The lower the volume or the lower the impact of the technology, the lower the risk of exceeding this notional threshold. This concept of a minimum biological threshold envisaged a number of biological scenarios, each with a certain degree of biodiversity, each of which could be maintained and passed on to future generations in perpetuity, but each reflecting different biodiversity tradeoffs.

THE VARIABLES ARE THE VOLUME
AND THE TECHNOLOGY

It became obvious to the team that the objective of the exercise was to try to line up a volume of production and a technological base that aligned with

Figure 8.1
Limits to the Economic Development of a Boreal Forest

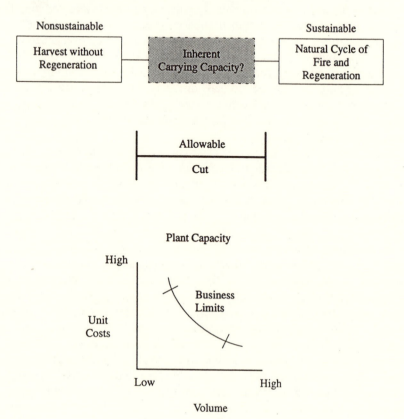

business limits, the breakeven point, and the ecological limits of the forest, however imprecisely they had been defined. This is illustrated in Figure 8.1.

Managing plant capacity is a critical element of business survival and economic sustainability. A fundamental business relationship is the one between volume of production and fixed costs. As the volume of production increases, the unit costs generally decrease because fixed costs for plant and equipment are spread over a higher base. Obviously, when a company produces a thousand units with certain capital costs for plant and other fixed overheads, it will have a lower unit cost than it would when it only produces a hundred units with the same plant and fixed overheads.

In order to be competitive in terms of costs, a company needs to operate at an appropriate volume of production relative to the original capacity contemplated when the plant was designed and built. If it was operating in this range, fixed costs would be within acceptable limits. Profit is earned when both fixed and variable costs (costs that vary with volume of production, such as materials) are below market price. As illustrated in Figure 8.1, there is a range of business activity that will be sustainable at varying levels of profitability, given past investment decisions about plant and equipment. Once the plant has been built and the loans secured, there is no going back and lowering these costs. They are sunk costs. This profitable range of activity represents a key business limit.

Walker knew that if the objective of the exercise was to marry business and environmental data, this breakeven range was one of the critical business limits. A company could not survive for long if it consistently operated below these limits. In Walker's mind, it was just like an aircraft flying at speeds below the airspeed for which it was designed. The wings will not generate sufficient lift, and the plane will fall like a stone.

Jack had been more explicit. "Sustainable development will require financial profit. Without profit, we will be unable to make the changes necessary to maintain excellence in our operations. Excellence is more than product quality—it also refers to the quality of our process and our people."

When Blackmore and Price modernized its lumber and pulp mills, each was designed to operate at a certain level of capacity, a minimum breakeven point where fixed and variable costs were to be recovered. Operation at this targeted level of capacity would result in a targeted rate of return on their investment. This plant capacity had been based on a projection of the company's annual allowable cut. The allowable cut is the annual volume of production the province allows the company to harvest. Every year the company provides the province with a map showing which areas will be harvested. The company's strategy is to harvest its whole "limit" on a 60- to 70-year cycle. At the end of this cycle, the company can begin harvesting areas cut in year one and left to regenerate for the next 60 years.

This allowable cut determines the volume of wood fiber available for the lumber mill, and ultimately the pulp mill, in the form of wood chips, a by-product of lumber operations. A critical element in the design of plant capacity was a best estimate of the annual allowable cut made some ten years ago. The company was now nervous about the security of the wood supply. As more and more areas were converted to riparian strips and reserves or removed from productive forest, the allowable harvest would shrink and the company believed it risked running out of wood to feed the lumber and pulp mills.

Operating under a regime of sustainable development would mean that the allowable cut would have to be married to the inherent carrying capacity of the northern boreal forest harvested. The question marks in the exhibit represent the reality that, given the infancy of the science of diagnosing the ecological health of a forest, there is no way to know with a high degree of certainty the size of the limits of this notional threshold. This has been the team's overall conclusion after analyzing the ecological effects of clear-cutting. However, while the size of this notional threshold is unknown, the extreme limits become more easily identified. Clearly, failure to regenerate as much as harvested will result in nonsustainable forestry (left margin of Figure 8.1), while letting the forest operate under a natural cycle of fire and regeneration is a fairly sure bet as to ecological sustainability but a poor bet as to economic sustainability (far right of Figure 8.1).

As illustrated in the previous section analyzing the effects of clear-cutting on a boreal forest, the operating reality is one of a large band of grey, largely because of scientific ambiguity. In a boreal forest, clear-cutting is not a clear-cut issue. From the perspective of sustainability, as contemplated in *Our Common Future,* the issue is not "to clear-cut or not to clear-cut" but rather when and under what circumstances so as not to exceed the inherent carrying capacity of each site. In short, generalities were meaningless.

The Variables Remain the Volume of Cut and Impact of Harvesting Technology. The team realized that when they cut through all the rhetoric the company's options were twofold. The company could reduce the volume of the allowable cut so as to reduce the risk of exceeding the notional biological threshold, or it could maintain the volume but employ a lower-impact technology for harvesting. For example, in the short run it could invest in a new generation of harvesters capable of removing the limbs and processing a tree into appropriate lengths of stump in the forest rather than beside the road. This would limit the removal of nutrient capital. These harvesters were also more adaptable for partial-cutting treatments in boreal mixed woods. The net effect on the ecoregion could be the same.

In theory the company could play with both the volume and technology variables. In practice, in the short run the company was limited to changes it could make in volume because of the heavy fixed costs that locked the company into a predetermined allowable cut. In the longer term, next modernization, the plant could be configured for a lower capacity and a lower allowable cut. This meant that the main variable was not volume of fiber cut but the methods and practices employed to cut the same volume on an annual basis (without jeopardizing the 60- to 70-year harvest cycle of the main species harvested — jack pine).

As the team had identified in their analysis of the effects of clear-cutting on the ecology of a northern boreal forest, some changes in practices *can* reduce or mitigate the effects of clear-cutting. Some of the technological variables were illustrated in the bottom of the exhibit. Each one could have a significant impact on the cumulative level of ecological stress experienced. For example, a reduction in the size of a clear-cut, especially on steep slopes prone to erosion, could significantly lower the impact on the ecosystem. If less of the tree mass were removed from the forest, there might be less nutrient loss. Different methods of site preparation after a clear-cut could result in less soil compaction. Timing of the harvest in the winter would also result in a significant reduction in soil compaction.

Managing for sustainable development would mean juggling all the many balls described in the exhibit under conditions of scientific uncertainty and continuous negotiation with the public. To juggle these balls, two levels of information would be required. Initial "one-time" information would be needed to establish an environmental investment strategy, and "ongoing" information on business and biological limits would be required to operate in a sustainable development mode on an ongoing basis. Right now the project team was working on a rudimentary information system to support the first level of strategic decisions. Later in the project they would turn their attention to the ongoing on-line system that would have to support a sustainable development operating mode.

SETTING STANDARDS AND DETERMINING THE CONVERSION COSTS

To position where the team had progressed in the process of developing an initial framework, Figure 5.1 is helpful. Looking at the box at the lower left corner, the team had completed an analysis of stakeholder needs and interests, developed a generalized framework for defining corporate environmental accountability and sustainable development, and begun to analyze how managing for sustainable development would be likely to change the way the company did business in the forests by focusing on the predominant harvesting technique, clear-cutting. So far, the underlying challenge had been accounting problems caused by scientific uncertainty and ambiguity.

The team recognized that rather than using an adjective such as sustainable they should be using a noun such as "sustentation" (which implies active human involvement rather than a state of being) to describe a given site and set of conditions. To the team, it was now apparent that sustainable was a vague adjective, given the scientific uncertainty and ambiguity. Rather than stop in their tracks, throw up their hands, and abandon the exercise, the team developed options for a range of sustainability for forest options (see *Stewardship Report to the Board of Directors,* Chapter 12, Table 12.2). After some days of spinning their wheels, the team saw the chart as a major breakthrough because it allowed them to proceed under conditions of scientific uncertainty. Their rationale was as follows. "While we cannot define sustainable with precision, we can position it within a predetermined range of scientific probability. For each possible position, we can then proceed to compute the detailed cost conversion factors that will enable us to analyze the broad investment options. It is the role of science to define the thresholds; it is the role of accountants to cost the conversion to the different operating modes appropriate to each assumption about where the ecological threshold lies."

Option 1 depicted a business-as-usual situation where wood fiber is viewed as the primary forest product. The company would comply with all regulations and define sustainable development as sustained yield. Blackmore and Price would assume their legal corporate responsibilities under their forest-management agreement. Option 1 could also be called the "rule of quarterly earnings." Option 2 envisaged a scenario where more money would be devoted to "nonwood values." Here the company would operate under a comprehensive management regime and accept more responsibility for bio-diversity, wildlife, and other ecological functions of the forest. Under this option, the company would go beyond compliance, focusing on the hot spots of public opinion revealed by the stakeholder analysis. The basic cor-porate strategy would be sustained economic yield and proactive stakeholder management of other groups who benefited from the boreal forest harvested. As Option 2 evolved, the team labeled it the "rule of two generations."

Under Option 3, the environment would be an equal partner in the mar-riage between business and the biology of the forest. Implicit in Option 3 would be the goal of the rule of two generations. Nonwood values would be a primary consideration. Under this option, in contrast to the scenario de-scribed in Figure 8.1, where the fixed cost and capacity demands of the mills came first and the ecology second, the ecology and mill capacity would be equal partners. Wherever possible, the company would try to emulate natural forest processes of disturbance; regeneration; and succession of species of trees, vegetation, and animals. Under this option, the company and others who benefit from the forest, including consumers, would have to subsidize noncommercial values such as aesthetics. While these options were a neces-sary step in the process, they were not specific enough to start analyzing the cost implications.

The next step was to translate these generalized options into specific stan-dards such as the size of clear-cuts, for which costs could be determined. The approach taken is illustrated in Figure 8.2, which illustrates some stan-dards that would be appropriate for Option 2. On the left of the chart are conditions that must be considered in setting specific standards. These stan-dards would address the concerns raised in the previous analysis of the ecological impacts of clear-cutting. Each one of these conditions would relate to a specific forestry practice that would have to be changed to move from the business-as-usual option toward sustainable development. Once these various conditions were defined, the cost accountants could start com-puting the incremental conversion costs to reach these standards for forestry practice.

The team started with the first condition that must be met, the preserva-tion of critical fish habitat (top left on the chart). As illustrated in the previ-ous analysis of the effects of clear-cuts, the slope of the terrain logged is a critical factor. One way to reduce the risk of exceeding this threshold is to increase the size of the erosion reserve relative to steeper slopes. This would reduce the productive land base, incurring an opportunity cost. These ero-sion reserves would affect road construction costs. For trout lakes, there

Figure 8.2
Options for Landscape Management: Option 2 — Enhanced Nonwood Values —
Standards for Sustainability

Condition	Guideline	Area Of Concern	Conditions: Roads and Landings	Conditions: Harvesting	Impacts
Fish					
Critical Habitat	Slope 0–15% 16–30% 30–45% 46–60%	Erosion Reserve 30 m 50 m 70 m 90 m	No Roads In Reserve 600 m No-road Zone	No Harvesting	Reduced Land Base
Trout Lakes	Slope 0–15% 16–30% 30–45% 46–60%	Erosion Reserve 30 m 50 m 70 m 90 m	No Roads In Reserve 600 m No-Road Zone	Maintenance Of Water Quality Modified Harvesting To 30% Of Volume	30% Loss Of Reserve Volume Reforestation Left For Natural Regeneration
Wildlife					
Moose	All Areas		No Restrictions	Clear–cut Average 130 m Wildlife Corridors	Long Amortized Period, Increased Operational Planning And Layout
Habitat Maintenance	Wintering Areas			Maintain 50% Cover	Increase Area Accessed, Additional Roads, Long Amortization Period
Aquatic Feeding And Calving Areas	Water Related	120 m Reserve	No Roads	No Harvesting	Loss Of Productive Land Base
Eagles And Ospreys	Nests	200 m 600 m	No Roads No Traffic During Nesting Periods	No Harvesting Modified Harvesting	Loss Of Productive Land Base Operational Restriction During The Nesting Period
Herons	Rookeries	300 m 1000 m	No Roads No Traffic During Nesting Period	No Harvesting Harvesting During Non-nesting Period	Loss Of Productive Land Base, Schedule Operations

would need to be erosion reserves with reduced harvesting. To enhance the habitat for other wildlife such as moose, the average clear-cut would be reduced in size; and wildlife corridors would have to be maintained between clear-cuts. This would require increased planning effort and could increase road construction costs. Reserves around aquatic feeding and calving areas would also result in the loss of productive land. Following a similar approach for eagles, osprey, and herons would result in a further reduction of the productive land base and necessitate a rescheduling of harvesting operations. The team was now ready to try to set standards for Option 3.

Computing the Cost Implications. The team then looked at the cost implications of each option on mill and pulp operations. For example, the removal of heritage forests from the wood supply would increase purchases from contractors and require changes in the road structure. The use of smaller clear-cuts would significantly increase road costs in the short run (in the long run, the number of roads in the management unit would remain essentially the same). Decreased harvesting in sensitive areas for trout spawning would both remove the efficiencies of scale and require more extensive roads and infrastructure. This would push unit costs up. Elimination of herbicides would require higher wage costs (hand pruning). Different regeneration technologies could change cost patterns.

Specifically, the team analyzed the cost implications of the following major changes that would follow a move toward implementing the rule of two generations:

- *Removal of productive forest.* The team estimated that 5 percent of the productive forest would be lost in a move to Option 1, 10 percent more would be lost in a move to Option 2, and an additional 11 percent would be needed to achieve Option 3. This suggested that the total land "cost" to move from business as usual to something approaching sustainable development as envisaged in *Our Common Future* would "cost" up to 26 percent of the productive land base. This fundamental change in land use would affect a wide range of operating costs.

- *Operating costs dependent on size of clear-cut.* Many operating costs are related to cut size. For example, hauling costs would rise initially then stabilize at some future time. This happens because during the early years of most mill operations, when the land is assigned to the company under a forest management agreement, it is cheapest to start clear-cutting closest to the mill and work outward (this is called "progressive clear-cutting"). However, this means that hauling costs will continually increase with time. Limiting the cost of clear-cuts will mean that while average hauling costs will remain fairly constant, they are likely to be higher initially. The costs of transporting crews increases inversely with the cut block size during harvesting, scarification, and planting. Road maintenance costs are directly linked to hauling operations and would again increase as the size of a cut decreases. Generally road costs are seen as a fixed cost, an expenditure necessary to access timber. Because the costs are amortized over volume, unit costs go up as volume decreases.

The team estimated road costs would increase a $1 per cubic meter under Option 2; $1.25 under Option 3.

* *Reduction in the use of herbicides.* The team noted that the public now accepted more readily the need to protect the forest from insects and disease. However, there are concerns about perceived toxicity of some of the sprays. Savings through reduced purchases of herbicides would be offset by the higher costs of nonspray treatments.

The net result was that Walker and his staff estimated that conversion to Option 2 would increase unit costs by $6.76 per cubic meter harvested (715,000) for a total of $4,833,000. Achievement of Option 3 would require an incremental unit cost increase of $10.07 ($7,200,000). The total unit cost increase to move from business as usual to something approaching sustainable development was then $16.83. The total conversion cost could reach $12,033,000.

These projected cost increases were most sobering. Pulp and lumber, being pure commodity products, could probably not absorb add-on values to the sales price. The team found it hard to imagine price increases being absorbed by consumers; and as a result, the cost would be likely to remain with the raw material producers, creating what they saw as devastating results for the company's raw material costs. In the marriage between business and the ecological limits of the northern boreal forest, the honeymoon had just ended. It was now becoming evident what it would really cost to practice sustainable development.

The obvious question, from a corporate perspective was, "What is the impact of these different options on our return on investment, on our costs, and on our price structure?" Walker and the others recognized the need for a reporting format that would provide management with an analysis of the basic variables. The format they developed is illustrated in Table 1.1.

At this point, the team felt comfortable with the framework they had developed. It was Walker, the accountant, who felt they needed to do more in terms of "valuing the asset," the asset being the forest, not the two-by-fours in work in progress. In Walker's mind the single most important asset Blackmore and Price had was the use of the forest. It always seemed strange that this never appeared on the balance sheet. Senior management at the head office in Toronto was never provided with a dollar estimate of the forest's increase in value if the company practiced sustained yield logging. In a time of acute recession when the company was feeling financial pain, Walker thought they might derive some comfort from an analysis of forest values over a 60-year planning horizon.

When Walker discussed this with Jack, the latter was receptive. "I was trained as a forester to look ahead in 70-year gallops. To survive in business I've had to cut back to looking 10 years ahead. Many of my board members are still captivated by quarterly earnings. Hell, if I wanted to impact the third or fourth quarter earnings I don't know how. About the only thing I could do is make things worse. I manage for the long haul. Can you tell me whether I'm making or losing on the forest?" Walker felt the need to define a currency for tradeoff decisions, decisions involving the removal of productive forest.

NOTES

1. J. P. Kimmins, Speech presented at the Canadian Pulp and Paper Association Conference, January 1991, p. 4.

2. Ibid., p. 25.

3. Ibid., p. 26.

Chapter 9

Valuation of a Forest

ACCOUNTING FOR THE COMMERCIAL VALUE

Walker knew he had to develop dollar values for the commercial facets of the forest under different assumptions about social values. This would allow the team to begin to quantify some of the cost implications of removing productive forest to achieve Options 2 and 3. Such an analysis might also alert the team to potential intergenerational liabilities. Walter realized he was embarking on an accounting exercise so integral to evaluating the earnings potential of a forestry management company that it should be included in every annual report. The forest was the company's single biggest asset, yet its projected value over time never appeared on a traditional balance sheet. Plant and equipment or work in progress paled in significance compared to the value of the forest to the company.

Account in Physical Terms First, Money Second

The United Nations case study in accounting for sustainable forestry management recommended that step one in valuing a forest would be to account for the forest in physical terms. As an experienced cost accountant, Walker was comfortable with this approach. In costing the various steps in the harvesting and manufacturing process, his starting point was always the physical flow of product. Step two would be to define the asset for which a company would be accounting—in this case, cubic meters of wood fiber and "other forest values." Step three would be to differentiate between what should and should not be valued in monetary terms. Step four would involve assigning a monetary value to the wood fiber and developing a proxy measure for other forest values such as aquatic habitat, wilderness, and genetic diversity. Step five would be to measure the changes in wealth over time. The CEO thought the time frame should be 40 to 60 years—an annual basis would be totally meaningless.

Table 9.1
Blackmore and Price Forest Products Ltd.: Area Change over Time (Percentage of Production Forest)

Age	1990	2015	2040	2065	2090	2115	2140
Jack Pine							
0 – 20	9%	11%	8%	8%	10%	10%	10%
21 – 40	1%	10%	10%	9%	9%	10%	10%
41 – 60	3%	3%	12%	10%	9%	10%	10%
61 – 80	7%	2%	4%	5%	6%	5%	5%
81 – 100	8%	5%	0%	0%	0%	0%	0%
101 – 120	4%	0%	0%	0%	0%	0%	0%
+120	0%	0%	0%	0%	0%	0%	0%
TOTAL	32%	31%	34%	32%	34%	35%	35%
Spruce							
0 – 20	3%	5%	4%	3%	3%	3%	3%
21 – 40	1%	3%	5%	6%	4%	3%	3%
41 – 60	2%	4%	5%	4%	4%	4%	3%
61 – 80	4%	2%	1%	6%	4%	4%	4%
81 – 100	6%	4%	1%	1%	5%	4%	4%
101 – 120	5%	6%	3%	1%	0%	0%	0%
+120	5%	2%	2%	1%	0%	0%	0%
TOTAL	26%	26%	21%	22%	20%	18%	17%
Poplar							
0 – 20	2%	11%	8%	9%	9%	9%	9%
21 – 40	6%	7%	10%	8%	9%	10%	10%
41 – 60	1%	3%	7%	9%	9%	9%	10%
61 – 80	5%	1%	0%	0%	0%	0%	0%
81 – 100	3%	0%	0%	0%	0%	0%	0%
101 – 120	3%	0%	0%	0%	0%	0%	0%
+120	0%	0%	0%	0%	0%	0%	0%
TOTAL	20%	22%	25%	26%	27%	28%	29%
Birch							
0 – 20	1%	8%	4%	5%	5%	5%	5%
21 – 40	1%	4%	8%	5%	5%	5%	5%
41 – 60	4%	0%	7%	7%	5%	6%	6%
61 – 80	8%	4%	0%	3%	4%	3%	3%
81 – 100	6%	5%	1%	0%	0%	0%	0%
101 – 120	2%	0%	0%	0%	0%	0%	0%
+120	0%	0%	0%	0%	0%	0%	0%
TOTAL	22%	21%	20%	20%	19%	19%	19%
GRAND TOTAL	100%	100%	100%	100%	100%	100%	100%

Walker started by following the recommended approach and first accounting for the forest in physical terms without assigning a monetary value.
Table 9.1 shows the planned restructuring of the age distribution of the
forest, as projected by Blackmore and Price's timber management plan.
This table shows how the forest would change under the company's stewardship. It also shows that right now there is an "age class imbalance" favoring
the overmature timber, as well as a shortage of area in immature age class,
primarily in the 20- to 40-year group. This shortage resulted from high fire
incidents and inadequate reforestation some 40 years earlier.

The table shows that cutting operations would be concentrated in the
mature and overmature age classes followed by reforestation of the harvested
area. These charts reflected Blackmore and Price's plan to balance the age
classes during the first rotation of the various tree species (70 years for jack
pine, 100 years for spruce, 60 years for poplar, and 70 years for birch). The
objective for Blackmore and Price would be to convert the overmature areas,
prior to their natural decline and before the economic viability was reduced
through insect infestation, rot, and tree mortality.

The obvious question in Walker's mind was, "What would be the commercial value of this forest over time if we practiced sustained yield forest
management?" He talked to Mike, the forester on the team, about the valuation alternatives.

"What are you trying to do here, Walker? If you want to simulate the
growth of the forest over time, there is forestry management software that
projects wood volume over time. Is that what you want?"

"No. In my mind the objective of the exercise is not to estimate volume as
much as to do a better job of accounting for the forest. We are not trying to
bring accounting into the domain of forestry management but rather to try
to bring a living forest into the domain of accounting. I would like to start
with a model that most closely resembles the traditional historical accounting
model and try to expand it to account for a living asset. Then I want to try
to push the model one step further and try to calculate a value of the ecosystem as whole."

Mike shook his head. "How are you going to do that? Are you going to
turn into one of those economists who puts a value on the spotted owls and
the blue herons?"

Walker laughed, "Not to worry Mike. All I want to do is compute the
commercial value of the forest over time. You know, what gets measured
gets managed. We're under intense pressure to reduce regeneration now
that the provincial subsidy is drying up. I want to be able to show the board
how the commercial value of the forest increases over time if we invest in
regeneration. I need a consistent valuation method similar to what we use in
financial statements. We value an asset like a building or a feller-buncher at
the cost we pay for it, then we depreciate it over time. If the forest is being
depleted by current forestry management practices, I want to be able to

quantify that depletion, just as I would quantify depreciation on other assets such as plant and equipment."

"You've got a problem there. It's going to take 30 years to know if we are doing damage. Plus I don't like using dollars to value the forest ecosystem. Under my proposed methodology, the company would take a random sample of virgin northern boreal forest. In conjunction with the forest industry associations, the company would develop some general measures and 'scorecards' for key components of natural capital such as animal populations and their habitat; plant life and plant habitat; wilderness; fertility of soil; carbon storage; other contributions to the global ecosystem; and biodiversity. The company would then develop a score for the pristine, 'untouched' wilderness. Developing a ranking system, the company would assess areas that had been clear-cut. We would monitor performance over time, comparing the actual with the ideal. That would give us values to use in tradeoff decisions that would get us away from the traps that numbers can create."

Walker listened to Mike's arguments. "I agree that we should initiate a long-term monitoring project. However, the reality is that in the short run we need to money for regeneration and other forest enhancements. Unfortunately, it is the dollar values that will get the board's attention. I suggest we proceed with both approaches and see which bears fruit."

They proceeded, following a strategy of trying to generate a range of values, some in dollars, others not. Walker reviewed the literature and considered four methods of estimating the value of timber and timber land:

- *Income method, discounted cash flow.* This method forecasts costs through a growth cycle. Stumpage prices at the completion of the growth cycle are discounted to arrive at a net present value of the forest.

- *Conversion return, discounted cash flow.* This method is similar to the income method except that revenues are forecast as conversion return values rather than direct stumpage prices. Conversion return values are derived by forecasting the end product prices and subtracting the cost to take the tree from the stump to the end product.

- *Market method.* This method establishes the value of a tract by comparing it to that of a similar tract that has recently been traded in for which there are documented market prices.

- *Cost method value by components.* The market value of each component of the tract is estimated separately by comparison with similar items that trade separately. Land, for example, is valued separately from timber.[1]

The team rejected the third and fourth methods because there were few comparable stands and because the land was leased rather than owned. The team selected a modification of the first method—income method, discounted cash flow—adjusted for the unique conditions of the forest management agreement between the company and the Province of Ontario. Given that this was to be an internal report, the team recognized that the method chosen would not have to withstand external scrutiny. The team decided to start with a relatively simple and conservative method that would most closely approximate the historical cost model of accounting for an asset such as a long-term capital lease. The team recognized that for internal reporting purposes, the important thing was consistency over time.

The team's approach would build on the basic historical cost-accounting model. This approach is used to account for the capitalized value of future lease payments where the substance of the transaction is deemed to be more of a purchase than a monthly rental. If a company signs a long-term lease that transfers the risks of ownership to the company, then it has essentially bought an asset, and incurred a long-term liability that should be recognized on the balance sheet rather than as "off–balance sheet financing." Accountants compute the present value of a long stream of future payments, using the arithmetic of compound interest to "discount" a dollar received tomorrow to a lesser value today.

The team would project known costs 60 years into the future to correspond with the growth cycle of the major species harvested. This projection would be very different from a forecast. A projection extrapolates present trends; a forecast tries to anticipate future trends. This lease model was a good fit in Canada where most forests are owned by the provinces and companies pay annual stumpage and royalty fees for harvest, subject to master agreements that are reviewed every few years to see if a company is complying with the required forestry management practices.

Table 9.2 illustrates what happens over a 10- to 60-year planning horizon. The starting point on the far left is the cubic meters of fiber in the forest today. After considering different ways to measure the forest — acreage, volume of timber, number of trees — Walker determined that volume was the most meaningful. The $35-million figure for this forest represented what Blackmore and Price would have to pay the Ministry of Natural Resources today to secure cutting rights for the next 60 years. In short, it represented the present value of all future payments to the ministry for stumpage. If Blackmore and Price gave the ministry $35 million, and the ministry invested the money, the ministry would be just as well off, relative to receiving stumpage or rental payments every year. The chart showed that the value of the forest increased every year because it was a living asset that moved closer to maturity. The chart also showed the economic benefits of planting more than is harvested.

Mike challenged Walker on his numbers. "Your volume projections may be overly optimistic. Given that the company is starting with an age class imbalance, there will be discrepancies between harvest and regeneration volume. In reality it will probably take much more than 60 years for regenerated

Table 9.2
Blackmore and Price Forest Products Ltd.: Sustained Yield in Cutting Operations and Fiber Valuation

	Original Forest		Regenerated Forest				Total Forest	
	M3	Stumpage $000s	M3	Stumpage $000s	Regeneration $000s	Total $000s	M3	$000s
Year 0								
Opening Inventory, January 1, 1991	41,612,500	35,266					41,612,500	35,266
Fiber Maturity Gain				10		10		3,385
Adjusted Opening Inventory	41,612,500	38,641		10		10	41,612,500	38,651
Harvesting	(500,000)	(1,520)					(500,000)	(1,520)
Regeneration	887,500		887,500	93	3,231	3,324	887,500	3,324
Closing Inventory, December 31, 1991	41,112,500	37,121	887,500	103	3,231	3,334	42,000,000	40,455
Year 10								
Opening Inventory, January 1, 1991	41,612,500	35,266					41,612,500	35,266
Fiber Maturity Gain		43,922		1,092		1,092		45,014
Adjusted Opening Inventory	41,612,500	79,188		1,092		1,092	41,612,500	80,280
Harvesting	(7,500,000)	(28,099)					(7,500,000)	(28,099)
Regeneration			10,887,500	1,406	48,701	50,107	10,887,500	50,107
Closing Inventory, December 31, 2001	34,112,500	51,089	10,887,500	2,298	48,701	51,199	45,000,000	102,288
Year 60								
Opening Inventory, January 1, 1991	41,612,500	35,266					41,612,500	35,266
Fiber Maturity Gain		508,240		591,394		591,394		1,099,634
Adjusted Opening Inventory	41,612,500	542,506		591,394		591,394	41,612,500	1,134,900
Harvesting	(41,612,500)	(543,506)		(28,409)	(3,231)	(31,640)	(42,500,000)	(575,146)
Regeneration			60,887,500	26,106	902,191	928,297	60,887,500	928,297
Closing Inventory, December 31, 2051			60,000,000	589,091	898,960	1,488,051	60,000,000	1,488,051

volume to match harvested volume. To reach 60 million M³ while investing only 42.5 million M³ implies a 41 percent increase in average production rates, even without the initial oversupply of mature timber."

"Mike, I already admitted that you foresters will do better projections of growth in volume over time. It is the overall commercial valuation, and the quest for security of supply that are the focus of the case."

Mike was not satisfied. "Walker, the real growth cycle of a forest is far more complex than anything indicated in this simple model. The reality is that uncut forest stands keep aging, the probability of their destruction by fire or insects keeps increasing. In this simplistic scenario there is no margin either for natural catastrophes or for the added pressure of increased public demands for land withdrawals. Even if a company starts with a perfectly balanced age class distribution, which as we both know is highly unlikely, there will be discrepancies between harvest volume and regeneration volume. I agree the principle of regenerating more than we harvest is a sound one over time, but I object to the way you have applied it in your simplistic model."

"Mike, your problem is that you will never make a good accountant. To fit a living forest into our accounting conventions, however bizarre they seem to you, requires some simplifications. The key to understanding the power of accounting is to understand that consistency and comparability are sometimes more important than being absolutely right. If we follow this valuation method over time, however simplistic, it will give the board something to chew on, a rough order-of-magnitude estimate of the value of the forest over time. If you think this model is hard to follow, just try to understand how accountants account for leases, pensions, or deferred taxes!"

A Walk through the Forest Valuation. In Table 9.2 two columns to the far right are critical for the board of directors and shareholders to understand—the two columns under the "Total Forest" heading. The first bottom line number is the M3 column which gives an estimate of the physical stock of timber as measured in cubic meters. This number accounts for the commercial dimension of the asset, a living forest, in physical terms. While economic valuations will vary with different assumptions, this physical valuation will stay constant. At this point there is no attempt to value other forest functions (in contrast to commercial functions). As illustrated on the top line of the chart, far right, the opening physical stocks are 41,612,500 cubic meters. To the right is the valuation of this volume of timber, a commercial value of $35,266,000.

At the far right, the second line down, Walker explained, shows the value of the forest increasing by a fiber maturity gain of $3,385,000 as the forest moves closer to harvest. This "gain" is really driven by the nature of present-value calculations—as a distant outcome gets closer to the present, the present value of a future dollar increases. Intuitively, $1,000 in 10 years is "worth more" than $1,000 in 50 years. In 50 years the money may be academic. The value of the forest is now up to $38,651,000, before adjustments for harvesting and regeneration during the year. Obviously, harvesting will reduce the commercial value and regeneration will increase the potential future value. The company's objective is to maintain a sustainable commercial value.

During the year, the company harvested 500,000 cubic meters of wood. The opening physical inventory is drawn down by this amount. However, during the same period the company planted seedlings that over the 60-year growing cycle will eventually result in 887,500 cubic meters of fiber, after adjusting for expected tree loss caused by insect infestation, poor soil conditions, and the like. This is the easy part because the valuation given is in physical quantities, not subjective, assumption-driven dollar valuations.

Overall, the chart shows that the value of the forest will increase from roughly $40 million at the end of the first year to $100 million at the end of year 10 and approximately $1.5 billion at the end of year 60. These increased values reflect the reality that wood fiber will be increasingly scarce in the year 2051. Because of the pressure to reduce reforestation costs, Walker also calculated the future value of the forest under a nonsustained-yield scenario.

Now that Walker had worked out a rough commercial value for the forest, he was ready to tackle the question of the noncommercial value of the other natural capital—animal populations, plant life, wilderness, fertility of soil, carbon storage, greenhouse effect, and biodiversity.

ACCOUNTING FOR THE NONCOMMERCIAL VALUE

Walker and the other team members had already identified the need for scientific data on habitat, on animal populations, and on numbers and diversity of species of plant life. They would look at the changes in these statistics over time and at other data from site monitoring and remote sensing to determine whether natural capital was increasing or decreasing in real terms. Walker and Mike had already agreed that while it would be best to value the components of the ecosystem in nonfinancial terms, this would not be possible for at least five years until the requisite database was in place. On a scale of one to ten, they would then be able to chart the changes in wilderness values if clear-cut sizes were modified. This would be one way to measure tradeoff decisions. But as Walker had pointed out, in a world where money counts, failure to assign a dollar value to these noncommercial attributes of the forest could lead to the board underestimating their long-term value to the company and to society.

The communications expert suggested they use an infinite value for these elements of natural capital. These would be the values environmental activists would ascribe to this natural capital. He pointed out that if a dollar value were assigned to the commercial value of the forest, environmental activists would say that the green balance sheet reduced a living, breathing

Figure 9.1
Options for Valuing the Noncommercial Functions of a Natural Resource

Method of Valuation	Description of Method	Common Example
Social cost value	Subjective evaluation of worth to society.	A bald eagle is worth $X to society.
Nonutilization value	Capitalized subsidy paid to a company not to use the resource.	Capitalized valve of subsidy paid to fishermen not to fish northern cod.
Remediation cost value	What will it cost to remediate known environmental degradation?	Cost of adding biomass to offset known nutrient loss.
Rehabilitation value	What will it cost to rehabilitate an ecosystem to its former diversity?	Cost of restocking streams, transplanting "lost" species.
Capitalized earnings of alternative sustainable economic uses	What will tourism and other sustainable forms of enterprise earn from the natural capital base if it is left intact?	Capitalized earnings of canoe outfitters using wilderness.
Compensation value	What will it cost to compensate identifiable users for the loss of natural capital?	Amounts paid to James Bay Cree for land flooded by James Bay 1 power project.
Future scarcity value	What would this intact natural capital be worth in a 100 years?	Wild guess of future market valve of intact rain forest in a century.
Infinite value	Recognizes limits what cannot be valued in dollar terms.	Few common examples.

forest to the common denominator of money. They were most vociferous about this. On the other hand, the CEO said that if the team did not come up with a dollar value, a proxy value for these other forest values, then "they hadn't done the job on sustainable development." He went on to ask, "How can we make tradeoff decisions when we don't have any numbers on this natural capital? Putting an infinite value on the rabbit population will not be helpful! We're living in the age of nonbusiness values, so compute some, however rudimentary at this stage of the exercise!"

Walker's review of accounting literature indicated that in the United States, as a result of the Superfund legislation, there was a growing body of knowledge that could be used to predict the "risk costs" associated with landfill cleanup. But there was relatively little work extending the business risk cost concept to natural capital.

Figure 9.1 summarizes the team's initial analysis of some of the options. From his reading of U.S. journals on environmental economics, Walker quickly realized he was out of his element. The journals referred to "internalizing externalities," complex cost–benefit analyses based on the principles of welfare economics, which were decades old. The focus of the environmental economist appeared to be on the value of the forest to society in very broad, macroterms. As an accountant trained to identify entity-specific costs, Walker was initially uncomfortable with the economists' definition of cost. However, Mike pointed out that in a multidisciplinary effort, Walker had to be open-minded.

Valuation Alternatives. Walker and the project team recognized they could value the forest at its subjective value to society. They decided that they would consider this approach and try expanding traditional accounting concepts rather than abandoning them for economic definitions of cost. The problem, as they saw it, would be that different economists could compute different subjective valuation for the habitat required for bald eagles or osprey.

Another approach in the news when the team considered its options was the "nonutilization" value of a natural resource. For decades, farmers have been paid by governments not to cultivate land. Recently, East Coast cod fishermen had been paid hundreds of millions of dollars each year not to catch dwindling stocks of northern cod. Before the early 1990s, people would have said, "It's impossible to estimate the value of the northern cod habitat, the value of the delicate web of marine life." In 1993 the Canadian taxpayers discovered that northern cod were worth at least $500 million annually. The objective of these expenditures was to pay the political price of preventing further damage to stocks from overfishing. An economist could say that this resource would have a value of at least $500 million per year. Walker quickly recognized that he could compute value for the "principal" — the cod stocks — based on the current estimates of how long the fishery would be closed and this $500 million annuity would be paid. Walker observed that the allowable-catch concept used to establish the level of harvest of the northern cod closely resembled the concept of the allowable cut in forestry. Walker noted that in the United States in late 1993, foresters in Northwestern forests learned that the northern spotted owl and the old-growth forests required for their habitat would be worth at least $1.2 billion. The president had offered $1.2 billion in aid and cutting incentives as he reduced by two-thirds the amount to be harvested in sensitive areas in Northwestern forests.

Walker and the team could estimate the subsidy that would have to be paid to the company not to harvest the sensitive areas reserved to preserve biodiversity. The principle of subsidies was well established. Accountants could try to determine the present value of a future stream of such subsidy payments to preserve the northern boreal forest in a pristine condition. The team thought seriously about this option. Its attractiveness lay in the fact that it would involve "real money," could be estimated by the company (they above all others could develop a subsidy claim for themselves and local communities). Walker noted that there was a growing body of precedent for how much compensation companies were seeking from governments for not harvesting old-growth rain forests or discontinuing mining start-up operations. In recent cases in Canada, companies were asking for compensation of about twice the amount of their capital investment. In the case of Blackmore and Price, this would lead to a forest value of almost $1 billion (twice the invested capital of $500 million). The team decided to continue to study this option.

Other valuation techniques the team considered were the remediation cost value and the rehabilitation value. The team recognized that the two concepts are similar; there were subtle differences that could have significant cost implications. The remediation value, in contrast to the subsidy value to fishermen or foresters, would represent the cost to remediate known environmental degradation. Taking the Superfund experience in the United States, one measure of the value of a water table in a specific site would be the cost to remediate or mitigate known environmental degradation. An alternative value would be the cost to rehabilitate that same site to its former level of ecological integrity. This would include the costs of restocking streams, transplanting species of birds that once lived in an everglade converted to housing developments, and so on. The logic would run something like this, "If society is willing to spend $50 million to rehabilitate a sensitive wetland so as to try to restore the former level of diversity of vegetation and wildlife, this habitat must be worth at least this much."

The team could also consider the capitalized earnings of other uses of the same land, such as tourist lodges, the use of the diversity of vegetation as a source of "miracle" drugs. The team noted that in the Pacific Northwest, the yew tree was routinely clear-cut when cedar and fir were clear-cut. As a species, the yew was deemed to have minimal value. However, recent medical research suggested that extracts made from yew bark might help cure some strains of cancer. The value of yew bark has now moved from a "nonquantifiable" value to a "real" market value. In valuing a forest, Walker and the team recognized they could assign a value for the potential economic value of other plant species that reside there. Walker also noted that American pharmaceutical companies had leased the right to harvest rare plants from sectors of the Costa Rican rain forests. These lease values again provided one market-based value for forest attributes such as diversity.

Another value was the compensation value of the forest. In other words, "What would it cost to compensate identifiable users of the forest for permanent loss of use?" The James Bay Cree were compensated by Quebec Hydro for the flooding of ancestral hunting grounds by the original James Bay Power Project. Compensation can involve a lump-sum settlement or annual payments. The present value of this future stream of payments could be estimated. This is a variation of the compensation paid to fishermen, with a vital difference. While the former involves paying stakeholders to temporarily refrain from doing something, the compensation value represents a payment to a user group for a permanent loss of the use of natural capital.

After reviewing the results of the team's initial brainstorming, it was obvious to Walker that they were a bit out of their element: It was time to consult with an environmental economist. Some initial networking in Canada and the United States provided a list of institutions that were engaged in innovative research in accounting for externalities, such as the Resources for the Future in Washington, D.C., or the Center for Economics Research, Research Triangle Institute in Research Triangle Park, North Carolina. Walker spent a fair bit of time on the phone with experts from both institutes. They spoke of their approaches to putting a dollar value of a forest through surveys of what people would be willing to pay for pristine wilderness, from the perspective of an armchair environmentalist who was concerned about preserving habitat for tomorrow.

Based on these initial consultations, Walker decided that over the long run, an economist would be a key member of the team. The scientists — silviculturalists, ecologists, organic chemists — would provide data on attributes of a health ecology. These would be the basis of any efforts to value the natural capital assets, as well as the damages to this natural capital, agriculture, and human health. The scientists would help analyze research on the relationships between specific effluent and the changes in the health of humans and natural capital. Then the economists would compute values for both the natural and human capital, as well as calculating the costs of externalities, or damages to this capital. The accountants would start where the economists left off, computing costs and liabilities based on these externalities. The accountants would also figure how to get this information into the internal and external information systems.

Walker realized from his discussions with the environmental economists that to develop good estimates of external costs would take considerable time and money. He was on a journey to develop nontraditional accounting systems, and this would be a later step. He decided to strike a contract with Bill Wentworth, an environmental economist, to act as an interim project advisor, and to scope out research projects for the future. However, Walker realized that given the state of the scientific ambiguity and uncertainty about the cause and effect relationship between clear-cutting and forest health, it would likely be premature to move too quickly on more sophisticated valuations, based on environmental economics. However, Walker and the team decided that they could continue to develop the accounting framework that could be used when better noncommercial values for the forest would become available. In short, they would focus on the overall framework, initially developing some fairly crude numbers for the noncommercial value of the forest, with the primary objective of experimenting with how they could be used to calculate intergenerational accounts at the corporate level. As Bill developed some more solid numbers, based on evolving methods in computing the economic values for natural resources, these better, more rigorous numbers would replace the team's initial attempts at valuation. Clearly, they were on a long journey where taking the next step was more important than any final outcome.

The team's overall conclusion was that there could be no one absolute value for the noncommercial facets of a living forest. In the same way, there was a range of relative values for a business — a going-concern value, a liquidation value, the net book value — each appropriate for a given set of circumstances. The team recognized there would be a range of coexisting values for a living forest, each reflecting different social values, each somewhere between a base value and an infinite value. The team recognized that to develop a more sophisticated methodology for the valuation of noncommercial values would be likely to take a decade.

"You see, Mike, if I had a value for the natural capital and a way to estimate potential depletion, I could then begin to calculate full, or fuller, costs that included the depletion cost of the natural capital."

"But Walker, it seems to me you have missed the obvious. If the growth of fiber represents the 'interest' on the 'principal' of natural capital and you know the earnings and the rate of return, then why can't you compute a crude value for the principal? You have also computed a rough rate of capital appreciation for the forest in your fiber valuation model. You know that according to your model the forest is appreciating from $40,455 million to $356,437 million in 30 years. That's an average appreciation of about $10.5 million. What's your guess on what the natural capital will earn the company, on average, over say the next 10 to 20 years?"

"Our normalized earnings over the next 20 years would have to be at least $85 million, or it's not worth staying in business. I see where you are going. Our long-term normalized rate of return should average, on a sustainable basis, at least 18 percent. Following your suggestion, using combined normalized earnings of $95 million ($85 plus $10 million per year), assuming a rate of return of 18 percent, results in a valuation of $530 million for the natural capital, the principal, upon which the company is economically dependent. In other words, $530 million, earning 18 percent a year would earn us the equivalent of forestry income, including pulp operations, and the appreciation of the forest value. Interestingly enough, this value is not far off the minimum compensation value the company would expect to cease harvesting in sensitive areas if this would make overall operations unprofitable."

Walker was beginning to see a potential interim solution. "Following the accounting rule of conservatism, or always assuming the worst-case scenario, let's say 10 percent of the total ecosystem could be at risk today. This would to a potential maximum risk value of $53 million, or 10 percent of the estimated minimum value of the ecosystem of $530 million."

Mike interrupted, "So our depletion allowance is $53 million. Walker, that's a number that will surely get the board's attention."

"No, it's not $53 million. Mike, opportunity is the flip side of the coin called risk. There are three variables — the size of the win or loss, the probability of its occurrence, and the timing of its occurrence. We haven't factored in the probability of occurrence, nor have we thought through the time element."

"What do you mean, the time element?"

"In determining environmental costs, which is the objective of the exercise from my perspective, there is a long delay between when the damage is done, when it is first recognized, when damages are established, when public pressure is brought to bear, and finally when a legal obligation to pay is incurred. In my view, it's as though someone has suffered a stiff neck in what was thought to be a fairly minor auto accident. It may take years for the symptoms of whiplash to surface, even longer to establish the extent of damage, and up to two generations to bring legal action for damages. The key question for accountants is when to recognize the damage. Accountants focus on the trigger event that leads to the ultimate charges. In the case of the car accident, should we recognize the damage costs when the accident actually occurred or almost two generations into the future when the lawyers come for their pound of flesh? Given accountants' assumptions about the time value of money, a dollar 40 years in the future is worth pennies compared to today's real money."

Mike was getting impatient. "So what's the bottom line. Is the $53 million a good number?"

Walker frowned, "It all depends on your view of what is the appropriate trigger event. If you believe it was when the accident occurred and we decided to use our best estimate of the potential cost, however crude, then it's a good number. If you believe that the only good number is the one 40 years down the road when the jury delivers the verdict, then it's a poor number that distorts more than it describes economic reality. Take your pick!"

"Walker, you know I don't know much about accounting. I want the best estimate as soon as possible after the accident. If there was a possibility that the other driver was injured, however remote, I want to know the potential out-of-court settlement now. I will factor that into today's decisions. Probably drive more cautiously."

"Let's recap where we are in the process — we have estimated the commercial value of the forest at $40 million and the noncommercial value of the ecosystem at $530 million. We have estimated that up to 10 percent of this ecosystem could be at risk. What we have yet to estimate is the probability of damage to the ecosystem based on the rate of development. I suggest we do this after we have evaluated the risks associated with pulp operations. Now, I'd like to experiment with preparing a green balance sheet where we can display the values we have computed so far. Once we get the final depletion numbers, we can plug these into this green balance sheet. In my view, the objective of the exercise would be to develop a framework to deal with intergenerational liabilities."

PREPARING A GREEN BALANCE SHEET

Walker went on to explain that the purpose of a green balance sheet would be to combine the commercial and noncommercial valuations of a northern boreal forest in one place so as to promote an informed assessment of a company's environmental stewardship by those with a stake in the forest. The most important component of a green balance sheet would be the intergenerational accounts that measured whether one generation was living beyond its ecological means, living off the principal of natural capital rather than off the interest. There would be three basic components of the balance sheet accounts—the wood fiber account, the investment to protect natural capital account, and the intergenerational liability and equity accounts.

The starting point of the green balance sheet exercise would be the information given in Table 9.2. Using basic present-value calculations, this table demonstrates that over time sustained-yield forestry management resulted in higher dividends to the next generation than harvesting without sufficient regeneration. Through sound silvicultural methods, the next generation would inherit an asset with a commercial value approaching $1.5 billion. Underlying this capital appreciation was the underlying assumption that, as a minimum, sustainable development required a company to regenerate as much as, or more than, it harvested. Table 9.2 illustrates that at the end of year 60 the company would have regenerated 60 million cubic meters of fiber while harvesting 42.5 million cubic meters. Table 9.2 suggests that the company was passing along a commercial asset that could provide the same earning potential to the next generation that this generation inherited.

The asset values computed in the table form the basis of Table 9.3. Under "Assets" are listed the commercial values computed in Table 9.2 for the original forest and the regenerated forest. These values increase from approximately $35 million to almost $1.5 billion in 60 years. The balance sheet also records budgeted investments to protect natural capital, estimated at $5 million per year. Based on the analysis of the ecological impacts of clear-cutting, the team estimated that the company would be likely to have to spend between $4.8 million and $12 million to lower the risk of potential damage to natural forest capital. Walker budgeted an annual investment of $5 million (unadjusted for inflation), giving rise to a budgeted investment of $150 million by year 30, $300 million by year 60. This is what should be spent if the company was committed leaving a valuable productive asset to future generations.

As is often the case in accounting, one side of a double entry is easier to understand than the corresponding other entry. Conceptually, the team

Table 9.3
Pro Forma Green Balance Sheet

	Opening	Year 1	Year 30	Year 60
Quantifiable Intergenerational Trust Accounts				
$000s – Budgeted Amounts				
Assets				
Original forest	$ 35,266	$ 37,121	$ 110,896	
Regenerated forest		3,334	245,541	$ 1,488,051
• Total forest	35,266	40,455	356,437	1,488,051
• Investments to protect natural capital		5,000	150,000	300,000
TOTAL ASSETS	$ 35,266	$ 45,455	$ 506,437	$ 1,788,051
Liabilities				
To next generation	0	0	0	0
Equity				
This generation				
• Investment to protect ecosystem		$ 5,000	$ 150,000	$ 300,000
• Regeneration (net of harvest)		1,804	112,451	353,151
Net Investment		6,804	262,451	653,151
Next generation				
• Original forest	35,266	35,266	35,266	35,266
• Dividends		3,385	208,720	1,099,634
	35,266	38,651	243,986	1,134,900
TOTAL LIABILITIES AND EQUITY	$ 35,266	$ 45,455	$ 506,437	$ 1,788,051

Other forest values account

Natural capital

– Animal populations, habitat				
– Plant life, habitat		$ 530,000	$ 780,000	
– Wilderness				
– Fertility of soil				
– Carbon storage/greenhouse effect				
– Biodiversity				

could visualize the buildup of timber assets through adherence to sound forest management practices. They would debit the asset side of the ledger. But where would they post the corresponding credit? In other words, "Who owns the forest?" Does it belong to this generation, the previous generation, the next generation, or the seventh generation from today? In accounting, a fundamental rule is "substance over form." To complete the green balance sheet, the team would have to reach a consensus as to which generation owned the forest and which was doing the temporary borrowing. The accounting under each set of assumptions of ownership would be very different.

The immediate question was where to credit the opening forest value of $35,266 million. Should the team treat this as a liability to the previous generation or as equity accruing to the current generation or the next generation? The decision on ownership would determine which generation would benefit from the fiber maturity gain that would rise to over $1 billion in 60 years.

The team found that once they had left the safe path of traditional accounting for corporate equity, they had entered an area of uncertainty. They had forest values—they just didn't know exactly what to do with them. One evening, a frustrated Walker asked his teenage daughter, "Who owns the forest?" Almost instinctively she responded that the future generations owned the forest. She handed him a quote from a journal book she used, "We do not inherit the earth from our ancestors; we borrow it from our children." Walker concluded that a credit of $35,266 to the next generation was both the most conservative and the most defensible approach from the perspective of best representing the spirit of *Our Common Future.* Walker's generation borrowed the forest to use for their own economic survival but had an obligation to maintain a living, productive forest subject to the same level of risk present when they originally inherited the right to use it. The concept of risk recognized that, given scientific uncertainty about the long-term effects of clear-cutting, the forest passed along to the next generation should be in no greater risk of irreversible ecological damage than the forest bequeathed by the founders of the company, J. R. Price and Eldon Charelebois Blackmore.

In the second column to the right in Table 9.3, the forest value in Year 1 would increase as original and regenerated forest moved 1 year closer to maturity and harvest. Previous analysis had suggested that at least $5 million should be spent to help ensure that the above "inheritance risk" level did not rise, thereby impairing the natural capital passed on to the next generation. In the liabilities and equity side of the entry, this $5 million is credited to the account of this generation. The project team debated crediting this amount to the account of the next generation but decided that in substance the expenditure was essentially a discretionary investment (i.e., not legally mandated by current regulations) made by the current generation. Accordingly, this generation should "get the credit" for this investment which had been made in advance of provincial regulations. In a sense, Walker viewed it as a cost of doing business today, a cost of sustaining natural capital, an investment intended to lower the risk of impairing natural capital passed on to the next generation.

The team determined that this generation should be credited with the value of regeneration in excess of amounts harvested. In Year 1, the amount credited to the account of the current generation is approximately $1.8 million. Again, the team debated where to credit the fiber maturity gain. Which generation should get the benefit of an increase in value as the forest moved closer to harvest? The team determined that in substance this gain represented a dividend due and payable to future generations for allowing the current generation to use the natural forest capital. Which generation gets the credit will determine whether one generation incurs a liability if natural capital is not maintained at "sustainable" levels of risk. Walker explained to Mike that the balances in Year 30 and Year 60 were developed following the same rationale.

"Walker, I can see that what you are doing is establishing a budgeted inheritance, based on prudent management of the estate. You have essentially established a benchmark value of what should be passed along to the next generation, if this generation treated the forest as an income trust and restricted itself to living off the interest. But what about these investments to protect natural capital?"

"Think of a trust where you have inherited a house in an excellent neighborhood. Right now the house is earning high rents. When it is passed along to our children, it should be earning good rents. This generation has full use of the house, can rent it for whatever the market will bear, pocket the difference between base maintenance costs and revenues, as long as the base productive value is not reduced, as long as natural capital is not irreparably damaged or eliminated. In addition, the current tenants have to contribute an annual payment of $5 million towards maintaining the value of the neighborhood. This annual contribution to the neighborhood would be credited to the account of this generation. If this generation falls behind in its payments, a liability is passed on to the next generation, an obligation that should be recognized in the accounts." Walker paused to catch his breath.

Walker explained that at the bottom of Table 9.3 is the "other forest values" account. Walker showed Mike how he proposed to use the $530-million threshold value of the ecosystem they had already computed. They agreed that this value "would put the commercial value of the forest in context." Walker explained that he had computed a value in 30 years following the same approach they had used to compute the $530-million value. Walker estimated that normalized earnings would be at least $100 million a year. Between Year 30 and Year 60 the annual rate of appreciation of the commercial value of the forest was approximately $40 million. Using a normalized rate of return of 18 percent, Walker estimated a potential value of the ecosystem in Year 30 of $780 million.

Mike wanted to know, "What's the link between the top and the bottom of the balance sheet?"

"Look at the top portion as the value of the house and the bottom half as the value of the neighborhood. There is a clear but somewhat indirect relationship between the two sets of values. To the extent that the value of the neighborhood rises, the value of the family house rises. To the extent that this generation runs the house into the ground, the value of the neighborhood drops. Let me show you one way to deal with these changes in values."

Walker explained that Table 9.4 showed how intergenerational liabilities could arise. The budgeted amounts for Year 30 are brought forward from the previous table. The "Actual" column represents present values calculated using the same methodology used to determine a commercial value for fiber (see Table 9.2). The company is in default because it is harvesting more than it is regenerating. By Year 30 it had harvested 19.25 million cubic meters of forest while regenerating only 15.38 million cubic meters. The company is showing an asset value of regenerated forest of approximately $112 million when it should be passing along to future generations an asset worth twice that amount. Also, the company has spent $100 million on investments to protect natural capital rather than the budgeted preventive maintenance figure of $150 million.

As a result, the assets that should accrue to the next generation have decreased from a budgeted amount of approximately $506 million to approximately $333 million. This represents a shortfall of approximately $173 million, which should be recorded as an intergenerational liability from this generation to the next. On the asset side, Walker explained that following the conventions of trust, or fiduciary accounting, this would be shown as a receivable from the company.

"At the bottom of Table 9.4 I have included the other forest values we calculated previously. In the actual column I have included the $780 million less a reserve for accumulated depletion."

Mike interrupted, "Where did that $195 million come from. I thought you said you needed a probability of damage to complete the calculation."

Walker nodded, "I do. Here I have focused on what we might do with the final number once we work it out. I have assumed that at Year 30 we are halfway through our cutting cycle so that half of the ecosystem might be at risk. Admittedly this is a simplistic assumption, but arguably no more simplistic than straight-line depreciation for a complex pulp mill. Anyway, let's accept this simplifying assumption for the moment. The missing part of the equation is the risk factor to apply to the $390 million potentially at risk (50 percent of $780 million). In 30 years, we have agreed, we will have the data to measure damage to the ecosystem. For this company in default, I have

Table 9.4
Intergenerational Accounts for a Company in Default – Year 30

	Budget	Actual	Adjustments	Final
Assets				
Original forest	$ 110,896	$ 110,896		$ 110,890
Regenerated forest	245,541	122,452		122,452
• Total forest	356,437	233,348		233,348
• Investments to protect natural capital	150,000	100,00	$ 195,000	100,000
• Due from company	0		173,089	368,000
TOTAL ASSETS	$ 506,437	$ 333,348	$ 386,089	$ 701,348
Liabilities			$ 173,089	
To next generation	0	0	195,000	368,000
Equity				
This generation				
• Investment (above)	150,000	100,000		100,000
• Net regeneration	112,451	1,492		1,492
Net change	262,451	101,492		101,492
Next generation				
• Original forest	35,266	35,266		35,266
• Dividends	208,720	196,590		196,590
Return on risk	——	——	——	——
	243,986	231,856		231,856
TOTAL LIABILITIES AND EQUITY	$ 506,437	$ 333,348	$ 368,089	$ 701,348
Other Forest Values Account				
Natural capital	$ 780,000	$ 780,000		$ 780,000
Less accumulated risk costs	.	195,000		195,000
NET NATURAL CAPITAL	$ 780,000	$ 585,000		$ 585,000

assumed a business-as-usual development philosophy and minimal efforts to preserve the ecosystem. This company has been consistently following the rule of quarterly earnings rather than the rule of two generations. I have assumed that at Year 30 the science suggests a 50 percent chance that the ecosystem has been irreparably damaged. In short, odds are that the company will be passing along damaged goods to the next generation. Accordingly, we recognize an intergenerational liability for $195 million in the accounts."

"I think you'd get the board's attention with these numbers. But Table 9.4 is being prepared 30 years from now when we have the data to make accurate estimations. How do we get the same impact now, how do we make the future explicit today, before we know with any certainty the outcome of that accident we were talking about? Right now we don't know the extent of damage."

"That's exactly what we are going to tackle after we review pulp operations and identify the risks to the ecosystem incurred during the manufacturing phase of operations. Once we have a comprehensive grasp of the risks, we will try again to develop some risk factors to use today."

NOTE

1. Robert E. Hoskin, William R. Sizemore, and James VanderWiede, "Timber and Timberland Valuation Methods," Durham, N.C., Duke University, May 1984.

Chapter 10

A Zero-Impact Factory

By this point in the project, the team had a rough framework, an approach, a philosophy. They had a sense of whom they were doing the accounting for, why they were doing it, and what they would account for. While they had yet to complete their work in accounting for other forest values, they had created a framework for analyzing environmental implications on return on investment, prices, and operating costs.

They had a rough definition of sustainable forestry management. Now they needed a definition of a sustainable pulp mill. At this point in the project, Len Hargrove, an organic chemist in charge of environmental protection at Blackmore and Price, joined the team. Their starting point was the environmental implications of the pulping process. The team agreed that their accounting would be driven by the organic chemistry.

THE ENVIRONMENTAL IMPLICATIONS OF
THE PULPING PROCESS

From Rags to Wood Pulp Wealth. Len said that to understand the demand for wood to make paper they had to review the history of paper making. Matthias Koops started experimenting with the idea of using wood pulp and straw as alternative fibers to make paper. Wasps had actually long known that wood fiber could be used to make paper, since they made the walls of their nests that way. Up to this point, the paper industry was still devoted to using rags as the raw material for paper, as it had done since A.D. 105. The rag man, calling down the street with his metal cart for old rags and scrap paper, was a familiar figure.

By the 1860s, paper from wood pulp was a serious possibility, a necessity. The rag supply couldn't match the appetite for paper. The United States alone was using 25,000 tons of rag by then, importing a quarter of it. Obviously, new sources of fiber besides cloth were needed; and wood pulp was an obvious choice. The first wood pulp mill in Canada was built in 1866, the Buntin Mill in Valleyfield, Quebec. It used blocks of maple.[1]

While wood pulp solved the quantity problem, it created a quality problem that condemned millions of books to early deterioration. The easiest way to make cheap paper was to leave a polymer called lignin inside the cell walls of wood fibers. Lignin helps to make the tree rigid, but it is acidic. This acid shortened the life of modern paper from several centuries for rag papers to about 70 years. This change from rags to wood pulp created the demand for pulp. This is where Walker wanted to start—the essentials of the pulping process. Len walked them through the chemistry.

The Pulping Process. Pulping refers to the operation that separates cellulose fibers in plant material into individual fibers and then bleaches or brightens them to form an intermediate product called *pulp*. This intermediate product then undergoes further processing to transform it into paper, the most familiar product of the pulp and paper industry. If the final product of a manufacturing facility is pulp, the plant is called a pulp mill. In that case, the pulp is shipped to another location for conversion to paper. If the pulp is sold on the open market to "converters" of pulp to paper or other products, then the pulp mill is referred to as a "market" pulp mill. If the pulp is converted into paper at the same mill, the plant is said to be an "integrated" pulp and paper mill.

Paper is a blend of different pulps and other materials such as clay, starch, and waxes. The properties of paper and its appearance are derived from the types of pulp and nonfibrous materials making it up, as well as the mechanical processes used to manufacture it. The products of the paper mill are widely varied—newsprint, facial tissue, cardboard boxes, writing paper, and high-gloss magazine paper, to mention a few.

The plant material used to produce pulp includes softwoods (trees with needles), hardwoods (trees with leaves), and such nonwood materials as straw, bagasse, bamboo, and flax. In the pulping of plant material, the natural fibers are separated either by dissolving away the lignin that binds them together with chemical agents or by shearing the binding material mechanically using physical force. Pulps produced in processes that use chemicals to dissolve the lignin are called "chemical" pulps, while pulps produced in processes that primarily use mechanical means to separate the fibers are called "mechanical" pulps.

The application of thermal and chemical treatments usually results in a reduced yield of pulp from the wood and a significant increase in the amount of contaminants discharged in the effluent (wastewater) from the mill. This effluent is "treated" in a wastewater treatment facility to remove contaminants before it is discharged into the environment. Since mechanical pulping has no "recovery" process to reuse or convert unwanted material removed from the wood during processing, all materials not converted into pulp end up as contaminants in the untreated effluent.

On a per-ton-of-production basis, the BOD (biochemical oxygen demand), COD (chemical oxygen demand), and toxicity of the untreated effluent from a mechanical pulp mill is greater by a factor of approximately 1.5 to 4.9 than that of the untreated effluent from a chemical pulp mill, even though the chemical pulp mill has a much lower yield of pulp from wood.[2] However, as mechanical pulp is generally brightened by hydrogen peroxide, no chlorine or chlorine-based chemicals are used, and no chlorinated organic compounds are generated, as is the case with chemical pulp.

Chemical Pulping Process. The process used by Blackmore and Price involved chemical pulping known as "kraft pulp" production. The kraft process is the dominant chemical pulping process in use throughout the world to produce chemical pulp because it produces a better quality pulp more economically than any other chemical pulping process discovered to date.

In chemical pulping, most of the lignin is removed before any attempt is made to separate the individual fibers. The subsequent separation process is much gentler; as a result, the fibers are longer and less damaged than those produced by mechanical pulping, and there are fewer fiber fragments ("fines"). Consequently, chemical pulps produce "stronger" paper; that is, paper with a greater resistance to tearing and a higher tensile strength.

Chemical pulps are commonly made by processes using sulphate, sulphite, or soda. In the kraft process, sodium hydroxide and sodium sulphide are the principal chemicals used to remove the lignin from the wood. This process was discovered in 1879 by a German chemist named Dahl. He found that it produced a very strong pulp compared to pulp produced by the sulphite process discovered some time earlier. Hence the pulp was called "kraft," the German word for strong.

WATER QUALITY CONSIDERATIONS

Source of Pollutants. Len simplified the process for the team and explained that mechanical and chemical pulping processes both are carried out in an aqueous (water) medium. The materials that are not recovered, such as fiber, together with the chemicals used in the pulping processes, are either dissolved in the aqueous medium or appear in the medium as small particles or colloidal material. These constituents are potential pollutants if they are not captured and reused within the process or destroyed by treatment methods external to the process.

The effluents from pulping and bleaching operations are combined and, in most cases, treated prior to discharge. Primary treatment removes suspended solids through screening and settling, thereby reducing the BOD of the effluents on the aquatic environment. Secondary treatment involves contact with bacteria that decompose organic substances in the effluent. This process removes oxygen-consuming substances, as well as some of the substances toxic to fish. In Canada, 49 percent of bleached-pulp mills employ secondary treatment, 43 percent employ only primary treatment, and 9 percent employ no effluent treatment.

Environmental Implications. The conventional bleaching process is the source of about half the BOD, all the organochlorines, most of the color, and much of the toxicity in the effluent from a typical bleached kraft mill. The amount of chorine used by pulp mills depends on the type of wood used, the pulping and bleaching systems employed, and the desired degree of product brightness. A wide variety of chlorinated organic chemicals is found in the kraft bleaching process, including chlorinated resin acids and chlorinated phenolics, which can be lethal to fish, and the chlorinated dioxins that have attracted so much media attention. The organochlorines are soluble in mill waste waters and are not completely removed by effluent treatment, even at the most up-to-date mills with the latest pollution-abatement technology.[3] For a perspective, the average Ontario bleached kraft mill produces about 2 tons of organic chlorine per day.

Len stressed that the main cause for concern about highly toxic and persistent organochlorines is the unknown degree to which they persist in the environment. Some of the chlorinated organic compounds are persistent and have been detected in water, sediments, and particles downstream of bleached-pulp mill outfall. Compounds with low chlorine substitution degrade within hours or days, whereas highly chlorinated organic compounds may persist from days to weeks or longer. Persistence may be longer in winter, especially under ice. Some chlorinated organic compounds can be biologically degraded or transformed, and transformation may lead to more persistent and bioaccumulative compounds. There is considerable controversy surrounding the effects of organic chlorines on the environment. According to Len, environmental leaders in industry are concerned about the perceptions in the minds of both the public and their customers. Progressive companies see a marketing opportunity in completely removing chlorine and chlorine-containing chemicals from the bleaching process, and they are working to develop new technologies.

By early 1993, the debate about chlorine was reaching a crescendo. The province had announced tough new rules intended to reduce the pollution from pulp mills. The new rules would call for a sharp reduction and eventual phaseout of chlorine use in pulp bleaching in the province. By the end of 1995, chlorine discharge limits would drop 40 percent; by the end of 1999 they would drop to 68 percent of present levels. Companies would also be required to draft plans to eliminate chlorine entirely by 2002. The rules also called for drastic cuts in acceptable levels of the other pollutants in pulp and paper discharge. The province estimated the cleanup would cost the industry $585 million by 1999 to meet improvements required by both the provincial and federal regulators.

Environmental activists greeted the new regulations cautiously. Environmental activists said that they would demand that company plans for eliminating chlorine be made public and that penalties apply to those who do not meet the 2002 deadlines. Environmental activists said they desired a "zero discharge regulation."

Industry leaders denounced the new rules. The industry estimated that dropping discharge levels of organochlorines would cost at least $800 million, including capital spending. In their view, this would be another blow to an industry already hard hit by the recession. As the CEO of Blackmore and Price said to the press, "They have painted a course for us that doesn't bear any relationship to the science."

From an accounting perspective, Len explained that there is uncertainty as to the long-term liabilities, if any, that may be associated with organochlorine discharge. "The scientific question is whether there are chronic toxic effects in the environment as a result of persistent organochlorines or other toxic substances in mill effluent. The role for you accountants is to look at the appropriate accounting commensurate with different scientific findings. Simply put, there are two possibilities: either there is no liability to future generations, or there is a liability. If the former proves to be true, there is no need to account for intergenerational liabilities, as they are nonexistent. If the latter is considered to be the case, then appropriate accounting for these liabilities must be undertaken on behalf of present and future generations. This is what full cost accounting for natural resources would require."

FULLER COST ACCOUNTING FOR RIVERS AND LAKES

In trying to account for full costs, they had two options — to focus on the costs of cleaning up past and present toxins, or to examine the cost of preventing future cleanups. In the CEO's view, the industry was in the middle of a major political debate. There was a push for zero discharge. According to the CEO, there was no such thing as zero discharge. A reasonable goal is the virtual elimination of all persistent toxins that bioaccumulate. The company could achieve this by a closed-loop system, by eliminating all chlorine compounds, but it would never get to zero discharge.

According to the CEO, their starting point had to be today's market. He saw that chlorine was no longer an issue. The company had to get rid of it, could not wait for the legislation. In his view, legislation was too cumbersome, too slow, always directed to the lowest common denominator and usually "missed the mark by a mile."

The CEO viewed chlorine as a time bomb, a nightmare. "It's a lethal gas

Figure 10.1
Water Quality Impact Scale

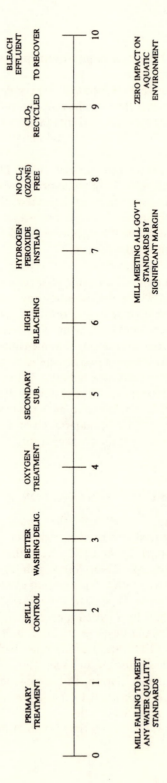

that if it leaked out of a train car would wipe out the whole town where we operate. I'd be the happiest guy in town if we could get rid of chlorine." He wondered if the company could go to 100 percent elimination of elemental chlorine and charge a premium. He noted that right now the company's paper was at 90 percent brightness. Perhaps the company could move to 70 percent brightness in 10 years and dump chlorine if the market would accept it.

A Waste-Reduction Approach: A Sustainable Pulp Mill. The team decided to take a waste-reduction approach. The focus would be on eliminating the amount of hazardous waste before it is generated in the process. Their goal would be to modify current pulp operations, to design a mill for the future that would reduce the quantity and hazard of waste generated. They would look at product innovation—lower brightness, chlorine-free paper. They would look at chemical substitution. They noted that some companies were experimenting with the use of ozone. They would look for a major process modification to increase efficiency and productivity in a new mill.

After considerable debate and discussion, this is how Blackmore and Price decided to present its case:

Water quality considerations. Bleached kraft mills produce effluent from the bleaching stage of the pulping process. Chlorine is present in the mill effluent because it is used together with chlorine dioxide and sodium hypochlorite chemicals in the bleaching process. A conventional mill produces about 50 kg of dissolved organic waste material for every ton of pulp produced. Oxygen delignification has been used as a partial replacement for chlorine in many mills. A typical mill that uses oxygen delignification produces 25 kg of dissolved organic waste material for every ton of pulp produced. This dissolved organic chlorine and the caustic used in bleaching cannot be reclaimed because the chlorine is chemically bound to the organic matter. There has recently been a trend toward replacing as much chlorine as possible with chemicals that are less environmentally deleterious, including oxygen, chlorine dioxide, ozone, and hydrogen peroxide. However, complete replacement of chlorine is not yet technically feasible.

The impact on water quality from various pulp and paper production technologies is illustrated in the scale shown in Figure 10.1.

The zero-impact bleached kraft mill. The ideal mill would have a bleach plant that did not use chlorine, chlorine dioxide, or sodium hypochlorite but instead used other oxidizing chemicals such as nitrogen dioxide, oxygen, ozone, hydrogen peroxide, or enzymes such as zylenase, to remove the lignin and brighten the pulp. The effluent would then theoretically be recyclable: the sodium in the effluent would be reused, and the organic matter could be burned to generate energy.

The zero-impact bleached kraft pulp mill would have virtually eliminated the organic waste from the bleach plant effluent. In order to make the transition from the existing bleached kraft mill to a sustainable mill with zero impact on the aquatic environment, it is necessary to satisfy at least two major criteria:

1. The mill must be able to produce a marketable product using nonchlorine bleaching agents.
2. The mill must find the best way to recycle the nonchlorine effluent back into the mill system.

In summary, Blackmore and Price's definition of a sustainable pulp mill is a zero-impact bleached kraft mill. In addition, the firm is looking for alternatives to landfill for storing some solid wastes from the pulp mill. It would like to move to energy self-sufficiency. The costs of achieving these objectives have been included in the overall capital costs, which are illustrated in Figure 12.3 Air and Water Pollution Scale presented in the Stewardship Report to the Board of Directors, Chapter 12.

Organizational Learning. In the process of this accounting exercise, the team started simulating options that had been only vague notions before the project started. For example, Len had been kicking around the idea of a zero-impact mill, doing the basic research; but the project had been on the back burner. During the accounting exercise, this new strategy took on a life of its own, a legitimacy, when they moved to the next phase of the project, detailed costing. The obvious question was, "How much is it going to cost to achieve a sustainable mill?"

Table 10.1
Blackmore and Price Forest Products Ltd.: Price Implications of a Zero-Impact Pulp Mill and Sustaining Nonwood Values (Incremental Price Increases Required to Offset Increased Production Costs)

	Pulp Commodity Prices (1)	Lumber Commodity Prices (2)
Silvicultural Enhancements		
– Option 2 (3)	4.5%	3%
– Option 3 (3)	11.0%	9%
Zero-Impact Pulp Mill	2.5%	N/A
Environment is Equal (4) (Option 3 plus zero impact pulp mill)	13.5%	12%

Assumptions:

1. Increase in sales value for Air Dry Short Ton (ADST) of pulp.

2. Increase in sales value per thousand foot board measure of lumber.

3. These price increases are incremental relative to the existing costs which industry is presently incurring for sustained yield silviculture and compliance with the regulatory framework for pulp mill operations.

4. The actual raw material "furnish" cost (i.e. cost of wood) to a mill could increase anywhere from 30% to 40% for the Environment is Equal option. It is this cost increase that results in the above commodity price increases. The issue to be explored is whether the nature of the commodity market is such that it would allow for these costs to be passed on to the consumer. If they could not, no company could absorb these costs and stay in business.

Costing the Bottom-Line Impact. The team then proceeded to simulate the impact of the removal of chlorine on return on investment, on prices that Blackmore and Price would have to charge for its pulp products.

When they told the CEO that the return on investment would drop by at least 7 percent from 22.7 percent to around 15.6 percent, he was shocked. "That's one mean drop in return on investment." His concern was that unlike previous modernizations, which generally paid for themselves and were good business, this hit to ROI might not be economically sustainable. His first concern was, "Who is going to pay for it?" His second concern was, "What are the intangible benefits of making this investment?"

Walker explained that the prototype statements they had in mind would focus on these questions. Their objective would be to stimulate a dialogue about who would pay. Walker proposed two prototype statements. The first, shown in Table 10.1, would disclose the adjustments that had to be made to prices of company products if enhanced sustainability were to be achieved. The second, shown in Table 10.2, would disclose the projected

Table 10.2
Rate of Return on Environmental Investments

Levels of Pulp Mill Sustainability	Range of Sustainability of Forestry Operations		
	Timber Is Primary Consideration (Option 1)	Enhanced Nonwood Values (Option 2)	Environment Is Equal (Option 3)
Average Pulp Mill	27.0%	24.4%	22.2%
Mill meets all air and water regulations by narrow margin	27.7% Blackmore and Price, Now	20.9%	18.9%
Industry leader	18.4%	17.3%	15.6%

Assumptions:

1. Annualized average earnings (20-year projection) of $85 million for an average pulp mill, $72.5 million for an industry leader. At the time this chart was prepared the average investor could get a 10% return on a bank debenture.

2. Average annualized capital employed (20-year projection) of $314 million for average pulp mill, $393 million for industry leader.

3. Middle range (between the average and the industry leader) is an average of the two extremes.

4. Option 2 (Enhanced Nonwood Values) assumes a linear incremental cost of at least $4.8 million per year, based on a 710,000 M^3 harvest.

5. Option 3 (Environment is Equal) assumes a linear incremental cost of at least $7.2 million per year, based on the same harvest.

rates of return over the next 20 years given different environmental investment scenarios.

Taking Stock. Although the team felt satisfied they had made real progress in accounting for sustainable development, Walker was not yet satisfied.
The CEO had said, "If you haven't accounted for those other forest values,
you haven't accounted for sustainable development." Walker knew that in
the ideal world he would be able to provide the CEO with a sensitivity analysis of both the abatement costs and the potential risk costs associated with
current and past mill effluent. The problem was he didn't have the tools to
do that today.

APPLYING RISK-MANAGEMENT PRINCIPLES
TO WATERBORNE POLLUTANTS

From an accounting perspective, the objective of the exercise had always
been to account for full costs and for any associated liabilities. So far the
team had not accounted for *full costs* but had accounted for *costs more fully.*
Walker was not satisfied because he knew others were accounting with ever
greater precision for the potential "risk costs" associated with every barrel
of toxic waste sent to landfill. Accounting for the risk costs associated with
natural capital and waterborne pollutants would be much more challenging.
For example, there are at least 1,000 known pollutants in the Great Lakes.
How could anyone assign responsibility for past industrial discharge that
may have ended up in the Great Lakes?

Walker knew he had to push his thinking far beyond the current regulations in force. These regulations did not require environmentally sustainable
operations, largely because of the nature of the regulatory process itself.
Walker saw regulations as a political compromise between scientific evidence
and business realities. The demands of sustainability were likely to be far
more stringent than the current regulations. Walker was still concerned
about the issue of past debts and future intergenerational costs.

Is There a Past Debt? Two issues would have to be addressed before any
determination could be made whether a pollution liability existed for past
discharges:

1. Was there tangible evidence today of past practices by the company which had
   polluted the environment? Clearly, if past pollution had, for example, harmlessly
   broken down or dissipated to the point where it could not be measured, then probably no liability would need to be recognized.

2. If the answer to the first question was yes, the next question would be, "Can
   anything be done to remedy the results of past pollution?" If, for example, toxic
   residues were found to exist in the river into which Blackmore and Price had discharged wastes but there was nothing that could technically be done to remove
   these residues, should Blackmore and Price recognize a liability?

In this latter situation, the integrity of the ecosystem may have been compromised (unknowingly and without breaking any laws of the day). Walker recognized the importance of incorporating into his environmental accounting model the means to account for an intergenerational debt, even though Len believed no such debts existed. Walker had developed a crude model for approximating liabilities on the forest site, and now he wanted to explore its application on the pulp side.

In Blackmore and Price's case, Len was adamant that there was virtually no evidence of past pollution caused by mill operations. Len recognized the harmful and in some instances cumulative effects of some toxins but argued that the degree to which they are (1) attributed to *past* rather than present polluting activity and are (2) capable of being remedied was ambiguous.

However, when Walker pushed, Len had to agree that there were many long-term effects scientists were not sure about. Len agreed to participate in thinking the unthinkable, in trying to account for the business risk costs associated with past, and present, toxic discharges.

As Walker, Mike, and Len were reflecting on what still needed to be done, Walker tried to summarize the remaining challenges. "Len, while you would not publicly admit to the existence of any liabilities, the sense I get listening to you is that there is a lot you scientists really don't know. You scientists just don't have the data on the long-term effects as toxins that bioaccumulate work their way up the food chain. You cannot state with absolute certainty that there is not a possibility, however remote, that past and present mill effluent is creating an ecological time bomb that may explode in 20 or 30 years. In other words, there are risks, just as there were risks associated with clear-cutting, for which we have to account. So far we have done a good job of bringing the sustainable word out of the clouds and figuring out how much it will cost to become a sustainable corporation. My concern is that in the course of calculating these costs, we have provided the board with lots of reasons not to spend. What we now have to prove to the board is how much it might cost not to spend."

NOTES

1. Phil Jenkins, "From Rags to Wood Pulp Riches," *The Citizen* (Ottawa), January 26, 1992.

2. Environment, *Canada, Effluents from Pulp Mills Using Bleaching: Priority Substances List Assessment Report No. 2* (Ottawa, 1991).

3. A. B. McKague, *Characterization and Identification of Organic Chlorine Compounds in Bleach Plant Effluents* (University of Toronto, 1988).

Chapter 11

Applying Risk-Management Principles to Costing Natural Capital

The CEO had said he was not convinced that further environmental investments would pay for themselves. However, Walker's hunch was that the costs of not doing anything could also run into the tens of millions of dollars. In other words, Walker suspected a full accounting of *both* the costs of zero impact *and* of doing nothing would show Blackmore and Price was caught between a rock and a hard place. His understanding of the Superfund experience in the United States confirmed this view.

IN THE LONG RUN, THE DEEPEST POCKET PAYS

Reading between the Lines of the Superfund Experience. Walker was no expert, but he had read the accounting literature, and he knew that the Superfund experience in the United States had led to liabilities that were likely to spiral into the trillions of dollars when all was said and done. Discussions with his peers across the border led Walker to believe that society would be likely to follow three simple principles over the foreseeable future:

1. *The deepest pocket pays.*
2. *There is no statute of limitations.* A company that polluted in the 1950s was still liable in the 1990s, liable under social values and rules vastly different from those in existence when the pollution occurred.
3. *Joint and several liability.* Even if the deepest pocket had contributed only a relatively small element of the total cumulative pollution, it could be assessed for costs disproportionate to its toxic contribution. The last one at the bar would pick up the whole tab.

Walker researched the matter and found that there were well-established risk-management principles, a large database of information for specific site cleanups, such as these associated with the Love Canal cleanup. Walker located some fuller cost models designed to help with specific environmental investment decisions rather than in setting an overall corporate environmental investment strategy. These analyses focused on building estimated cleanup costs into decisions on new technological investments rather than calculating the costs of protecting a broader range of natural capital. However, Walker quickly realized that the same basic principles should apply in both applications. His research had first led him to *Financial Analysis of Waste Management Alternatives,* which had been produced by ICF Technology for Corporate Environmental Programs at General Electric Company in 1987.

This leading-edge work was intended to provide GE management with tools to make the most cost-effective waste management decisions. GE recognized that like most capital decisions, waste handling and disposal decisions, were evaluated using familiar engineering and economic models. These models calculated payback in terms of measurable short-term capital and operating estimates that did not factor in any environmental costs. The perceived problem was that a plant manager would accept these project decisions, even though longer-term liabilities would not have been considered by the responsibility center making the decisions. Managers could be encouraged to think, "Oh, cleanup costs are somebody else's problem."

The GE workbook provided site managers with the tools necessary to include fuller costs and the related longer-term liabilities associated with possible future claims for corrective action, remediation, personal injury, and property damage. GE felt these costs could be avoided if they could be predicted and quantified. The overall philosophy was that it is easier to eliminate waste through plant and product redesign than to treat it at the end of the productive cycle, or the "end of the pipe." The GE workbook provided formulas and software to use in analyzing the fuller costs of waste produced.

Walker's research located other models, such as the *Total Cost Assessment* model developed by the Tellus Institute for the Environmental Protection Agency (EPA). The total cost model was intended to provide tools to help overcome economic and financial barriers in the capital budgeting process that stack the deck against environmental investments. The model broke new ground by providing a way to factor indirect, or less tangible, savings into the financial analysis of environmental projects. These savings would enhance the estimated profitability of investments in prevention technology. These factors could be decisive in choosing a waste-elimination rather than an end-of-the-pipe solution. The total cost model included a case study on the pulp and paper industry that stimulated Walker's thinking. The case study illustrated that materially different rates of profitability would be calculated using the total cost, rather than the conventional approach.

The total cost model factored in the following "less tangible benefits" from

- Enhanced product quality
- Increased revenue from enhanced company and product image
- Reduced health maintenance costs from improved employee health
- Increased productivity from improved employee relations

The other key feature of this model was its longer time horizon, usually 5 or more years. This reflected the reality that certain cost savings from pollution abatement take years to materialize. Conventional analysis normally confined cost savings to a 3- to 5-year time horizon.

When Walker and the team reflected on this model, they realized that to account for a 10,000-year-old asset, a northern boreal forest, the time horizon would have to be extended considerably beyond 5 years. The risk costs of damaging such a living asset, over a 60- to 100-year horizon, while intangible, could nonetheless run into the hundreds of millions of dollars.

These were costs that would probably never be discussed with stakeholders but costs management needed to be aware of. There were a host of stakeholders out there, consumers whose business was critical for Blackmore and Price's survival, activists who could influence the marketplace for wood products, and the politicians who set the regulations.

Identifying the Business Risks. Walker went through the list of stakeholders, trying to identify which stakeholders could cost Blackmore and Price over the next 60 years. Walker used his analysis of the components of the boreal forest ecosystem, as well as the ecosystem functions such as storage of CO_2. The question addressed by the team was, "Relative to each component of the ecosystem, how and when might these stakeholders affect sales, bring an individual or class action against Blackmore and Price, or try to influence politicians and bureaucrats?" In Figure 11.1, for each component of the ecosystem, Walker and the team looked at the potential intergenerational liabilities, and the time frames associated with each potential liability. The greatest single business risk associated with the perceived impairment of natural capital had to be the loss of consumer dollars. The communications expert confirmed the extent to which consumer demand for chlorine-free paper could affect the market. The expert estimated that in the 5- to 10-year time frame, the "do nothing," business-as-usual option could eventually cost sales.

Walker had set up his time horizons to run parallel to the growth cycle of the major species harvested, jack pine. He and Mike had already agreed that within 20 to 40 years, Blackmore and Price would be approximately halfway through its 60-year cutting and reforestation cycle. Mike had talked with the silviculturalists, both within the company and at the federal fores-

Figure 11.1
Sources of Intergenerational Liabilities

Natural Capital	Short-Term (Next 5–10 years)	Medium-Term (Next 20–40 Years)	Long-Term (Next 40–80 Years)
Components of Ecosystem			
1.1 Micro Climate	Loss of Customers		Climate Change
1.2 Soil			Loss of Nutrients
1.3 Vegetation		Endangered Species	
1.4 Microbial Life			Reduction in Diversity
1.5 Wildlife		Endangered Species	
1.6 Fish and Water		Endangered Water Quality and Habitat	
1.7 Sensitive Areas (Wetlands, Spawning Grounds)		Endangered Wetlands	Endangered Areas
Ecosystem Functions			
2.1 Sustained Life of Biomass			Loss of Biomass
2.2 Carbon Storage and Greenhouse Effect			
2.3 Biodiversity			Loss in Diversity
2.4 Aesthetics, Recreation		Endangered Spaces	
Human Health and Wellbeing		Damage to Human Health	

try research stations. There was a fairly good consensus that *if* there were going to be heightened public perceptions of unanticipated ecological stresses associated with clear-cutting, they could start surfacing in the medium-term time horizon. The thinking was that symptoms of unanticipated ecological stresses would be detected by scientific studies as the younger trees approached maturity.

Walker contemplated the longer haul, 40 to 80 years into the future when they would be harvesting the replanted crop. He envisaged a world where there might be up to ten billion people struggling for scarce resources. Any company that was perceived to have impaired ever scarcer natural capital would likely be castigated in the court of public opinion—not by the rules of 1990 but by the rules of 2050. Since Blackmore and Price was in for the long haul, its deep pocket could be tapped heavily.

Walker was now ready to confront the toughest part of the exercise, coming up with some dollars and probabilities of occurrence to put against these categories of risks.

It Goes against the Grain to Produce "Fuzzy" Numbers. By temperament and training, Walker was not an economic forecaster. However, he recognized that a progressive company had to project current trends into the future. This would be different from forecasting, something he considered to be akin to reading tea leaves. He would project the long-term implications of present known trends. There was one thing he knew for sure—the forest would be under increased pressure from human beings. With an exploding world population, there would be either a renewed pressure to preserve existing forest land or, as the CEO had pointed out, even pressure to convert forest land to agriculture.

THE RISK-MANAGEMENT COSTS ASSOCIATED WITH OTHER FOREST VALUES

The team tried to contemplate potential legal costs that could be levied against Blackmore and Price, by interested groups. These claims would not necessarily represent the intrinsic value of the capital, but they would represent public perceptions. As the communications expert had said so often, "Perceptions become reality." The precedent was well established.

Walker put on his doomsday cap and prepared Figure 11.2. He saw the need for monitoring and measurement costs of at least a million dollars a year throughout the 60-year period. These were a given. As the risks of the technology employed increased, these costs would rise. He saw ongoing public relations costs. These would run a million dollars a year. Then he saw legal and expert-witness costs that would rise over the 60-year period. Walker envisaged an endless progression of public hearings on forest use. He estimated that these legal and expert-witness costs would start at $1 million a year, move up to $1.5 million in the medium term, and peak at $3 million a year toward the end of the 60-year term.

In the short run, he estimated there could be up to a 30 percent chance of a 10 percent loss of customers *if* Blackmore and Price did not develop a line of chlorine-free paper and create a "leadership image" with consumers. The company could also lose customers if it did not invest in landscape management. In the medium term, Walker identified the remote possibility of a class action on water quality downstream of the pulp mill. He estimated the conversion cost of switching three communities, with a total population of about 25,000 people, to alternative water sources. With 10,000 households and a potential conversion cost of $5,000 per household there was a potential risk cost of $50 million, with a 10 percent chance of occurrence. This probability of occurrence was the softest of soft numbers. Any value between 0 and 20 percent chance meant the probability was more than "remote," but far less than probable.

He then looked at the risk of endangered species. The company could be perceived by some environmental activists to be liable for reductions in

Figure 11.2
Cumulative Risk Costs of the Business-as-Usual Option

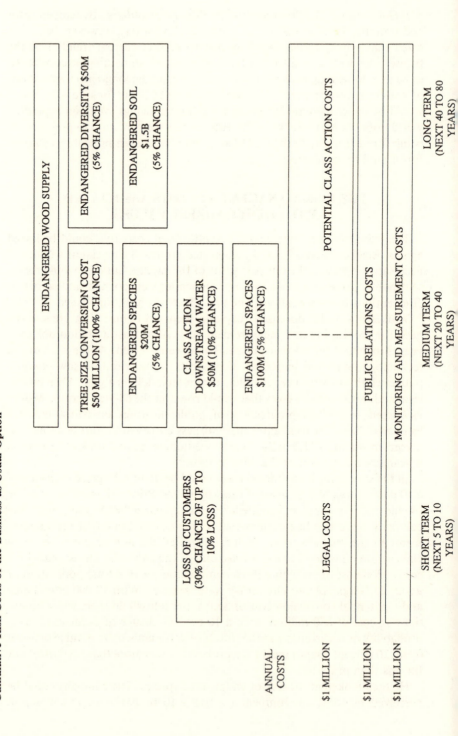

moose populations, blue heron populations, eagle populations, osprey populations, and populations of other "sensitive" species. He figured that environmental activists would assess the company for the costs of resettlement to suitable habitat, the costs of "repatriating" others of the endangered species back into the habitat. Either way, Walker estimated there could be up to a $20-million cost, with a 5 percent chance of occurrence.

From discussions with Mike, Walker estimated that there were about 50 highly sensitive areas in the logging limit such as spawning grounds and wetlands. For each one of these 50 endangered spaces, Walker conservatively estimated a potential remediation cost of up to $2 million. He felt this to be conservative, given that the average cleanup cost for landfill was running over $25 million, based on the Superfund experience. Walker estimated there was a 5 percent chance of this $100-million bill coming due.

Looking at the long term, Walker could foresee the remote possibility of a potential claim for endangered soil for $1.5 billion. This was Walker's logic. The commercial value of the trees was going to be $1.5 billion in 60 years. In 40 to 80 years, there would be sound measurement techniques, a database to measure soil fertility. If there were to be evidence of soil depletion on the Blackmore and Price logging limit, it would be thoroughly documented and probably enforceable in court in 40 to 80 years. Walker also figured that anyone making a claim would argue that the soil was worth at least as much as the commercial value of the forest of $1.5 billion. Walker and Mike estimated up to a 5 percent chance of such a claim occurring.

Walker estimated a potential claim for reduced diversity of $50 million, with up to a 5 percent chance of occurrence. In the longer term, there would be accurate measurements of changes in biodiversity and in genetic diversity. Blackmore and Price could be held liable.

Walker estimated an old-growth conversion cost. Walker recognized that the efficiency of most logging technology in the bush depended on the size of the tree. Generally, as the trees shrank in size, the company's efficiency would go down. New, efficient technology could be developed for these regenerated, smaller-sized trees, but there would be a conversion cost. Walker and Mike estimated the conversion cost to be $50 million with a 100 percent chance of occurrence.

From Blackmore and Price's perspective, the biggest single risk was that associated with the security of wood supply. If the company were to be perceived by the public as irresponsible in the past, in the 1990s, or in the early years of the new century, its timber rights could be reduced. The bottom line fell approximately at the halfway point of the 60-year cutting cycle. Blackmore and Price could risk losing cutting rights to an asset worth approximately $365 million. Blackmore and Price would cease to be a going concern. In other words, the single biggest sanction would be to be denied access to the natural resource upon which the company was economically dependent.

When Walker put all these doomsday scenarios on the table, he knew that the risk cost to use in management decisions would be the cost of insuring against these major interruptions to business as usual. If an insurance company could estimate an all-perils approach to these risk costs, that insurance cost would be the relevant cost the CEO and the board should consider. As Walker reflected on these risk costs, he realized he had calculated a range of contingent costs associated with the business-as-usual strategy. However, these were the fuzziest numbers he had ever produced in the sense that they were speculative, imprecise, and difficult to defend if challenged. Yet, the dilemma was that to report no risk costs could be just as misleading to the corporate braintrust in Toronto.

Mike, Len, and Walker were sitting in the conference room trying to integrate all the data they had assembled. Mike was impatient and wanted a sense of closure, "So Walker, where are we at? You said we had to identify the scientific risks, translate these into business risks, and then we would be ready to color our world shades of grey. I believe those were the words you used. One thing though. Did making all those estimates of business risks make your head spin?"

Walker laughed. "If you nonaccountants only knew all the hairy estimates I have to make at year end just to prepare a normal financial statement. Estimates for bad debts, pension accruals, foreign exchange losses, other accruals. It's a myth that financial statements are objective—they are as subjective as hell. Accounting is no science. More of a best guess at a given point in time. So to answer your question—no those estimates are just an extension of what I get paid to do anyway. But let's cut to the car chase, as you would say Mike. We have identified risks to the environment, we have identified real business risks in the hundreds of millions of dollars in the next 20 to 40 years. These risks will arise in the court of law and, perhaps most important, in the court of public perceptions."

"Now what do we do with these potential business risks?"

"We do what we accountants do with any potential impairment to an asset's value. We estimate the potential damage, using professional judgment, then write down the value of the asset, recognizing a cost of operations. I have thought about this a great deal, and I am going to propose a set of probabilities associated with each shade of grey. When we start establishing risk factors, the important thing is that the relative differences between the various rankings are approximately right and lead in the direction of a sound decision. They do not have to be absolutely right. In other words, if business as usual is a lot riskier than sound environmental management, then it is critical that the relative weightings reflect that one path is far less risky than the other. What's relevant to the decision is incremental reduction in risk in moving from Option 1 to Option 2. It is the different weighting here that is material or germane to the decision at hand. And because of the accounting convention of conservatism, or assuming the worst-case scenario, we can't underestimate the costs of business as usual."

"I think I see your point. As long as we are approximately right, we will not distort decisions. We are just trying to present some rough orders of magnitude; and if we disclose our assumptions, then we have done our job. We do this all the time in our volume predictions for forest growth," Mike added.

"Right. I see a continuum of probabilities ranging from virtual certainty of occurrence to a situation where the occurrence is inconceivable. Traditional accounting conventions deal with the normal situations where we have to estimate usual, or even somewhat extraordinary, costs of doing business. However, here our focus is on the remote but conceivable costs of doing business. The traditional accounting model stalls out on the concept of remote. I suggest the following weightings:

- *"Remote, but conceivable.* I propose we assign a possibility of occurrence of two out of ten times, or 20 percent. Implicit in this weighting is a recognition that risk of environmental degradation is an inherent part of modern business. There is an inherent threshold limit of risk that has to be recognized, that will always exist given the political nature of the regulatory process in a democracy. Regulations by the state will always gravitate towards the lowest common denominator.
- *"Remote, but the risks have been identified and are being managed (i.e., unlikely).* I propose we assign a probability of one in ten, or 10 percent. We have lowered the risk because we are managing both the chance of occurrence and the size of potential loss (i.e., we have a good containment strategy in terms of both managing the serious occurrence and public perceptions).
- *"Remote, managed, and almost inconceivable.* Here a company manages and monitors the risk, adjusts its behavior when early warning signs appear, lowers the level of uncertainty to a minimum threshold. Here I would assign a probability of one in twenty, or 5 percent."

"But Walker, what do you have to back up those weightings?"

"All the foregoing analysis of business risks suggests that not changing course is going to cost over the next 20 to 40 years. I'm saying that based on all these conceivable but remote risks the company would be experiencing but not managing, there has to be a fairly high cost. Using 20 percent of our natural-capital calculation of $53 million would lead to an annual risk cost of $10 million. Is that unreasonable, given that today's practices could lead to the cancellation of our timber lease in 20 years? If we lost our lease, I estimate that the value of our corporate goodwill would drop at least $200 million. Amortizing that over 20 years is about $10 million a year. But you guys are the experts in forestry and pulp operations. You tell me which category you would match with our three business options."

Mike thought about it for a while. "From a forestry perspective I'd say the three choices line up pretty well with our three options. As you said before, what counts is the incremental difference in risks between the two options. However, I'd definitely argue that Option 2 is more than twice as safe as Option 1. My gut feeling is that we get the best tradeoff between risk reduction and cost between the first two options. You know the old adage — we fix 80 percent of the problem with the first 20 percent cost increase and last 20 percent with another 80 percent increase. I know it is not that extreme, but that is the general idea. Overall, I think your weighting scheme achieves our objective of translating tomorrow's business risks, which are spawned today, into today's decisions."

Len concurred with Mike's assessment. They agreed to adjust the relative weighting to reflect this perception. Option 1 would carry a two-out-of-ten risk factor (20 percent); Option 2 would carry a one-out-of-fifteen risk factor (7 percent), and Option 3 would carry a one-out-of-twenty risk factor (5 percent). They agreed that Option 3 was so radical a departure from today's regulations that they could not conceive of losing their case in the courts, even in the court of public opinion.

ACCOUNTING FOR INTERGENERATIONAL COSTS AND LIABILITIES

With this conceptual framework in place, Walker and the team were now ready to complete Table 11.1. They started to fill in the blanks for Option 3. The annual costs of silvicultural enhancements and the quest for a zero-impact mill were likely to be at least $22.3 million. The resulting environmental advantage of pursuing this option could range from 0 to 5 percent of sales, depending on the overall market reductions of wood supply and any premiums consumers would pay for chlorine-free paper and other wood products. The reduction in wood volume (through a reduction in wood supply) that could occur if Option 3 were followed on a wider scale could drive up the price of lumber products. When softwood lumber prices began "exploding" in early 1993, one of the contributing causes cited was the impact of the environmental movement in increasing the tracts of National forest lands being declared "off limits" to forestry companies. This could translate into an environmental advantage to the company. Following the conservative notion of accruing all liabilities but not counting on possible gains, the team estimated a very conservative environmental advantage of 1 percent of sales of $500 million, or $5 million. The risk costs associated with Option 3 would be minimal, $2.7 million, or 5 percent of the $53 million value of the ecosystem potentially at risk (i.e., $530 million value of the total ecosystem times the 10 percent portion at risk).

For Option 2, the team estimated there would be minimal competitive advantage because they guessed that Option 2 would soon be the minimum

Table 11.1
Analysis of Incremental Environmental Costs ($000)

	Option 1	Option 2	Option 3
CAPITAL COSTS:			
• Silvicultural enhancements	0	$ 0.0	$ 0.0
• Zero–impact mill	0	8.0	200.0
• Alternatives to landfill	0		5.0
• Energy self–sufficiency	0	0.0	0.0
		$ 8.0	$205.0
ANNUAL OPERATING COSTS			
• Silvicultural enhancements		$ 4.8	$ 12.0
• Zero–impact mill	0	4.0	10.0
• Alternatives to landfill	0		0.3
• Energy self–sufficiency	0	0.0	0.0
		$ 8.8	$ 22.3
Environmental advantage(deducted from cost)	NIL	NIL	$ 5.0
Risk cost(added to cost)	$ 10.6	$ 3.7	$ 2.7
NET INCREMENTAL INVESTMENT COST	$ 10.6	$ 12.5	$ 20.0

acceptable standard in the marketplace. Achieving this minimum would neither restrict wood supply in a significant way nor provide a competitive advantage to companies achieving Option 2. The team estimated that the risk cost of Option 2 would be $3.7 million, or 7 percent of the $53-million value of the ecosystem.

For the business-as-usual option, the team estimated nil environmental advantage and a minimum risk cost of 20 percent of the $53-million value of natural capital. This risk reserve of $10.6 million translated into slightly over 2 percent of sales. The team felt that, if anything, this reserve was low relative to total sales.

Walker looked at the table, wondering if the numbers were plausible and did a reasonable job at depicting reality. "What these numbers show, if we take them as very crude approximations of economic reality, is that Option 1 has hidden costs. When these are made visible, the gap between Option 1 and 2 narrows fairly quickly. Our reporting challenge will be to present these numbers to the board in a way that is fair to Option 2 yet reflects the softness of the calculations. However, my gut feeling is that there is little real business risk in biasing the calculations in favor of Option 2. In my judgment, this is the course to follow, the one that is most consistent with enlightened-self interest." Walker and the team were now ready to develop a

Figure 11.3
Full Cost Accounting under Conditions of Scientific Ambiguity

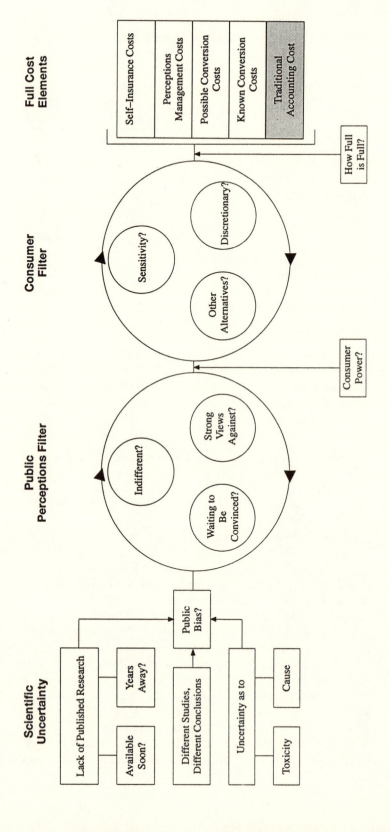

reporting format that would present this information to the board of directors. However, before they returned to the mechanics of reporting, they wanted to reflect on the ground they had covered to date.

By now it was clear to the team that accounting for sustainable development meant accounting for full costs and intergenerational liabilities when scientific uncertainty would be the norm. The accountant's ideal scenario called for an emerging consensus among the scientific community that might or might not support the environmental assertions of a reporting company. Under this situation, the company practice would either be deemed to be sustainable or to be a liability for deferred remediation would be recognized. The team recognized this would be rare and that they would usually be working under conditions of extreme scientific uncertainty.

The position in which the team had found itself is illustrated in Figure 11.3. There had been an absence of published research for many of the environmental impacts of clear-cutting. There had been studies under way that would yield conclusions someday; in other cases it would be years before definitive conclusions might be available. One of the problems caused by this situation was the possibility that the research might come too late relative to the fragility of the ecosystem being managed.

Another scenario the team encountered was "different studies of the same phenomena; different conclusions." This led to one expert disputing another expert. From an accounting perspective, this posed serious problems. Sometimes there was uncertainty as to the toxicity of discharge or uncertainty as to the cause of toxicity. This was the situation with regard to the removal of chlorine from mill effluent. There was scientific evidence supporting assertions of damage to fish but uncertainty as to the cause of the toxic effects. The position of industry was that until the regulators could prove what they were trying to fix there was no point spending $800 million fixing it.

The team recognized that from an accounting perspective, the science was just the beginning of the complexities they faced in developing fuller costs. They had to consider the public's perceptions of the science. Was the public indifferent, just waiting to be convinced by either industry or environmental activists, or did the public already have a negative image of industry practices such as clear-cutting? They recognized the interplay between the science and public perceptions.

For example, when there was a lack of published research and the public had strong views against a practice such as clear-cutting, then the team had recognized a higher probability that perceptions would fill the scientific vacuum. The company would be likely to face the reality of conversion costs to different practices or technologies. Another factor was the vulnerability of the product or service to consumer sensitivities. For example, companies in the tourist business were highly vulnerable to "discretionary" trips by environmentally sensitive consumers. If hotels in a convention city were dumping untreated sewage, even if there was great scientific uncertainty as to its toxic effects in the open ocean, an accrual for the costs of conversion to a more benign treatment system would be warranted. The team had to acknowledge that "perceptions become reality at the cash register."

The column in the right of the Figure 11.3 translated these factors into a determination of full cost. The starting cost element the team considered was the traditional accounting cost on an aggregate or unit-cost basis. This cost element included the cost of everything the firm paid for – all fixed and variable costs calculated under the conventions of accrual accounting. These were the costs in the published financial statements, the unit costs that were used in a traditional analysis of costs. The next cost increment the team identified was the cost of conversion to reach Option 2 (enhanced noncommercial values). These costs represented the "known" conversion costs to lower-risk development (i.e., smaller clear-cuts on steep slopes). The next level of cost increment had been the Option 3 increment (environment is equal), which represented possible conversion costs to try to achieve the goal of the "rule of two generations." In many cases, how far a company would be pushed into Option 2 or 3 would be largely determined in the court of public opinion where science would probably be less persuasive than emotion. In other words, the team had factored public perceptions into their estimations of accruals for potential intergenerational liabilities and costs.

The next level of cost increment was the "perceptions cost." This represented the ongoing costs of stakeholder management through consultation, opinion research, and image enhancement; the costs of scientific monitoring; the legal costs; and the costs of developing nontraditional accounting systems and reporting environmental results externally. These were baseline costs of doing business in a global economy where there are alternatives available to environmentally sensitive consumers.

The last element of cost was the risk cost of corporate "self-insurance" for natural capital such as wildlife or habitat. This was what a company would have to pay an insurer to absorb any and all intergenerational liability claims over the next 20 to 40 years for real and perceived damage to natural capital. These costs would vary inversely with expenditures on Options 2 or 3. Under Option 3, these risk costs would drop to virtually nothing. According to the matching principle in accounting, these self-insurance costs would have to be matched against current revenues. These risks were incurred today because of current practices and volumes of production and technology. While the injury was sustained today, the bruises would not become evident for 20 or 30 years. Adding all these elements together would result in fuller costs that would begin to include the cost of any natural capital consumed. Awareness of these fuller costs would lead to more informed investment decisions.

Walker recognized that to fully develop this model would take 5 to 10 years of further research, testing, and refinement. However, his dilemma was that his company was faced with large investment decisions today, not 5 or 10 years in the future. Walker's analysis of future vulnerabilities suggested that to report no potential intergenerational costs and liabilities associated with the business-as-usual option would be understating the risk cost component of full costs.

He accepted that his numbers were extremely crude. However, he did have a strong gut feeling that he was on the right track. He believed that with further research more meaningful numbers could be generated. In large part, they would be based on legal precedents regarding the use of the commons — actual cleanup costs for natural capital, as well as actual legal habitat remediation and restoration costs.

The team envisaged a computerized model that would simulate the costs and contingent opportunities associated with different technological and volume options, as well as the business risk costs associated with not making these environmental investments. He believed that a risk profile could and should be developed for each industrial sector. For example, the pulp and paper association could develop a risk profile for the average forestry and pulp operation. The association could rank individual companies within this overall framework, highlighting the leaders and the followers.

When computing the risk costs and contingent opportunities, Walker recognized that he could have estimated the future liability then used present-value tables to compute the value today. He had deliberately chosen not to do so because he knew that whatever interest rate chosen with present-value calculations "a dollar in 20 or 40 years is worthless today." In other words, the time value of money was inherently stacked against giving investments in the environment a fair chance.

The team was now ready to consider how to report their findings. They wanted to prepare a one-page summary that would pull everything together from a management information point of view. It would show the costs to convert to the different options. It would also show the environmental investment costs and contingent opportunities associated with each option, as well as the estimated risk costs of doing nothing. Option 1, business as usual, would have the lowest investment cost but the highest risk cost. Option 3 would illustrate the inverse situation. Management needed this information to strike the best tradeoff between what was good for business and what was good for the environment.

The team wanted to present the net investment cost, after accounting for risk costs and increases in market share. They debated whether to present the rate of return on a net (after adjusting for risk costs) or gross basis (no adjustment for risk costs). They resolved to present the calculations on both a traditional and a nontraditional basis. The numbers in italics in brackets would represent the risk-adjusted calculations. The team now felt they had started on the road to developing a nontraditional accounting system that would help the board navigate through the 1990s.

Chapter 12

Reporting to the Board on the Stewardship of the Forest

There were five audiences – the board of directors, customers, shareholders, employees, and those stakeholders on the Blackmore and Price Advisory Council. Each had different information needs, different levels of "access clearance" for sensitive proprietary information, and very different agendas. Walker knew he would have to work closely with the CEO in terms of sorting out who would get what information. What would make the exercise tricky were the internal politics and the sticky question of access to confidential information. Walker felt ambivalent because the information that he knew would be critical to decision making was the very information he was most reluctant to disclose to those outside the company. The project team decided on a time-phased approach to implementation that recognized the company's nervousness with breaking new ground. As Walker suggested to the team, "We want to be in a position to be a leading second when this type of information first hits the capital markets. However, in the interim, this information will come in very useful in dealing with individual interest groups. We will know what their demands will cost."

OVERVIEW OF THE REPORTING STRATEGY

Table 12.1 describes the team's overall approach to reporting. Their strategy recognized that each category of stakeholder would need different information in a different format. Each stakeholder group would also have different access to confidential financial data that could jeopardize Blackmore and Prices's competitive position. The board would get the complete Stewardship Report now. All other groups would be provided with elements of the report over the next 5 years, on an experimental basis, once the board was more comfortable with the reporting mode.

Table 12.1
Blackmore and Price's Reporting Strategy

Class of Stakeholder	Decisions To Be Taken	Information Need	Reporting Format	Access To Confidential Data
Board of Directors	Environmental investments	Financial analysis of options	Options analysis	Unrestricted access
	Strategic directions	Risks of do nothing option	Risk costs	
		Market analysis	ROI analysis	
	Assessment of corporate stewardship	Growth in wealth: • Forest wealth (natural resources) • Productivity • Innovation	State of the forest report	
Customers	Buy or not to buy	Resource managed in renewable manner	Label: • Renewability • Index • Sustainability Index	Unrestricted access
	Pay premium	Production in sustainable way		Unrestricted access
			Price implications	Profit margin, unit costs restricted
		Full costs		
Shareholders	Buy, sell, hold shares	Sustainable rate of return	Analysis of risk, opportunities	Restricted access
Employees	How to protect jobs, health, aid in company's survival	Sustainable jobs	Trend analysis of work force adjustments	Profit margin, unit costs restricted
Environmental activists other forest users	Lobby or not to lobby Buy or not to buy	Environmental impact	Simulation model	Profit margin, unit costs restricted
		Costs of conversion		

The Board of Directors. The board of directors would get everything in a big-picture format with unrestricted access. The board needed information on strategic options—the costs and benefits of environmental leadership, the risks of the status quo. They also needed information to assess the CEO's overall stewardship of Blackmore and Price.

Customers. Customers needed information that would enable them to compare the relative sustainability of competing products, such as wood and steel building products. Customers concerned about the environment would also want to know the full costs.

Shareholders. Shareholders should get information on the major business risks and opportunities facing the company, as well as the long-term projected rate of return. In the ideal world, they would get much of what the board would get, but in a more summarized form, without information that would harm the competitive or legal position of the company.

Employees. Employees would want to know how well their company was doing in the environmental area. They would also want a preview of the projected work force in the near future. They would recognize that future modernizations, in part driven by environmental requirements, could affect their jobs.

Now that they had an overall framework, they were ready to prepare the reporting package for the board.

"WE'VE GOT TO TELL THE BOARD WHY BUSINESS AS USUAL IS NO LONGER AN OPTION"

In Theory, the Board Gets Everything. Walker knew that in theory the board should get everything the CEO got but in a summarized, condensed fashion without the extraneous detail. Walker also knew that in practice it did not always work that way because of the realities of the Blackmore and Price's corporate structure. Blackmore and Price was one operating division of a corporate empire that included real estate, mining, brewing, and Blackmore and Price's small part of the more extensive forest operations. To say the least, it was an uneasy alliance. All corporate roads led to two hubs of power—the head office in Toronto and survivors of the Blackmore dynasty in Montreal. As in any marriage, there were chronic tensions and some infighting.

In preparing the final report for the board, the team had to modify and repackage some of their previous analysis. Their biggest reporting challenge was how to present the work they had done on the risk costs and the related intergenerational costs and liabilities. The team decided the objective of the exercise was to show the board three things: first, that the forest was an asset, just like real estate, that is appreciating over time; second, while the forest has a commercial value to the firm, the ecosystem upon which the company is dependent has an even higher value; and third, current business

Table 12.2
Options for Sustainable Forest Operations

	Option 1 Timber Is Primary Consideration	Option 2 Enhanced Nonwood Values	Option 3 Environment Is Equal: Nonwood Values Are of Equal Consideration
Operating Philosophy	Full compliance with all guidelines established by the Ministry of Natural Resources	Full compliance plus selective response to public concerns	The volume of production, the technology employed is to be determined by ecological rather than economic criteria
Operating Definition of Sustainable Development	Sustained economic yield with regeneration equal to harvest with acceptance of a risk that guidelines may not be ecologically sustainable in the long run	Commitment to sustained economic yield. Commitment to explore public perceptions on the forest's ecological sustainability and accommodation of the long—term needs of all forest users	Emulation of natural forest processes of disturbance, regeneration and succession. The sustainable use of the forest means sustainable use of the tree species and ecosystems found there not simply replacing one felled tree with another
View of Corporate Accountability	Company accountable to Ministry and public for compliance. Company to pay for shared costs stipulated in Forest Management Agreement (FMA)	Company accountable for more than compliance; will respond to public advice, may incur some costs beyond FMA requirements	Stakeholders should be responsible for and pay for all forest management. The relative cost sharing must be determined. Accountability to the people through privately audited statements

practices are creating risks of environmental degradation, and business as usual creates more relative risks than the other options. When these costs were factored into return-on-investment analysis, the costs of not changing course could be just as high as moving toward the ideal of the sustainable corporation. The balance of this chapter is the package they presented to the board.

STEWARDSHIP REPORT TO THE BOARD OF DIRECTORS

31 DECEMBER 1993

BLACKMORE AND PRICE FOREST PRODUCTS LTD. KIRKLAND, ONTARIO

Contents

Proposed Investment Strategy
- Overview
- Underlying Assumptions
- Table 12.2 – Options for Sustainable Forest Operations
- Table 12.3 – Condensed Stewardship Accounts
- Figure 12.1 – Change in the Value of the Forest over Time

Sustainable Forestry Management
- Company's definition of sustainable development
- Figure 12.2 – Range of Sustainability for Forest Operations

Sustainable Pulp Operations
- Water Quality "Considerations"
- Figure 12.3 – Air and Water Pollution Scale

Proposed Investment Strategy

Overview. As illustrated in Table 12.2, Blackmore and Price Forest Products Ltd. has three broad choices. Option 1 is business as usual. Option 2 is charting a middle course. Option 3 is making the environment an equal partner.

From its analysis of the costs of sustainable development, Blackmore and Price proposes to move toward a strategy of full compliance plus selective response to public concerns (Option 2) over the next decade. This will in-

Table 12.3
Blackmore and Price Forest Products Ltd.: Condensed Stewardship Accounts

Option 1 Timber Is Primary Consideration		Option 2 Enhanced Nonwood Values		Option 3 Environment Is Equal: Nonwood Values Are of Equal Consideration	
Full compliance with all guidelines established by the Ministry of Natural Resources.		Full compliance plus selective response to public concerns.		The volume of production, the technology employed are to be determined by ecological rather than economic criteria.	
Sustained economic yield with regeneration equal to harvest with acceptance of a risk that guidelines may not be ecologically sustainable in the long run.		Commitment to sustained economic yield. Commitment to explore public concerns about the forest's ecological sustainability and accommodation of the long–term needs of all forest users.		Emulation of natural forest processes of disturbance, regeneration and succession. The sustainable use of the forest means sustainable use of the tree species and ecosystems found there not simply replacing one felled tree with another.	
Incremental price increases to offset increased production costs:		**Pulp**	**Lumber**	**Pulp**	**Lumber**
• Silvicultural enhancements		4.5%	3%	11.0%	9%
• Zero–impact pulp mill		<u>2.5%</u>	N/A	<u>2.5%</u>	N/A
		<u>7.0%</u>		<u>13.5%</u>	
<u>Incremental operating costs</u> (millions)		$ 8.8		$22.3	
Environmental advantage	NIL	NIL		$(5.0)	
Risk cost	$ 10.6	$ 3.7		$ 2.7	
Net investment cost	$ 10.6	$12.5		$20.0	

Rate of Return on
Environmental Investments (Full Cost Basis)

Levels of Pulp Mill Sustainability	Range of Sustainability of Forestry Operations					
	Timber is Primary Consideration (Option 1)		Enhanced Nonwood Values (Option 2)		Environment is Equal (Option 3)	
Below average pulp mill	27.0%	(23.7%)	24.4%	(23.0%)	22.2%	(21.4%)
Average pulp mill	22.7%	(19.7%)	20.9%	(19.9%)	18.9%	(18.2%)
	Blackmore and Price (Now)					
Industry leader	18.4%	(15.8%)	17.3%	(16.1%)	15.6%	(14.8%)

volve a level of regeneration sufficient to support sustained economic yield and a commitment to explore public concerns on the forest's ecological sustainability, as well as accommodation of the long-term needs of all forest users. In the view of corporate management and given the public pressures surrounding land use, Option 2 is the only sustainable alternative that will allow the company to remain competitive.

This strategy reflects both the risks and the opportunities of the company's current land tenure arrangements. The Province of Ontario owns the land, Blackmore and Price leases the right to harvest for 20 years, on a renewable basis. Blackmore and Price is proposing to invest in an asset where the benefits of this investment will not be realizable for 40 to 60 years. If the lease were terminated, which in the opinion of management is highly unlikely, the company risks losing its investment.

If the company *does not invest,* it risks losing the right to harvest the forest, an asset that could be worth at least $1.5 billion in 60 years. On a straight-line basis, the commercial value of this forest is increasing at an average rate of $25 million a year. If Blackmore and Price is not perceived to be investing in the future of the forest, it risks losing the right to capitalize on this sustained increase in forest value over the next 60 years. If, because of public perceptions about Blackmore and Price's forest management practices, Blackmore and Price were to not have its lease renewed, the company would not be able to continue as a going concern. In other words, corporate plant, equipment, and intangible assets worth an estimated $750 million in 20 years would have to be written down to a net realizable value significantly below their value as a going concern. The writedown could be in the range of $200 to $300 million. In management's view, the *risk of not investing* is higher than the risk of investing ahead of regulatory changes.

In the area of pulp operations, Blackmore and Price proposes moving cautiously toward the stated goal of a zero-impact mill. Blackmore and Price's objective is to buy time while the scientific research solidifies the cause-and-effect relationships between current toxic discharge and perceived environmental damage on water quality and fish habitat. Blackmore and Price will work toward partial elimination of elemental chlorine and will engage in the requisite research for a long-term environmentally benign solution that will take the company into the next century. At present, the science and technology are not sufficiently well developed to support a comprehensive redesign of the existing plant and equipment used in pulping operations.

The financial implications of pursuing this goal are illustrated in Table 12.3. The return-on-investment analysis illustrates that on a fuller cost basis which includes costs associated with the potential degradation of the forest ecosystem, the difference between Option 1 and Option 2 becomes almost negligible. Table 12.3 also shows that the incremental investment costs between Option 1 and Option 2 narrow considerably after taking into account

Figure 12.1
Change in the Value of the Forest over Time

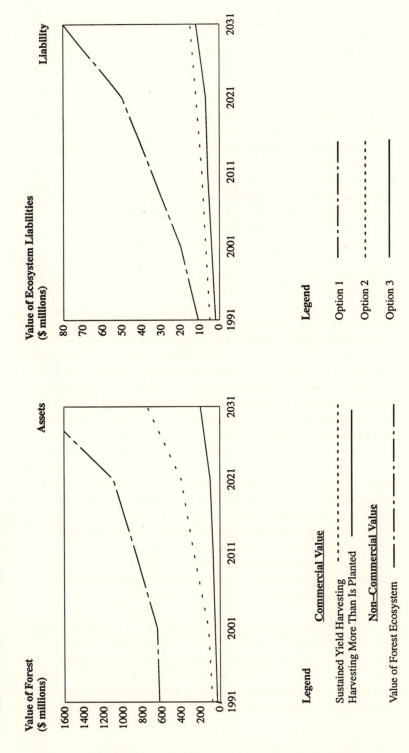

the risk costs illustrated in Figure 12.1. The return-on-investment calculations, in italics in Table 12.3, represent returns, after factoring in the risk costs of development options that take fewer precautions to protect the forest ecosystem. Blackmore and Price plans to change course to move toward environmental leadership. As illustrated in Table 12.3 on a fuller cost basis, there is no significant change in return on investment, over the long-term, of moving from Option 1 to Option 2.

Figure 12.1 illustrates this reality. Today, the commercial value of the timber is approximately $40 million. In contrast, the noncommercial value of the forest ecosystem upon which the company is economically dependent is worth upwards of $530 million. That value reflects minimum threshold values for habitat, soil fertility, and diversity of vegetation and animal life—in short the principal or natural capital that over time produces as interest the fiber with a commercial value to the company. Each business option has a different risk profile or environment footprint relative to the risk of damaging the ecosystem worth at least $530 million today.

Business risks give rise to future environmental obligations, obligations that surface one or two generations into the future but were caused by today's forestry practices. As illustrated in Figure 12.1, the risks associated with Option 1, business as usual, could climb to over $80 million in 30 years. Pursuing Option 2 or Option 3 keeps the lid on these obligations, probably keeping them below an estimated ceiling of no more than $25 million. Furthermore, what is most disturbing about the risks associated with business as usual is their rate of increase. After 30 years, they may start to compound, while the risks associated with the other two options are likely to level off at a threshold level over the longer term. In short, Figure 12.1 confirms that Option 2 is the one most compatible with enlightened self-interest.

Underlying Assumption. The underlying assumption is that the company has two broad options—to reduce the volume of production or to maintain the existing volume of production but modify the practices and technologies employed. The existing plant capacity is taken as a given. There is a minimum level of production that must be achieved to break even. The variables for Blackmore and Price are the forestry practices employed and the technologies used. Different scenarios are simulated, each reflecting a different definition of "sustainable" and the use of different technologies, equipment, and forestry practices.

SUSTAINABLE FORESTRY MANAGEMENT

The Company's Definition of Sustainable Development

From Blackmore and Price's perspective, sustainable forestry means a dedicated land base, secure tenure, efficient timber utilization, immediate reforestation, protection and tending of the forest, and recognition of other uses. Specifically, this means a sustainable volume of wood is to be harvested from a given area in a given period of time. This volume is the annual allowable cut. The company's objective is to harvest timber of a sustained quality, quantity, and economic value. This translates into a predictable continuous supply of quality raw material, which is fundamental to the company's economic viability. It is Blackmore and Price's belief that if a major productive forest area were withdrawn from timber management activities, the wood supply and socioeconomic environment of the province would be negatively affected.

The theory of sustainable development looks at development within the ecological bounds of the area harvested. The difficulty lies in determining those boundaries. Ideally there would be a definitive statement of limits. The reality is that sustainability appears to be in the eye of the beholder. That is, whether a forest is deemed sustainable depends on the user's definition. To help address this complex question, Table 12.2 provides a framework for analysis. It illustrates Blackmore and Price's perceptions of the range of definition of sustainability.

Blackmore and Price recognizes that maintaining genetic and species diversity and diversity of ecosystems while meeting its wood fiber needs will pose a real challenge. The company believes that it is essential to make the optimum use of available productive sites, using tree improvement programs to grow the best trees in the shortest rotations. The company recognizes that this is an expensive long-term strategy that requires dedication. It believes that sustainable forestry is attainable only through integrated management that balances forest use among timber, wildlife, and recreational interests.

Blackmore and Price recognizes that the company's definition of sustainable development is narrower than that of the environmental activists. Some indigenous peoples refer to "the rule of seven generations." These groups talk of "sustained life" as meeting the objective of protecting and maintaining the quality of the earth, air, and water that give life to the forest, which in turn protects and replenishes the earth, air, and water and creates an independent home for all biological life forms within it. The company's definition of sustainable development is more restrictive and limited.

It is essential that society identify the various components that need to be sustained to determine what it wants from its forests. From this determination follows the question of what must be done to achieve these goals, how much money will be required to implement and sustain them, and where will the money come from. Blackmore and Price is committed to developing the required management practices, including timber harvesting and renewal techniques that are scientifically and socially acceptable for a boreal forest. To achieve this commitment, Blackmore and Price strives to communicate with a wide base of the public so that all parties can understand the complex long-term nature of sustainable forestry. The company's objective is to build effective bridges to the users of the forest and to the nonusers in urban centers. Blackmore and Price sees this accounting of the forest's sustainability as a key bridge between the company and others who use and benefit from the forest.

Detailed charts are available that show the planned restructuring of the age distribution as projected in the company's Timber Management Plan. These charts provide essential information on the forest now and how it will change.

At present, there is an age class "imbalance" favoring the overmature segment, as well as a shortage in the immature age class, primarily the 20–40-year group. This shortage resulted from high fire incidence and inadequate reforestation 40 years ago.

Cutting operations are concentrated in the mature and overmature age classes, followed by reforestation of the harvested areas. The plan is to balance the age classes during the first rotation (70 years for jack pine, 100 years for spruce, 60 years for poplar, and 70 years for birch). The objective is to convert the overmature areas prior to their pathological decline and before their economic viability is reduced by insect infestation, rot, and mortality.

Investment to Protect Wood and Nonwood Values. An annual investment of approximately $4.8 million would be required to move forest operations to a status of enhanced sustainability described in Option 2. This investment illustrated in Figure 12.2 would allow the company to offset cost increases largely caused by modifying the size of clear-cuts, the timing of clear-cuts, and the spatial positioning of harvesting. By decreasing the size of clear-cuts, increasing the time span between adjacent harvests, and increasing the buffer zone between cuts, the company can significantly lower the risks of damage to habitat and wildlife. These adjustments lower the chances of failing to meet the expectations of the next generation when the company's timber license comes up for renewal.

Reflected in this $4.8 million cost are the following adjustments:

- *Withdrawal of production forest.* Some heritage stands of red and white pine will be withdrawn from the production forest.

- *Lower-impact development.* A higher level of restrictions on harvesting and renewal techniques. Specifically

    Clear-cutting. Use of clear-cutting and size of clear-cuts to be partially determined by ecological rather than economic criteria. Maximum size of any clear-cut to be 130 hectares. Soil disturbance and road building to be minimized. Timing of clear-cuts to be adjusted.

    Regeneration. Research on how forest renewal based on natural regeneration and natural processes of forest succession could be allowed to occur. Planting should strive to replace naturally occurring mixes of species. The result would be longer rotations and a higher hardwood component.

    Fish habitat. No harvesting in critical habitat areas, increased reserves and buffers around trout lakes with full maintenance of water quality and only modified harvesting (to a max-

Figure 12.2
Range of Sustainability for Forest Operations

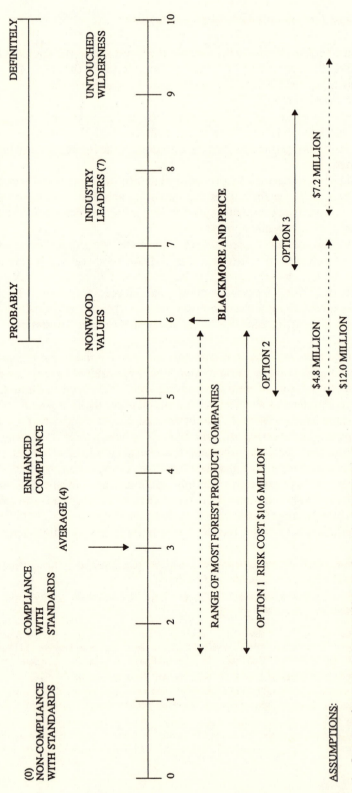

ASSUMPTIONS:

1. Incremental costs assume an annual harvest of approximately 694,000 m3.

imum of 30 percent of the wood volume), modified harvesting to 30 percent of the volume around cold water streams, and modified harvesting to 50 percent of the volume around cool and warm water streams.

Wildlife. To protect moose, reduce average clear-cut to 130 hectares with the extensive network of moose corridors; prohibit harvesting around aquatic feeding and calving areas. For eagles and ospreys, modified harvesting; and for heron rookeries, no harvesting during nesting period.

Aesthetics. Seasonal noise restrictions to promote canoe tourism on rivers and modified harvesting in viewscape areas. Modified block cutting along highways.

Heritage sites. Increased reserves and buffers around native sites and archaeological sites.

Herbicides. Partial elimination of herbicides and insecticides.

SUSTAINABLE PULP OPERATIONS

Water Quality Considerations

The Average Bleached Kraft Mill—Why It Produces Effluent. Bleached kraft mills produce effluent from the bleaching stage of the pulping process. Chlorine is present in the mill effluent because it is used, together with chlorine dioxide and sodium hypochlorite, in the bleaching process. A conventional mill produces about 50 kg of dissolved organic waste material for every ton of pulp produced. Oxygen delignification has been used as a partial replacement for chlorine delignification in many mills. A typical mill that uses oxygen delignification produces 25 kg of dissolved organic waste material for every ton of pulp produced. This dissolved organic chlorine and the caustic used in bleaching cannot be reclaimed because the chlorine is chemically bound to the organic matter. There has recently been a trend toward replacing as much chlorine as possible with chemicals that are less environmentally deleterious, including oxygen, chlorine dioxide, ozone, and hydrogen peroxide. However, complete replacement of chlorine is not yet technically feasible. The impact on water quality from various pulp and paper production technologies is illustrated in the following scale.

The Zero-Impact Bleached Kraft Mill. The ideal mill would have a bleach plant that did not use chlorine, chlorine dioxide, or sodium hypochlorite but instead used other oxidizing chemicals such as nitrogen dioxide, oxygen, ozone, hydrogen peroxide, or enzymes such as zylenase to remove the lignin and brighten the pulp. The effluent would then, theoretically, be recyclable. The sodium in the effluent would be reused, and the organic matter could be burned to generate energy.

The zero-impact bleached kraft pulp mill would have virtually eliminated the organic waste from the bleach plant effluent. In order to make the transition from the existing bleached kraft mill to a sustainable mill, which has zero impact on the aquatic environment, it is necessary to satisfy at least two major criteria:

Figure 12.3
Air and Water Pollution Scale

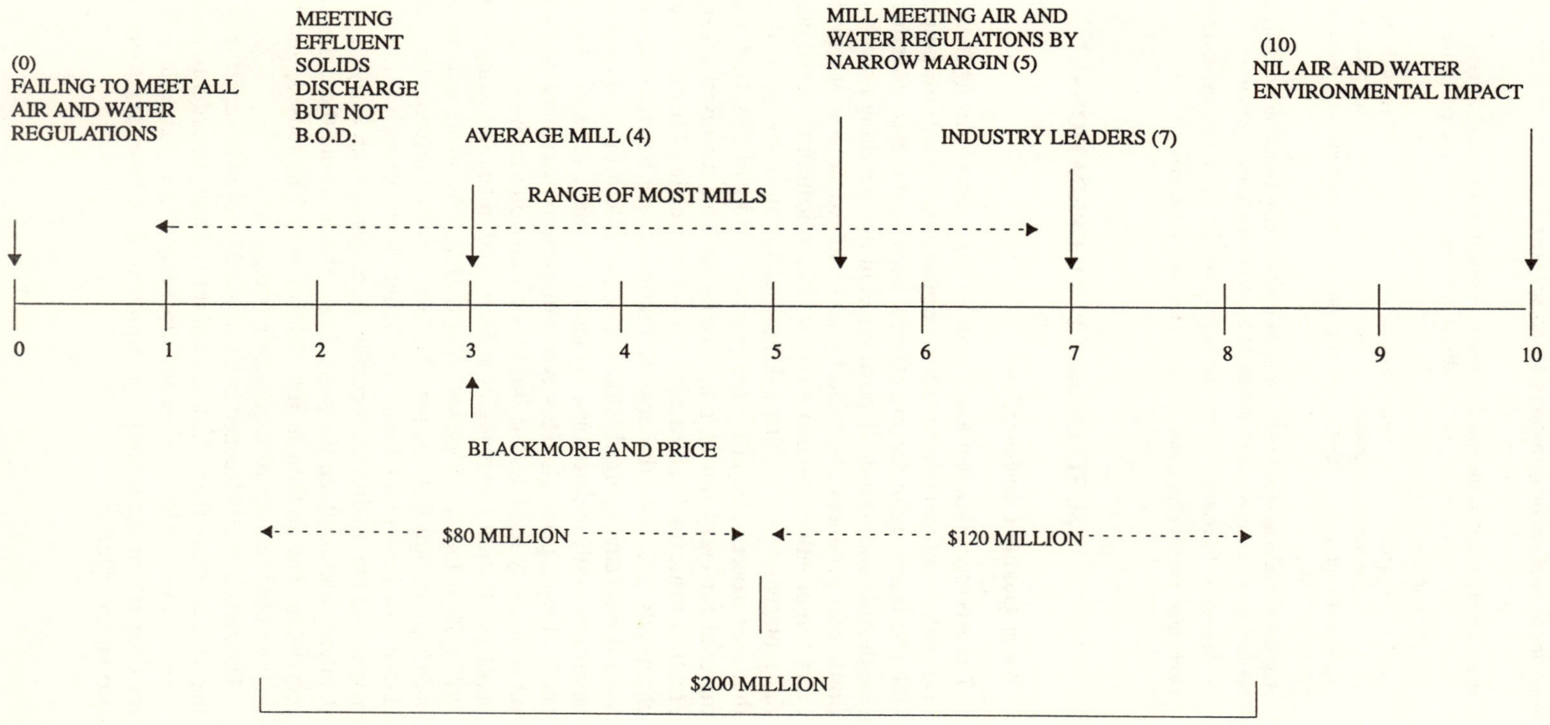

MEETING EFFLUENT SOLIDS DISCHARGE BUT NOT B.O.D.	MILL MEETING AIR AND WATER REGULATIONS BY NARROW MARGIN (5)	(10) NIL AIR AND WATER ENVIRONMENTAL IMPACT
(0) FAILING TO MEET ALL AIR AND WATER REGULATIONS	AVERAGE MILL (4)	INDUSTRY LEADERS (7)
	RANGE OF MOST MILLS	
	BLACKMORE AND PRICE	

0   1   2   3   4   5   6   7   8   9   10

$80 MILLION

$120 MILLION

$200 MILLION

1. The mill must be able to produce a marketable product using nonchlorine bleaching agents.
2. The mill must find the best way to recycle the nonchlorine effluent back into the mill system.

In summary, Blackmore and Price's definition of a sustainable pulp mill is a zero-impact bleached kraft mill. The balance of this report illustrates what it will cost to reach zero impact, including the necessary tradeoffs. In addition, the firm is looking for alternatives to landfills for storing some solid wastes from the pulp mill. It would like to move to energy self-sufficiency. The costs of achieving these objectives have been included in the overall capital costs which are illustrated in Figure 12.3, Air and Water Pollution Scale.

Chapter 13

Reporting to Shareholders and Others Who Benefit from the Forest

LET'S TELL THE STORY TO THE PUBLIC

Managing the Expectations of Shareholders. Walker and the CEO knew that their challenge was to change the earnings expectations of shareholders, moving them from the short term to the long term. Shareholders would want prospective financial information on possible future earnings. The problem was that the market might not be ready for such honesty.

However, they were again caught between a rock and a hard place. They knew that if they did not prepare investors for the inevitable decline associated with heavy environmental investments, they would lose shareholders as soon as earnings dropped. The CEO hoped that if they pushed long-term earnings, tried to attract institutional investors, and stressed growth in forest assets, they might just come up with a package that would maintain share prices.

They also wanted to appeal to investors willing to trade off a lower rate of return for the satisfaction of knowing they were earning this return from an environmental leader. Walker and the team debated as to how much information to provide to shareholders on silvicultural investments, forest management, and pulp operations. Much of the material would have to be fairly technical if they were going to address the issues in a meaningful way.

Shareholders would need information on a sustainable rate of return. In the ideal world, they would get the same return on investment analysis the board of directors would get. However, Walker was extremely nervous about disclosing information on projected rates of return. He cautioned the CEO, "If we disclose that and nobody else does, we're going to look like hell. They'll look at some mill in an unregulated province or state and say we can get 27 percent there, why go with Blackmore and Price?" The team recognized that Blackmore and Price provided a much better investment opportunity on the long haul, but they also knew they could take a beating on the capital markets. They agreed that ideally shareholders should be provided with an analysis of the risks and opportunities. This would provide investors with an early warning of environmental investments approximating $250 million over the next 5 years. Investors would also be provided with the risk costs associated with current practices.

According to Walker, "If the company adopted our approach to risk costing, it could dispense with the current approach to accounting for contingent liabilities. Investors would be provided with the company's best estimate of its running environmental tab and therefore be shielded from unpleasant financial surprises. If all companies had to do this, the environmental leaders would start reaping a real dividend in increased access to capital; the pressure on the laggards would be fairly brutal. To me, that's what capitalism is all about, funneling capital to the winners under a full-cost basis of accounting and choking off the rest."

However, the CEO cautioned that the market was not ready for such honesty. In the interim, Walker would explore a way of providing investors with a description of the company policy on sustainability and selected charts on projected costs of enhanced sustainability. According to Walker, "This kind of information is really already required by the Management Discussion and Analysis required by securities regulators in North America. We just haven't been leading the charge in supplying it." After looking at the reports prepared by other companies, they decided that the informed shareholders wanted to know the facts. Their hunch was that the more sophisticated institutional investors were tired of glossy pictures and optimism. "It doesn't take a genius to ask, 'How come every year I get glossy pictures and big promises but my dividends keep shrinking?'"

The team decided to provide shareholders with a short supplement that would contain the general information under the headings of "Sustainable Forestry Management" and "Sustainable Pulp Operations" from the full Stewardship Report presented to the board. They felt this would be a reasonable first step. It would begin to sensitize shareholders to the complexities of forest and watershed management without disclosing sensitive information. According to Walker, most of the information presented was required by the existing regulations of the Ontario Securities Commission in Canada and the Securities and Exchange Commission in the United States. These regulatory bodies required a discussion and analysis of the major risks and opportunities facing a publicly traded company.

In addition to the basic material in the sections of the stewardship report on sustainable forestry and pulp operations, they agreed to include the following indicators of sustainable development:

- Socioeconomic impacts
- Resources used
- Efficiency of resource conversion
- Wastes generated
- Research activities

The public relations people suggested calling their report "Charting a Middle Course—Status Report on Sustainable Development." In the message from the president, Jack wrote:

Sustainable development is not a question of choice between growth and the environment, it is the establishment of a decision-making process that integrates the efficient conversion of resources with concern for long-term environmental consequences. Simply put, sustainable development is a question of balance.

REPORTING TO CUSTOMERS AND EMPLOYEES

Customers. Within 5 years, customers would get a product label, giving a renewability scale, a sustainability scale, and the price implications of enhanced preservation of other forest values and chlorine-free paper products. On a scale of one to ten, one being zero assurance of renewability and ten being 100 percent assurance of renewability of the resource, consumers would know whether the basic raw materials (i.e., wood fiber) used in a two-by-four or pulp products were renewable. The sustainability index would measure the sustainability of the manufacturing process, looking at persistent toxins released to the environment. Consumers would also get information on the price implications of fuller costs. These "shadow" prices would be provided for informational purposes only. The team felt confident that a forest-products company would measure much higher on this scale than, for example, a manufacturer of steel girders. In contrast, a two-by-four was a renewable resource that required no "net energy" to produce. It also served as a "carbon sink." Before the company could publish such information, industry standards would have to be established both for the pulp and paper industry and for other industries, especially those supplying complementary products such nonwood building materials. The objective would be to provide consumers with information that would facilitate inter-industry and intraindustry comparisons. These ecological "footprints" would be the basis of ecological thrift. Consumers would also have to be provided information to assess the risks of environmental damage associated with product production and use. Information on the renewability index, sustainability, would not be "classified"; but information on the profit margin and unit costs would, of course, always be restricted.

Employees. The CEO was concerned that Blackmore and Price was not making any money. His initial reaction to the analysis prepared by Walker was that the situation was going to get worse before it got better. "Walker, we're not making enough money to support everybody — the shareholders, the bondholders, the environmental activists." Clearly, if Blackmore and Price was going to survive, it would need a strategic alliance with employees. Jack had been thinking about trying to negotiate a wage rollback. It had been happening in other pulp mills across the country — in New Brunswick, in Ontario, and in Quebec. It was not an option he relished. For years, Blackmore and Price had worked to maintain good relationships with employees and with the union. Other mills had wage disputes caused by wage disparities between sawmill workers and pulpmill workers, but Blackmore and Price had been lucky.

"Walker, how are we going to get our workers to bite the bullet? What these guys don't see is that if we can't make paper here, we're going to move south of the border. It's time for some reality."

The team debated the question of confidential information on profit margins and unit costs. They recognized that there was a risk to disclosure of cost information — it could come back to haunt them during the next wage negotiations. The dilemma was that unless Blackmore and Price provided reasonable disclosure to employees they would not recognize the urgent need for internal adjustments. They would need facts on where the money came from during the boom years and where it had gone during the bust years when Blackmore and Price was bleeding. In the end the team decided to make a presentation to union leaders, explaining their targeted modernization strategy, as well as the problems with the competitiveness of their cost structures. No hard copy was handed out.

CREATING A SUSTAINABLE PARTNERSHIP

The team's vision was an informed dialogue between Blackmore and Price and other forest users such as environmental activists. Through this sharing of information, environmental activists and other users would begin to focus on options that would both sustain the forest and sustain jobs in the Blackmore and Price mills. Over 2500 people depended directly on Blackmore and Price for work. Without Blackmore and Price, regional unemployment would rise significantly. Walker envisaged developing a simulation model that would show relationships without disclosing confidential information "imbedded" in the program. Walker saw a learning exercise that could result in greater understanding between the various groups. In the interim, the information developed for the board, as well as other presentations on forest use, would be readily available for discussions with the company's forest advisory group. As Walker said, "Information is ammunition, and you never know when some group will start shooting at you."

The team they envisaged would provide knowledgeable environmental activists with detailed specifications on landscape management goals. This is illustrated in Figure 8.2.

For knowledgeable activists and other forest users, information on the broad options would not be good enough. Knowledgeable users would want, and could assimilate, information on the size of clear-cuts, the sensitive areas set up around trout streams or moose habitats, and the like. They would want to model different scenarios with different buffer zones. This would require simulating different tradeoffs, each with a different set of cost parameters. Walker envisaged eventually providing these users with access to a simulation model.

The company had set up a forest advisory group, complete with hunters, trappers, academics from forestry schools, aboriginal groups, and environmental activists. Initially the foresters had been skeptical. After a few meetings and a few bottles of wine, the foresters were almost ecstatic. They could not believe the kind of informed, knowledgeable dialogue the group was capable of having. The foresters were now sold on the process and sensed that more information could lead to a shared understanding of the challenges of sustainable forestry.

Clearly, having a forum to debate issues did not eliminate all problems. There were some fundamental stumbling blocks and different philosophies toward risk, biodiversity, and buffer zones required by blue herons or osprey.

Figure 8.2 would be the basis of today's discussions. But what would be the basis of tomorrow's dialogue? What information tools would Blackmore and Price need after it had made the full conversion to sustainable development? This is illustrated in Figure 13.1. There would be an ongoing consultation process involving scientists, standard setters, regulators, and others with a perceived stake in the forest. The result of continuous consultation would be a series of evolving standards that would change with new scientific evidence. These would be site specific, based on the resiliency and fragility of the northern boreal forest.

A critical element in the standard-setting process would be ongoing measurements of the attributes of forest health. Actual measurements would be compared with the expected standards. The forest company would use data from remote sensing, soil samples, measurements of rates of regeneration, and the like. The scientists would then project these trends "into the next generation" so as to estimate whether current trends would be sustainable for at least two generations. The standards that emerge from continuous consultation would have defined an upper limit of cumulative stress compatible with preserving a healthy living forest.

If the result of the projection was "probably sustainable" for two generations, no corrective action would be required. If the projection results exceeded targeted levels of risk, corrective action would be required. There would be modifications in either the scale of operations, the technology em-

Figure 13.1
Measuring Forest Health

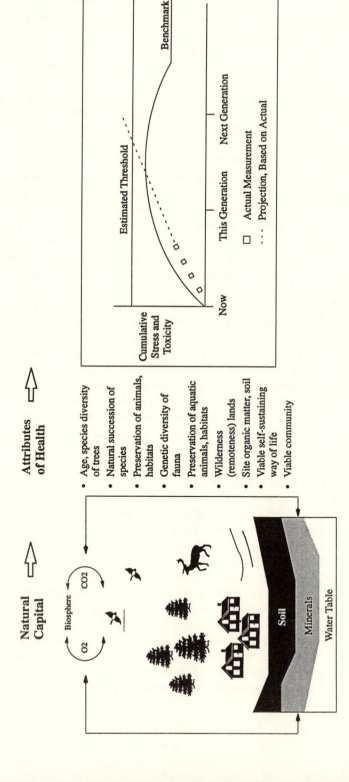

Natural Capital ⇨

Attributes of Health ⇨

- Age, species diversity of trees
- Natural succession of species
- Preservation of animals, habitats
- Genetic diversity of fauna
- Preservation of aquatic animals, habitats
- Wilderness (remoteness) lands
- Site organic matter, soil
- Viable self-sustaining way of life
- Viable community

Biosphere

CO_2

O_2

Soil

Minerals

Water Table

Cumulative Stress and Toxicity

Estimated Threshold

Benchmark

Now

This Generation

Next Generation

□ Actual Measurement

- - - Projection, Based on Actual

ployed, or the specific practices followed. The cost implications of each modification would be estimated and fed back into the consultation process where the debate would focus on who would pay rather than the necessity for change. Under this regime, the accounting would be relatively easy once the ecological thresholds were established, monitored, and continuously adjusted for new scientific information and interpretations. If the required adjustments were made, intergenerational assets would be recognized. If they were not, intergenerational liabilities would be recognized for the estimated levels of deferred remediation. The team estimated it would take at least 5 to 10 years to move to this mode of operations. These would be the tools required by a corporation governed by enlightened self-interest.

Walker, Len, and Mike paused to reflect on the journey they had taken during the past 2 years. Each had learned extensively from the others and returned to his or her own discipline with some new insights. Walker reflected on how he now viewed his own profession—how he viewed accounting.

ACCOUNTING MEASURES WEALTH

Walker recognized that the common thread in all the twists and turns during the past 2 years had been a search for a better way to measure wealth—wealth in the forests, wealth in the labs, wealth from the company's image in the marketplace. Walker had recently attended a comptrollers' conference. One of the sessions was devoted to business valuation. The presenter had talked about the traditional value/earnings relationship illustrated in Figure 13.2. The exhibit showed that if a company realized sustained earnings over time, its value would go up. If a company kept losing money over time, there would be virtually no enterprise value. The company would be lucky to get basement prices for the sale of its fixed assets. With sustained earnings, there would be a chance to realize the value of intangible assets such as patents or trade secrets and other elements associated with a going concern. Over the long haul, a company would generate goodwill—the difference between the net identifiable tangible and intangible assets and what a purchaser would pay for a going concern that was making money. Walker knew from his own clients that this goodwill value would pay for the retirement of many small businessmen. Their plan was simple—build a profitable company then sell it off before moving to Florida to play golf.

But now, Walker saw things differently. As illustrated in Figure 13.3, he saw that corporate wealth included *both* the natural capital that a company was dependent on and the dollar value of the business. They were two sides of the same coin. Sustainable utilization of natural capital was the base of all earnings. Over the longer term, there would be depletion that ideally would be offset through investment in remediation and restoration activities. In the case of the forest, this could mean fertilizer to offset the loss of biomass.

The enterprise value would increase as earnings were invested in tomor-

Figure 13.2
Traditional Value/Earnings Relationship

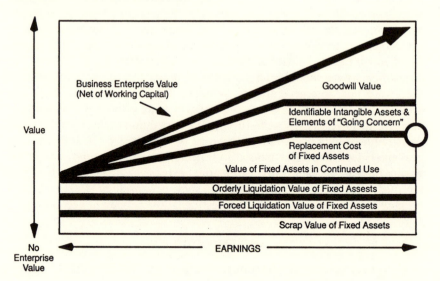

Figure 13.3
Wealth and Earnings Invested in Tomorrow Relationship

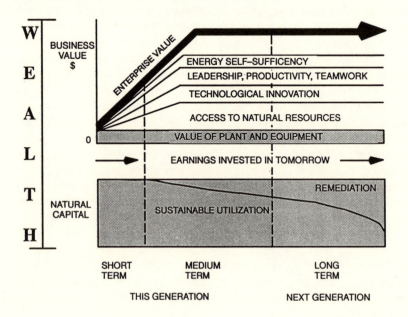

row. The value of plant and equipment was a base value. As the company invested in the future, the dollar value of its rights to the access to natural resources would be likely to increase. The dollar value of technological innovations would increase over time as earnings were reinvested in product development and in new processes such as chlorine-free paper. The intangible value of the leadership, teamwork, and all that went into productivity would increase as the company continued to earn and reinvest earnings. Energy self-sufficiency would increase the resale value of the company. Overall, the enterprise value would be likely to climb over time then level off. This leveling off would recognize the limits imposed by the base of natural capital. Such limits, if exceeded, would ultimately lead to a reduction in the enterprise value over the longer term. Walker knew of real estate companies that instead of having a positive net value for plant and equipment now faced a negative net book value caused by cleanup costs. When Walker showed his analysis to the CEO, he realized he had touched a responsive chord. The CEO understood that Walker was talking about investing in tomorrow. The CEO recognized that in today's fast-paced business environment investing in today was investing in yesterday. And a company never made money investing in yesterday.

"You know Walker, this illustrates something that has troubled me for years. I go to these conferences and I hear other CEOs talking about their stock bonuses and their earnings bonuses. If there were ever an incentive to run a company into the ground it's those bonuses. When they drag me out of here, I'd like to have a bonus tied to share prices 10 years in the future. What you are really talking about is investing in tomorrow. Most companies don't invest in tomorrow because they're busy paying off yesterday's debts. And Walker, I'm going to buy you dinner at the club. You've proved to me you are a creative accountant."

Walker recognized he had just scratched the surface in terms of developing new tools for corporate survival and sustainability in the 1990s. With the signing of the North American Free Trade Agreement, he knew that Blackmore and Price would be thrust with a vengeance into a brave new world. He resolved to work on the tools, the inertial navigation system that would be required to help guide Blackmore and Price into the next century. But in the process of visioning these new tools, he realized he had reaffirmed the traditional definition of profit. Profit equals revenues minus expenses. The only difference was that now he had expanded the definitions of a company's assets and the corresponding expenses to be included in the calculation of profit.

PROFIT IS TOMORROW'S ACCESS TO RESOURCES

Profit Is a Lot More Than a Leftover. For over 20 years, Walker had been involved with financial statements for Blackmore and Price, for his

Figure 13.4
Profit Is a Lot More Than a Leftover

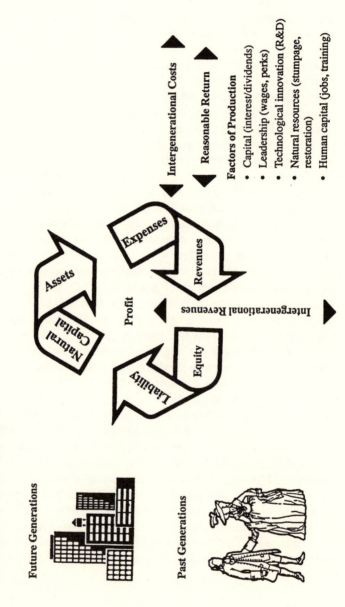

Intergenerational Costs

Reasonable Return

Factors of Production
- Capital (interest/dividends)
- Leadership (wages, perks)
- Technological innovation (R&D)
- Natural resources (stumpage, restoration)
- Human capital (jobs, training)

Expenses

Revenues

Assets

Natural Capital

Profit

Intergenerational Revenues

Liability

Equity

Future Generations

Past Generations

own clients on the side, and for community organizations. For every financial statement, Walker had tabulated assets, liabilities, and equity and got them to balance. He had tabulated expenses or expenditures, compared them to revenues, and calculated a residual. He had always visualized two big boxes, the left-hand box was revenue, the right-hand box was expenses, and the residual was the difference between the two boxes.

However, now Walker had a different view, as illustrated in Figure 13.4. He wondered if perhaps there was no ultimate profit or loss, but a stable level of purchasing power that allows a company to transform natural resources into products and services that meet human needs to remediate the unintended but inevitable consequences of industrial activity, provide an equitable return to all factors of production, and maintain the productive capability of the firm.

The starting point for creating economic wealth was the boreal forest that had been thriving for at least 10,000 years. There was human and cultural capital. There were trained workers, the infrastructure of roads and transportation. All these were essential to run a business. These get translated into assets — fixed assets; intangible assets; cash in the bank; inventories of lumber, chips, and pulp.

In a sense, liabilities and equity were revenue in advance — cash in the bank without a sale. This was the spark plug that ignited the engine, that allowed an entrepreneur to transform natural capital into economic assets like buildings and sawmills. Economic assets were then transformed into expenses. Business buys assets because they are expenses to be spread over a number of years. For example, a building is really just an expense spread over 40 years. These expenses get translated into revenues — every cost is incurred for the purpose of earning revenue.

The residual was profit. Walker now saw it not as a residual but as something to be recycled for corporate survival to maintain a fragile competitive advantage. Profit was in part a return to investors. They have a right to a dividend, after calculating the costs associated with the potential depletion of natural capital. The bondholders received their return in the form of interest. Part of this residual could be seen as a return for leadership and teamwork, a bonus to Blackmore and Price's management and employees for performance.

There should be a notional return for technological innovation. Money would have to be ploughed back into research and development, to developing chlorine-free paper. Profit would be needed to finance that innovation. There is a return on risk or uncertainty.

Then there was a return to the community, a return measured in jobs. There was also a return in other intangibles returned to the community in the form of training people and building a community infrastructure. Part of that residual is a return on natural resources. To the extent that the company is not paying the full price, unrecorded costs will be passed on to the next generation. These have to be accounted for.

The net result was that if all the reported earnings were to be paid out in dividends, this would deplete the reserves of the company and deplete its ability to remain sustainable. Failure to maintain technological innovation would result in higher short-run profits but would come back to haunt a company in 5 to 10 years. The real bottom line question was then "How much of reported profit is really profit?" Walker now realized that only a small portion of reported profit was real, free, and clear profit. The bulk of what he had used to call profit was really a misallocation of costs between generations.

In his own mind, Walker had developed a view of profit somewhere in between the medieval view of a just return to factors of production and the view of the Age of Profits, where society imposed few sanctions on free enterprise. Walker realized that the concept of sustainable development required a subtlety that was foreign to conventional business outlooks. It imposed some countervailing principles on business in the same way the Church had imposed restrictions on commercial activity in the Middle Ages. Based on what he had recently read about the father of accounting, Luca Pacioli, Walker's multidisciplinary approach to accounting for wealth was consistent with the approach Pacioli, the consummate Renaissance man, might have applied to accounting for the environment. For Pacioli, double-entry bookkeeping was always seen in the context of world view where divine symmetry and balance permeated human existence, shaped and circumscribed the commercial facet of life. In short, for Pacioli, there were always other values that defined and limited business values.

Walker saw that business — the struggle and the competition — is in a way analogous to the struggle in the forest, the struggle in the vast food chain. There were many different creatures, each interacting, some in symbiotic ways, others in a predatory manner. All were linked together. Blackmore and Price was part of somebody else's corporate food chain. Blackmore and Price or any other business had to survive the struggle and the stresses of the economic food chain. However, the goal was more than survival, to maintain tomorrow's access to the resources needed to survive in the corporate food chain. Self-interest, albeit enlightened self-interest, was a means to an end, the actualization of values such as service, contribution, and sustaining and creating wealth. Walker now accepted that without the broader context of "other values," there could be no meaningful business values.

Chapter 14

How Do I Apply This
in My Work?

The obvious question for a reader is, "What basic steps should I follow to develop the nontraditional accounting systems necessary for survival in a new century?" There are two major facets of this journey—the how and the why. This first section of the chapter summarizes the steps followed in the case study, focusing on how they can be generalized to apply to other industrial sectors. It provides a road map of specific steps to be followed and the changes in the culture of a corporation that must be achieved if the nontraditional accounting tools are to achieve their intended benefits. The second section of this final chapter deals with the situation where the reader believes in the concept but the rest of the team does not. The final section looks at the next wave of nontraditional accounting issues, exploring accounting issues for a new century.

First, the road map for developing nontraditional accounting systems. Now that all the pieces of the model have been reviewed in depth, it is useful to return to Figure 5.1. To the left is the starting point, the need to establish an environmental investment policy. The type of investments that will have to be made will determine the exact nature of the nontraditional accounting systems to be developed. The case study presented has looked at the investments applicable to a resource industry with a manufacturing component. It was a highly visible industry that is daily in the news. This industry decided to invest a considerable amount of time and money in developing the requisite nontraditional tools. An industry with a lower profile might have decided to invest less.

At present, the model assumes there will be strong similarities between accounting for a living forest and arable land; between accounting for waterborne and airborne pollution. Both are much harder to account for than the cleanup costs of known contaminated sites where accountability and cost are relatively more easy to establish. The existence of this road map, supplemented by software, would lower the costs of development. However, those embarking on the journey should be cautioned that every company is unique, and the necessity of tailoring any generalized models available will be required.

Once a decision to proceed has been made, along with a project budget, the next step will be to develop a project's terms of reference. Basic project management procedures, such as creating terms of reference, are especially important for an inherently ill defined "mission impossible" type endeavor. The specifics of the terms of reference will vary with each application; but at a minimum they should include a statement of objectives, a description of the desired outputs, and development time frames.

However, whatever the application, the early focus of any project to develop nontraditional accounting systems should be on the five key corporate decisions that require additional information on the costs and benefits of enhanced protection of a corporation's environmental assets. This focus on key strategic decisions will give a project the necessary focus, as well as a sense of realism.

Picking the Right Team. The next step is to choose a multidisciplinary team. Within any company there will be pockets of expertise that normally work in relative isolation. Management talks to management; scientists talk to scientists most of the time. The objective here is to create a project team that will cut across organizational and professional boundaries. In an environmental accounting exercise, the reality is that any one discipline will seldom have enough pieces of the puzzle to put together a complete solution. The use of experts in accounting is not new. To account for pension liabilities, accountants have to depend on actuaries. Accounting in the petroleum industry requires dependence on geologists. However, there is an exceptionally high level of interdependence between the scientists, the engineers, the economists, and the accountants in an environmental accounting project.

The difference here is that this interdependence is highly interactive and may involve interaction with two or three other disciplines simultaneously. For example, in this case study, the accountant could not proceed without fairly steady input from the engineers, scientists, economists, legal people, and public relations people. How well this process will work will largely depend on the personalities, attitudes, and breadth of experience of the participants. If team members are narrowly focused technicians who have great difficulty reaching beyond the confines of their own disciplines, the project will falter from the start. The ideal team member is an inquisitive individual with strong communications skills that allow him or her to speak in nontechnical language. He or she will have general experience in a broad range of corporate activities while retaining a strong technical expertise in his or her core professional discipline. In the overall team, there must be the right mix of dreamers, practical technicians, tinkerers, talkers, and finishers.

Listening to Those with a Perceived Stake. Once a strong team has been assembled, their first task is to consider the needs, wants, and emotional "buttons" of those who believe they have a stake in the company's operations. The generic model in this text should provide a good starting point for the broad classes of those with real and perceived interests in a company's operations. The fundamental issues such as access to sensitive propriety information will surface in almost every application. Also, the team will have problems defining exactly what those with a stake really need in terms of information for informed decisions. During this phase of the project, the marketing people may take the lead.

Defining Corporate Accountability. The next step will be to confront the daunting task of defining the breadth of corporate accountability. The bottom-line issue in every application will be accountability for "noncommercial" facets of an ecosystem upon which a company is economically dependent. Here economic dependence means dependence on natural resources for raw materials as well as dependence on the environment for the storage and treatment of toxic residues from production. Unless a company has achieved the ideal of zero impact on the environment in terms of persistent toxins that accumulate over time, then the company is economically dependent on the ecosystem. Therefore, a nickel refinery will be economically dependent on the atmosphere that receives sulfur dioxide emissions. A power company generating electricity with fossil fuels will be economically dependent on the atmosphere that receives its emissions or the sites where radioactive wastes are stored.

The challenge for all nontraditional accountants will be to analyze the company's impact on those environmental assets upon which it is economically dependent for continued production and its continuation as a going concern. The approach taken in this model of starting with a credible model of the specific components and functions of an ecosystem can be applied elsewhere. There will be a wide variety of models, each more or less appropriate for specific sites or applications. The ideal starting model is one that has gained some degree of general acceptance in the scientific and environmental activist communities. The team would then "match" these ecosystem components and functions with the concerns of specific subgroups of stakeholders. In the forest industry, stakeholders are concerned about clearcutting; in the steel industry, stakeholders may be more concerned about airborne pollution.

The approach advocated of defining corporate accountability in terms of three broad options should be useful in many applications. These options define the basic potential "contracts" between a company, society, and the environment — business as usual, an uneasy marriage between business and biological limits, and making the environment an equal partner. This multioption approach should help most projects avoid painting themselves into a corner. During this phase of the project, the lead will be shared between the lawyers, the ecologists, and the senior managers. It is an uneasy time of lengthy discussions.

An issue that is certain to surface during these discussions of corporate accountability is the definition of full cost. During the initial phase of any project to develop nontraditional accounting information, a company will be likely to have a one- or two-day brainstorming session where experts fly in from around North America and present their different models for full costing. There will be environmental economists, accountants, and scientists. Each will have a different definition of full cost. During this phase it is critical to get these different definitions on the table and agree on the definition to be pursued. During these discussions, the life-cycle concept will surface. What is a company's responsibility for the environmental damage caused by consumer use of a product? What is the company's responsibility for the ultimate recycling of a product? Here there are few easy answers. Who is to blame for the health effects of smoking—the cigarette manufacturers or the smokers? The author's advice is that companies should clearly be accountable for effects that could largely be eliminated during the design phase of any product's development. In other areas there will be shared accountability, and the accounting for intergenerational costs and liabilities should reflect this. For example, in this case study, who bears responsibility for the costs of paper products ending up in municipal landfill sites? The author suggests that project teams initially focus on the areas where corporate span of control and accountability are clear and unambiguous then move into the grey areas. In the grey areas, it will probably be more important that costs be recognized than to define with great precision the fine points of legal and moral responsibility.

The Search for Specificity. The next step of translating a broad definition of accountability into specific standards of practice is one of the most difficult phases of the project from a technical perspective. However, it is also the single most important step. It is here that slogans and rhetoric must be translated into standards and work plans to which people can be held to account. In a religious context, it is the equivalent of translating a set of shared beliefs into a tangible code of ethical conduct that defines both explicitly and implicitly what an individual can and cannot do. This is where the rubber has to hit the road. If it does not, the effort to develop nontraditional systems is doomed to becoming a shelf project.

In every application, there will be endless debate focusing on, "What is a sustainable corporation?" This chapter, in later sections, provides some general criteria. Here the practical production-orientated team members who know a company's present operations and the ecologists and scientists have to lead the project. If all has gone well, at the end of this phase the team will have identified exactly which practices and technologies will need to be modified. During this phase, there will be less arguing but a lot more wheel spinning until the team begins to establish some firm ground. Here it sometimes can be helpful to start with the most "extreme" option first, the environmental partnership option, and then work backwards into the grey zone surrounding the middle-of-the-road options. As a rule of thumb, if this "extreme" option does not mean a major rethinking of the ways a company is doing business, then the team has probably not identified standards that in hindsight will prove to be sustainable over the long haul.

At this point in the process, the team will experience the heartburn caused by scientific uncertainty, silence, or ambiguity. The experts will lose a bit of their credibility, as other team members push them for the definitive answers they may not be able to provide. In part an underlying problem is the fundamental difference between the outlook of, say, a public relations expert and a trained scientist. In the scientific community, there will be an acceptance that there is a continuum of risk associated with a particular toxin couched in the language of probability. For a particular toxin, there could be a one-in-a-billion chance that one exposure could cause cancer. Is this toxin safe? The public will want black and white pronouncements, not shades of grey. As a last resort, the team will probably need to fall back on common sense, a "gut feel" about the proper size of a clear-cut, the extent of persistent toxins that can safely accumulate in an ecosystem decade after decade. In the last analysis, the key question may well boil down to "How long is long?" Does a company want to follow the rule of seven generations, or will it follow the rule of quarterly earnings? Perhaps the rule of two generations is a more realistic goal. Implementation of this rule, as discussed in the final section of this chapter, would involve a far different corporate culture. The challenge at this phase in the project will be to separate the rhetoric from the facts. Leadership may come from the nontechnical person on the team who listens to all the competing arguments and acts as a "jury of one's peers," or the "reasonable" person.

Once the team has passed this phase of the journey, the calculation of the costs of conversion to operations that are more sustainable will be relatively straightforward. When the cost accountants know exactly how business will be conducted differently, they can begin to compute the relevant costs fairly readily. There will be established cost patterns—standard unit costs, activity-based costs—that can be modified and projected into the future under different sets of assumptions. The accountants who are leading this phase of the project can compute conversion costs and expected returns on investment.

Computing the risk costs will prove much more challenging. Inherently these will be "fuzzy," ambiguous numbers. The approach suggested is to start with the crude benchmarks provided in this case study and tailor these to specific applications. The fundamental approach taken in the case study is to make some rough estimates. The focus is on "how much the ecosystem is worth to a company intent on remaining a going concern over the next 20 to 40 years." This value will necessarily be far narrower than the value society would put on this asset. However, the advantage of the approach advocated is that it is far more relevant to the aspirations and anxieties of a given company. By thinking locally, they may be encouraged to think globally. As a rule of thumb, in calculating the value of the ecosystem upon which a company is economically dependent, the minimum threshold value should be the traditional value of the assets used in production, including fixed assets such as plant and equipment, productive processes, land, and other commercial rights and assets. The logic here is that for every corporate asset there is an "invisible, shadow" ecological asset and liability. In a sense, the value assigned to these invisible, shadow assets can be a somewhat arbitrary base value. What is more critical is that the risk values assigned to the various options reflect the underlying ecological risks of each course of action. As long as these reflect the underlying ecological realities, the model will "work" in the sense of leading to informed judgments that are most compatible with enlightened self-interest.

In this case study, the team focused on the risk cost approach, rather than the damage costing approach. It should be stressed that using the risk cost approach was an interim solution to developing an overall framework. Over the longer haul, the damage costing approach should be used to compute the external costs associated with today's practices. Ideally, over time, the scientific members of the team would be able to provide estimates of the physical damages to the natural capital, as well as human health, caused by current forestry practices and mill effluent. These estimates of damage would be based on observed cause and effect relationships between specific toxins and the impairment of human and ecological health.

The environmental economists could then compute a range of likely monetary costs associated with the estimated damages to health. The role of the accountants would be to take the monetary estimates and determine the requisite environmental costs and liabilities to be included in the corporate management information systems. Estimates of a range of these liabilities would also be reported in the published financial statements. This approach to measuring intergenerational liabilities would replace the contingent liability approach, which is the norm today.

The risk cost approach would still be used for applications where the requisite cause and effect relationships and scientific research were insufficiently developed to support the damage costing approach. For example, for an electric utility, the damage costing approach is good for estimating the costs of damage to crops and human health in the more immediate area of power generation. However, the damage costing approach does not work well for estimating the damage costs associated with the emission of greenhouse gases that cross national borders. Here a risk cost approach might be more useful.

Preparing a Balance Sheet of Intergenerational Liabilities. In this last phase, the team would measure the "noncommercial values" that would be an integral part of preparing a green balance sheet to account for intergenerational equity. Teams approaching this phase of the project should be warned that for the unwary this phase can easily become extremely frustrating to both accountants and nonaccountants. The teams are advised to skirt this sink hole carefully, briefly resting the paddle in the infinite value of natural capital. In everyday life we do not need to know the meaning of life or the resale value of our family house in 100 years to decide to fix a leaking roof. At this phase of the journey, it is critical that the professionals take the back seat to the "reasonable" person.

Companies may want to embark on preparing and publishing a supplementary state-of-the-environment report. This is a board-level decision that is largely taken for public relations purposes rather than to provide new information to support board decision making. What a company decides to include will be largely driven by its corporate culture rather than the technical aspects of accounting for sustainable development.

CONVINCING THE REST OF THE TEAM

It should now be clear that basic accounting conventions, rules, and practices *could* be redefined to better account for the environment. Perceptive readers may wonder whether the problem is with the accountants, not their principles. Accounting *could* look two generations into the future instead of one year in arrears. The definition of assets *could* be expanded to include natural capital. Accountants *could* view wealth as more than retained earnings. The obvious question is, "Why would accountants want to look two generations into the future?" In other words, if accounting for sustainable development is the means to a desired end, what is this "end?" The "why," the desired ends, are threefold:

- *Better decisions.* Informed environmental investment decisions that recognize the importance of the "noncommercial" facets of an ecosystem upon which a company is economically dependent. In the light of so much scientific uncertainty, the objective is more prudent decisions.
- *Better stakeholder management.* A disciplined approach of dealing with nontraditional owners (i.e., stakeholders other than consumers, shareholders, employees, or management) of shared resources.
- *Dealing with murky science.* A reasonable approach to dealing with scientific uncertainty, ambiguity, and silence (i.e., "murky" science).

But the real objective is to create a sustainable corporation. As illustrated in Table 14.1, a sustainable corporation acts out of enlightened self-interest rather than nearsighted self-interest. It is a corporation that looks at making money over decades of creating wealth rather than realizing profit over the next three months. Table 14.1 illustrates the attributes of such a corporation.

Table 14.1
Partners in a Sustainable Corporation

	Key Players in a Sustainable Partnership				
Key Concepts	**Senior Corporate Management**	**Accountants**	**Auditors**	**Visible Stakeholders**	**Invisible Stakeholders**
Long-range vision	Vision a sustainable present	Value the vision	Challenge the vision	Invest in the vision	Demand a future from business and consumers
Accounting for stakeholder management	Create a "realism in reporting" culture	Create numbers that bridge, rather than compartmentalize	Keep the numbers honest	Use proprietary information responsibly	Demand a full accounting
Expanded definition of assets	Define the scope of environmental stewardship	Value natural capital, define the accounting entity broadly	Audit for sustainable development, not just compliance	Tradeoff the present for tomorrow	Push for expanded accountability
The rule of two generations (Limits to Growth)	Create a risk minimization regime	Value the competitive advantage of lower risk development	Challenge nearsighted strategies	Accept limits to growth in earnings	Demand a recognition of the risks
Sustainable profit	Foster a culture of wealth preservation and creation	Model a reasonable return, not a leftover	Blow the whistle on profit stripping	Reinvest in the future	Demand intergenerational equity
Poverty is bad for business	Consider equity of access to resources	Equity is debiting poverty	Benchmark equity	Consider investing in wealth transfusions	Bring equity into the marketplace

1. *Long-range vision.* All levels of management, as well as investors and others with a perceived stake in the company, are prepared to take a long-term view of business.

2. *Accounting for stakeholder management.* Accounting information is seen as the currency of a meaningful dialogue between a diverse group of stakeholders, each with a different but legitimate proprietary interest in the operations of a corporation.

3. *Expanded definition of assets.* Under this concept, accountants and managers would see that they are managing for the forest, with all it contains in terms of habitat and soil nutrients, rather than managing for the trees in work in progress.

4. *The rule of two generations (limits to growth).* Responsible environmental stewardship is seen as managing the risks inherent in modern industrial development, working to minimize these risks through cost-effective technological and social solutions. This concept recognizes that for a given ecological region there will be defined limits to growth beyond which the risk of damage to natural capital may increase significantly. Accounting is expected to look two generations into the future rather than one year into the past.

5. *Sustainable profit.* For a sustainable corporation, profit is more than a residual or leftover. It is what is left over after a comprehensive investment in tomorrow, in natural capital, human capital, community capital, and technological innovation. Reported profit will hardly ever equal sustainable profit.

6. *Poverty is bad for business.* This concept recognizes that for long-term corporate survival, poverty is one of the most pernicious inhibitors of economic well-being. This concept recognizes that a prosperous corporation can act as a "wealth exchange" between developed countries and developing countries, between those who have and those who do not. Such a corporation factors this dynamic potential into long-term decisions on plant investment, product development, and marketing. Enlightened self-interest means that equity of access to jobs and products leads to growth in consumer demand.

In the real world, few corporations will have all these attributes. The challenge for a reader is then to begin to convince other members on the management team that there are alternative cultural norms that might lead to a higher probability of corporate survival over the next decade. Once the culture begins to change, there may be greater acceptance that accounting for sustainable development could lead to better decisions. When a reader is acting in the "voice in the wilderness" mode, the following guidelines may prove useful:

- Senior management and the board will have to provide the required leadership. The ideal scenario is a "push" from top corporate management.

- Wherever possible, advocates for nontraditional accounting should make a clear and explicit link to healthy, sustained earnings.

- Whenever opportunities present themselves, advocates should focus on specific, tangible environmental decisions with which management is currently grappling. Here the objective is to create a demand for new information.

- The nonconverted, who might choke on the whole concept, might be more easily hooked by a series of "what if" questions.

For example, a financial analyst in the environmental affairs branch could ask the cost accountants in a forestry company, "What would it cost if we reduced the size of clear-cuts 10, 20, or even 30 percent?" Such limited questions would be easier to "sell" than the whole model. While some experienced cost accountants might be initially skeptical of the whole concept, few would fail to respond to a well placed and relevant question. After they accept the challenge of valuing a forest 10 years in the future, it is not a big leap to value it 60 years into the future.

Once management has acquired an initial taste for such nontraditional accounting information, they may be willing to embark on the journey. With each decision, management could push deeper and deeper into the model, developing a greater appreciation for the importance of information on the risk costs of business as usual, the costs of conversion, estimates of a potential competitive advantage. Over time, following this course of progressive incrementalism, management may pass a point of no return where it no longer needs to be convinced of the merits of accounting for sustainable development. And at that point in the journey, they may turn to the reader who eased them into the river and ask, "Where is this journey leading?"

The next phase of accounting for sustainable development would mean providing management with the tools required to strike this three-way balance between economic, ecological, and equity considerations. Corporate decisions could help shape the size of the wealth transfer zone or the transfer of wealth between a corporation and the community in which it operates. The wealth transfer zone refers to the extent of economic benefits created by a transnational corporation operating in a developing country.

Sustainable corporations could recognize that over the next two decades the world may be on a hinge of history, a unique turning point. The extremes between rich and poor may grow exponentially. There could also be a recognition of the mutual vulnerability of both the developing nations, a recognition driven largely by enlightened self-interest. The board and senior management could consider the equity of access to resources questions when reviewing the corporation's product line. They could also consider the potential of a corporation to help transfer wealth when setting corporate investment priorities. They could consider the equity implications of their wage rates and their corporate policies on investing in local community infrastructure.

Accountants must play a role in sensitizing management to these issues. Accountants could report how much a company was reinvesting in the community where a factory is located—in terms of education, training, and essential infrastructure. If accounting is not part of the bridge between the three solitudes of wilderness, business, and poverty, it will be part of the abyss that separates them.

Afterword

There are many ways to read this fictional documentary of Blackmore and Price. This story can be read as an attempt to expand the borders of accounting. It can also be read as an attempt to better understand the dynamics of business survival in the turbulent 1990s.

Throughout this story, the focus has been on accounting. But accounting is really little more than a mirror into our souls, our values, and our philosophy of life. Accountants value what society values, what society considers important. Accountants value fixed assets because our society values tangible assets. We do not account for air or water because our society does not value them in the same way.

The essential story is one of finding new values to bridge the three solitudes of wilderness, business, and poverty by understanding the invisible threads that bind natural resources the way we bind business and some notion of economic equity. This is a search that began for me some 43 years ago.

I vividly remember touring a Mexican silver mine as a boy of four. I was standing by the entrance of the mine as the conveyor belt disgorged ore from the depths of the mine below. I was awed and overwhelmed by the wealth of the earth. The chunks of ore glistened with silver and gold flecks.

A Mexican, his dark skin contrasted against his white linen suit, lifted a chunk of ore with his good arm. The other arm ended in a stump. He handed me a piece of the ore to keep. I asked my father, "How come the people are so poor when the country is so rich?"

As life unfolded, I found that this was a question that would recur in many forms, pushing for a satisfactory answer. After I graduated from college with a degree in economics, I worked with Puerto Rican migrants in the Gold Coast of Florida to organize a fishing cooperative.

I will never forget walking west from the Gold Coast, from Pier 66, from the lavish yachts and Cadillacs, walking west across the tracks that divide the Gold Coast from the world of the migrant peoples. I stayed with Ep, a 70-year-old bean picker who lived in a simple wooden shack without running water. There were two lightbulbs hanging from the ceiling. The refrigerator was usually empty, except for an immense block of government surplus cheese. Ep still worked in the fields.

Every day at dawn, Grower Brown, who operated one of the rich vegetable farms, would have a beat-up school bus collect Ep and the other migrant pickers. At dusk, the bus would return and drop them off. One day as I watched the bus unload, an immense black man with cowboy boots and snappy clothes emerged from the bus carrying a double-barrelled shotgun. I recognized W. H. Johnson. He was the director of the local Office of Economic Opportunity in Broward County. I was surprised to see him on the bus.

I asked, "W. H., what are you doing on the bus?" He turned, his wide brow furrowed in anger, "I was born a migrant. These are my people. I had to sit with a shotgun on my lap, out in the tomato fields, so Grower Brown would let them take a 15-minute lunch break. The days I am not out there with my shotgun, they don't get a break."

Some years ago, I had the opportunity to work in the West Indies. In the predawn hours, vendors streamed into the market, their vehicles laden with produce from the rich tropical rain forests — bananas, mangoes, limes, and grapefruits. By early morning, the marketplace was teeming with customers and vendors haggling over prices, a living, thriving commercial exchange. The gap between world of nature and the world of commerce was almost transparent.

And now I have spent two years probing into the soil chemistry, this invisible web of life that encompasses a northern boreal forest. A question that has been below the surface of my inquiry is my place as a human being in this forest. I look at the felling of trees, the cutting, the harvesting. I look at human activity and compare this harvest of trees to that of the beavers. Both the loggers and the beavers are harvesting trees, processing them, changing natural habitat. What's the same and what's different about the cutting and harvesting by each set of creatures? I look at the differences between habitat alteration in terms of scale and time. Humans can alter more widely in a shorter time. The beavers dam up a pond; humans dam up James Bay.

What this suggests to me is that human commercial activity parallels survival activity in the natural world. But there will be a gap, at times an abyss, between the natural world and the world of business. And it is our tools, our values, and our view of our place in the grand scheme of things that determine how wide this gap is. This book is intended to be one small step in bridging that gap.

Selected Bibliography

Canadian Institute of Chartered Accountants. *Reporting on Environmental Performance*. Toronto: The Institute, 1993.

Environmental Protection Agency. *Total Cost Assessment: Accelerating Industrial Pollution Prevention through Innovative Project Financial Analysis*. Washington, D.C.: The Agency, Pollution Prevention and Toxics Division, 1992.

General Electric Company. *Financial Analysis of Waste Management Programs*. Fairfield, Conn.: GE Corporate Environmental Programs, 1987.

International Institute for Sustainable Development. *Business Strategies for Sustainable Development*. Winnipeg: The Institute, 1992.

International Institute for Sustainable Development and Deloitte Touche Tohmatsu International. *Coming Clean: Corporate Environmental Reporting*. Winnipeg: The Institute, 1993.

Price Waterhouse. *Environmental Accounting: The Issues, The Developing Solutions*. New York: Price Waterhouse, 1992.

United Nations Transnational Corporations and Management Division. *Environmental Accounting: Current Issues, Abstracts and Bibliography*. New York: United Nations, 1992.

World Commission on Environment and Development. *Our Common Future*. New York: Oxford University Press, 1987.

Index

ABOUT THE AUTHOR

DANIEL BLAKE RUBENSTEIN, Principal in the Office of the Auditor General and a Chartered Accountant in Canada, has specialized in environmental accounting for sustainable development for the last five years. He has recently finalized a research project on accounting for sustainable development for the United Nations Conference on Trade and Development.